WITH GREAT POWER

WITH GREAT POWER

HOW SPIDER-MAN CONQUERED HOLLYWOOD DURING THE GOLDEN AGE OF COMIC BOOK BLOCKBUSTERS

SEAN O'CONNELL

APPLAUSE
THEATRE & CINEMA BOOKS

Essex, Connecticut

APPLAUSE
THEATRE & CINEMA BOOKS

An imprint of Globe Pequot, the trade division of
The Rowman & Littlefield Publishing Group, Inc.
4501 Forbes Blvd., Ste. 200
Lanham, MD 20706
www.rowman.com

Distributed by NATIONAL BOOK NETWORK

British Library Cataloguing in Publication Information available

Library of Congress Cataloging-in-Publication Data available
ISBN 978-1-4930-6619-3 (cloth : alk. paper)
ISBN 978-1-4930-6620-9 (electronic)

∞™ The paper used in this publication meets the minimum requirements of American
National Standard for Information Sciences—Permanence of Paper for Printed Library
Materials, ANSI/NISO Z39.48-1992

For Stan and Steve. Excelsior!

And for Muggsy Bogues, Andrew Garfield's favorite Charlotte Hornets player.

CONTENTS

Chapter Eleven

Chapter Twelve

Chapter Thirteen

Chapter Fourteen

Chapter Fifteen

Chapter Sixteen

ACKNOWLEDGMENTS

It takes a village to write a book. No, wait. It takes a village to raise a child. Still, the process of writing a book also relies on countless emotional and spiritual boosts from an enormous support system, and I had so many people in my corner while writing *With Great Power*, encouraging my progress and inspiring me to continue. I'm not sure the human language contains words that are powerful enough to express my appreciation for these people, but hopefully the following sentences convey my heartfelt gratitude.

I'm able to pursue my creative endeavors and write books about subjects I adore only because my family encourages me to chase my dreams (and I hope I inspire them to do the same). My wife, Michele, meets my every crazy whim with endless support and enthusiasm. I can't tell you how many times I've turned to her over the years and said such ridiculous things as, "I think I want to be a film critic" or "I think I'm going to write a book." Some spouses might shoot down these seemingly half-baked suggestions or counter such a pitch with a calm, rational explanation as to why the idea is terrible/fruitless/a waste of time. Not Michele. Every single time, she responds to my suggestion with, "That sounds great! You should totally do that." And that's why I'm a film critic who has written two books.

It was "easier" to write a book at this stage of my life because our boys, P.J. and Brendan, have become young men with their own passions. Working parents recognize the balancing act of being there for your kids while also trying to cross items off your to-do list. Attempting to write a book can be the equivalent of adding a second job to your already jam-packed day, and I'm blessed that my boys took Dad's distraction in stride. They probably don't realize how much I appreciate the time that they gave me to write on nights and weekends, when I'd rather be watching a basketball game with them, introducing them to a movie I think they'd love, or just soaking up all the family time we have together. But each time they poked their head into my office to ask me how the book was going or tell me something interesting they read somewhere about Spider-Man, they provided a spark that ignited my creativity all over again. Hopefully, they know that everything I do, I do for them.

This book would not have been possible without the constant assistance and invaluable guidance from my friend Merisa Lavie at Sony Pictures Entertainment. We've worked together on movie projects for years, but Merisa was a needed ear during the earliest pitch stages of this book, and she repeatedly helped me get my foot into the door of so many publicists and agents who eventually sat me down in front of their clients. Most of the interviews that helped shape this book started with me texting Merisa for advice, and I'll never forget that. Merisa also introduced me to the patient and resourceful Tahra Grant, Sony's senior vice president of corporate communications. Tahra worked with me for the entirety of 2020 to secure interviews I never thought would be possible when I started this journey. Thank you both, so very much, for all of your help.

My close publicist friends put me in touch with new publicist friends, and I owe a sincere debt of gratitude to the constant communications I had with Steve Elzer, Guido Gotz, Simon Halls, Garth Burkhard, Candice McDonough, Rachael Reiss, Brianna Smith, Emily Hunter, Kristin Nava, and every publicist who answered my inquiry e-mails.

Thank you to everyone who agreed to be interviewed for the book, with a special shout-out to Avi Arad, who spent hours on the phone, walking me through his complete history with Marvel and Spider-Man and helping me realize there actually was more than enough information for a book here.

My three brothers in film—Jake Hamilton, Kevin McCarthy, and Gabe Kovacs—reinvigorate my passion for film on a weekly basis, and they all endured far too many texts from me with book-progress updates. They'd read chapters, listen to potential questions I wanted to ask subjects, and geek out with me over interviews I'd completed. Our movie podcast, ReelBlend, was the ideal escape from the pressures of the book's deadlines, and I'm still so thankful we started that show. It has changed our lives.

Special thanks go out to Megan Brogan, Tom Tinney, Michael Kamens, K. C. Procter, and Kyle Hall, who all lent helping hands or read individual chapters at random periods of development, patiently answering my nagging question, "But is it interesting?" Thank you, as well, to my CinemaBlend family—particularly Mack and Jessica Rawden. You guys allow me to hold my dream job and give me a daily platform to write about something that is very important to me: movies. You supported me when I set out to write my first book and encouraged me when it was time to write another. CinemaBlend is the greatest entertainment website because of the people who keep the wheels spinning every day. I'm in awe of their abilities and am so proud to work side by side with each and every one of them.

My literary agent, Joshua Bilmes, helped me shape, refine, and sell this book. His feedback makes my writing better, and I hope *With Great Power* is merely the beginning of a long and fruitful partnership. Finally, a huge thank-you goes out to John Cerullo for giving me my shot with Applause Books. Let's do another one!

CHAPTER ONE
AN AMAZING TIME TO BE SPIDER-MAN

arvel Entertainment stockpiles its universe with fascinating characters from all walks of life. There are gods (the mighty Thor), and there are monsters (the Incredible Hulk). Comic book readers, television audiences, and moviegoers routinely flock to heroic stories told by Marvel's imaginative creators, whether they involve an intelligent African king from the advanced nation of Wakanda, a defrosted World War II soldier who fights for freedom with his trusted shield, or a Canadian mutant with blades in his hands whose skeleton is coated in an indestructible metal alloy called adamantium. By every metric, though, the most popular, influential, and successful character in Marvel's diverse stable is an orphaned teenage bookworm from Queens, New York, who happened to get bit by a radioactive spider.

Peter Benjamin Parker. The friendly, neighborhood Spider-Man. He's a dichotomy, by design. The costumed superhero is a global sensation, even though Parker himself could pass for the unassuming boy next door. An agile physical specimen with the proportionate strength and speed of a spider, Parker also gets babied by his overprotective aunt because she's worried he's too fragile. And this unselfish savior who consistently sacrifices life and limb often goes unappreciated by the people in his own stories, thanks in part to a biased newspaper publisher with a serious ax to grind who pushes the false narrative that Spider-Man is a masked menace.

The contradictions inherent in the character help explain why Spider-Man's appeal is global. They tell us that Spidey is imperfect. They prove this superhero is more like us than you'd initially think. No matter your background, you can recognize yourself—or someone you know—when you read the exploits of Peter Parker and his alter ego. That relatability is now and always has been the defining factor in Spider-Man's worldwide popularity.

"The reason that the character's success is so extraordinary is because of how ordinary he is," said Tom Rothman, chairman and CEO of Sony Pictures Motion Picture Group, the studio that distributes Spider-Man's feature films.[1]

Andrew Garfield, the Oscar-nominated Brit who played Spider-Man in two feature films as well as the 2021 team-up sequel *Spider-Man: No Way Home*, summed up the character's allure when he said, "He's covered head to toe. You don't see skin color, you don't see sexual orientation, you don't see any of those things. So everyone can project themselves into the suit, and I think that's why he's probably the most beloved superhero universally, throughout every culture, throughout every race."[2]

"There's so much affinity for this character. It means so much to so many people," adds Tobey Maguire, who helped define the Marvel hero for an entire generation by playing him on screen in three Sony movies. "Once the sort of goofiness of being in Lycra or spandex goes away, you are like, 'Oh wow, this is cool. This is a responsibility, a blessing, [and] something that I get to do that I'm grateful for.'"[3]

"Spider-Man is the biggest Marvel character," concludes Kevin Feige, president of Marvel Studios and the architect of the Marvel Cinematic Universe (MCU). "He is the jewel in the crown. Such an amazing icon. He's a very different kind of hero because he is, quite simply, the greatest superhero of all-time."[4]

Praise doesn't get much higher. A superhero's definition of "success," however, differs from the rest of ours. To them, success usually boils down to saving an innocent person from peril, foiling a maniacal villain's plans, or preventing catastrophic damage to a city, nation, or planet. Textbook savior stuff. In the fickle film industry, it's box office receipts, merchandise sales, lucrative corporate partnerships, and the tough-to-quantify magnitude of "pop-culture influence" that measure a superhero's value and are pivotal to defining a character's worth. Saving a school bus filled with children is good. Selling a toy, T-shirt, or comic book to every kid on that same bus is even better in the mind of a corporate executive.

Spider-Man stands head and shoulders above his competition in most of these categories. The hero's cultural reach extends from comics and clothing to video games, toys, and animated television shows. He's such a marketing force that his influence was used for a punch line in the opening scene of the 2018 animated feature *Spider-Man: Into the Spider-Verse*, where the hero (voiced by Chris Pine) explained, "Look, I'm a comic book, I'm a cereal, did a Christmas album, I have an excellent theme song, and a so-so popsicle."

That's only a humble brag because it's true. According to *The Hollywood Reporter*, Spider-Man's global retail sales exceeded $1.3 billion in 2014, while the digital commerce data analysis service Slice Intelligence reported that Spider-Man was responsible for the second-largest quantity of online toys, games, and apparel purchased between 2015 and 2019. (Only Batman topped the wall crawler, claiming 28 percent of all sales compared to 13.5 percent for Spidey.) Major toy manufacturers such as Hasbro and Hot Toys don't willingly share annual sales figures. But data collected in 2017 by the market research firm NPD Group showed that the four Spider-Man films released by Sony Pictures between 2004 and 2014 generated a grand total of $1.21 billion just in toy sales.[5]

Beginning in 2018, Spider-Man also started to conquer the competitive video game market. The wall crawler starred in playable console games over the years but few compared to the open-world Spider-Man game designed by Insomniac Games and published through Sony Interactive Entertainment that year. *Marvel's Spider-Man* offered an original story that allowed users to play as either Peter Parker or a relatively new Marvel character, Miles Morales, as they took on a series of classic Spider-Man antagonists. But outside of the game's baked-in plotline, *Spider-Man* players could (and did) spend countless hours simply swinging around the game's stunning re-creation of New York City, stopping small crimes, interacting with starstruck citizens, halting high-speed car chases and, essentially, living Spider-Man's day-to-day life. *Wired*, *Time*, the websites The Ringer and IGN, and numerous other gaming publications put this immersive Spider-Man game on their "Best Of" lists for 2018. Statistics posted in 2020 revealed that *Marvel's Spider-Man* moved more than 20 million units, making it one of the most lucrative titles in Sony's video game arsenal.[6] So when Sony was tasked with launching its new gaming system, the PS5, in November 2020, the sequel game *Marvel's Spider-Man: Miles Morales* was a centerpiece in the company's marketing campaigns.

Overall, though, Spider-Man's strongest financial impact to this day is felt in the feature-film realm, where nine different Spider-Man movies collectively boast more than $7.5 billion in worldwide ticket sales. Movies adapted from Spider-Man comic books went on to become the highest-grossing domestic releases in 2002 (Sam Raimi's *Spider-Man*), in 2007 (the director's sequel, *Spider-Man 3*), and again in 2021 (with Jon Watts's *Spider-Man: No Way Home*). Of the five highest-grossing film franchises in Hollywood history, Spider-Man now plays a role in three: the MCU, the four-film *Avengers* franchise, and Sony Pictures Entertainment's ongoing Spider-Man series. This ranks the character ahead of James Bond, the Transformers, every on-screen Batman, and Peter Jackson's complete J. R. R. Tolkien series on Hollywood's box office hierarchy. Audiences adore Marvel's web slinger, and the numbers prove it. When Sony unleashed the first official teaser for *Spider-Man: No Way Home* on August 23, 2021, the clip broke the 24-hour all-time record for most global views with 355.5 million trailer views.[7] That helped it eclipse the previous record holder, *Avengers: Endgame*, which drove 289 million views. That fan interest translated into ticket sales. *Spider-Man: No Way Home* set box office records on opening weekend. It eventually became the highest-grossing Spider-Man movie of all time. And by the end of its theatrical run, it also claimed the title of highest-grossing film in Sony Pictures Entertainment's studio history.

A Friendly, Neighborhood Superhero

These financial statistics, while impressive, don't paint the entire picture as to why Spider-Man is more beloved than his comic book counterparts. They don't explain why readers collect multiple Spider-Man comic book titles, wear officially licensed Spider-Man gear, and buy tickets to films centered around different interpretations of the character. They don't get to the heart of the reasons why children instinctively curl their middle and ring fingers in towards their palms while extending their pointer and pinky fingers, pretending to shoot imaginary webs from their wrists or why adult cosplayers spend thousands of dollars to re-create their own Spider-Man costumes, eager to pretend that they are the wall crawler, if even for a moment.

This book will help readers better understand the universal appeal of Spider-Man by breaking the character down to his foundation and spelling out all of the cool aspects that make Spider-Man tick. It will trace Spider-Man's path to the top of the Hollywood food chain by documenting every step on that journey and highlighting Spider-Man's influence on the evolution of the comic book movie genre. The book includes interviews with almost every one of the Hollywood creatives who spent years figuring out how best to translate the magic and wonder of Spider-Man to the big screen.

Amy Pascal is one of those integral collaborators, having spent more than half of her professional career working on Spider-Man movies. "At this point, I feel like his aunt," Pascal jokes.[8] The veteran Hollywood producer and former chairperson of the Motion Pictures Group for Sony Pictures Entertainment was instrumental to the plotting of Spider-Man's cinematic journey at Sony, backing all three Sam Raimi *Spider-Man* films and both of the *Amazing Spider-Man* movies directed by Marc Webb. She additionally holds a producer credit on all three Spider-Man films created through the Marvel and Sony collaboration (a deal she helped facilitate) as well as *Venom*, its 2021 sequel, and the Oscar-winning animated feature *Spider-Man: Into the Spider-Verse*. When Pascal elaborates on what it takes to understand the core of the character, you'd be wise to listen.

In her opinion, Spider-Man connects with global audiences because he's pop culture's most relatable hero. He isn't a boy wizard like Harry Potter. He wasn't born a Jedi like Luke Skywalker. Spider-Man doesn't defend a fictional city like Gotham or Metropolis but instead lays his life on the line for the citizens of a recognizable New York City, a place that many of his fans call home.

"He's not a God," summarizes Pascal, "He doesn't have magical powers. He doesn't come from money. He's a completely relatable character, and he always has been. And I think the trick [to making a good Spider-Man movie] is making all the stories come out of his character, and not putting him into a plot that you can't relate to, or where he gets lost."

The defining characteristic mentioned by Garfield, the fact that Spider-Man's mask helps make him identifiable to all ages and races, too often gets overlooked when discussing reasons for the hero's global popularity.

"[Growing up] all I had was Spider-Man," said Destin Daniel Cretton, director of Marvel's 2021 origin film *Shang-Chi and the Legend of the Ten*

Rings, when commenting on the lack of diversity in comic book role models available to him as a kid. "Because he had the mask on, I could dress up like Spider-Man for Halloween. I had a handful of other characters that looked like me on screen, but there were maybe two or three that I could choose from, and superheroes were not a part of that."[9]

Yet, when his mask comes off, Peter Parker encounters the same problems that everyday folks might face on a daily basis. Peter's unpopular at school, perpetually picked on by a bully named "Flash" Thompson. Parker has the potential to be a brilliant student, but his grades often suffer because he masquerades as a crime fighter. "Peter Parker. Brilliant but lazy," summarizes Dr. Otto Octavious (Alfred Molina) during a decisive scene in Sam Raimi's 2004 sequel *Spider-Man 2*, and while that's not entirely accurate, it does cut directly to this character's core. Parker's often short on cash and relies on a freelance gig at a newspaper to barely make ends meet. He's unlucky in love. And he covers his fears with razor-sharp sarcasm, making him one of our funniest superheroes.

Personally, I admire the fact that Spider-Man refuses to quit. Perseverance in the face of overwhelming odds is a popular blue-collar hero trope, and it's the one I try to borrow from Spider-Man and apply to my own life. Even when he's exhausted, outmatched, frustrated, or overwhelmed, Spidey digs down deep to find that last burst of effort, ensuring that he does the responsible thing. He has made costly mistakes along the way and has paid tremendous emotional prices because of them. The story lines that are associated with Spider-Man's failures over the years—up to and including *Spider-Man: No Way Home*—tend to have the greatest impact with fans because they remind us of how human this character can be. These gray areas help audiences to believe either that they could be Spider-Man themselves or that Spidey at the very least resembles someone they know from their own lives.

This helps clarify why fans become abnormally protective of how Spidey is presented in animated productions, television shows, and feature films. You can start a heated debate in the Spider-Man fan community simply by asking individuals to defend their favorite actors to play Peter Parker on-screen. Such passionate fan reaction (or a lack of it) often explains why certain versions of Peter Parker soared high but others stumbled.

Hollywood director Sam Raimi really seemed to understand this kinship Spider-Man fans have with their hero. When he had temporary guardianship over Spidey and his universe, he often spotlighted Spidey's symbiotic relationship with the people of New York, whether they were throwing him a celebratory "Thank You" festival in *Spider-Man 3* or carrying his limp body over their heads in a sacrificial, Christ-like gesture after he stopped a speeding train in *Spider-Man 2*. "You wanna get to him, you gotta go through me," a defiant New York tough guy tells Otto Octavius when the villain arrives on the train to abduct the badly injured web slinger. And in a similarly memorable moment of loyalty and protection, this one in the 2002 origin film *Spider-Man*, the wall crawler (played by Tobey Maguire) is saved by irate city dwellers who start throwing bricks, pipes, bottles, and wrenches at the Green Goblin (Willem Dafoe) when he has Spider-Man trapped. It's not just the fact that ordinary citizens step in to help the helpless hero. These folks amplify their possessive attachment to this costumed teenager by shouting, "I got something for your ass! You mess with Spidey, you mess with New York!" and "You mess with one of us, you mess with all of us!" The scene works both as an on-brand representation of the standoffish New Yorkers who share Spidey's ZIP code and an accurate snapshot of the temporary societal unification that gripped Manhattan in the post–September 11 era.

Without question, Stan Lee and Steve Ditko's prized creation has helped create and cultivate the current golden age of comic book blockbusters, and knowledge gained from the *Spider-Man* franchises continues to be applied to all comic book movies today. But this hero's Hollywood story wasn't written overnight. Spider-Man carved out a twisty path to the top of the comic book movie hierarchy, one marked with unexpected obstacles, unprecedented partnerships, and numerous, valuable moviemaking lessons.

"The Worst Idea I Have Ever Heard"

Spider-Man might be a global superpower now, but the hero sports a humble origin story that befits the character's blue-collar roots. Spidey faced an uphill battle to become the current king of the comic book genre and was almost annihilated by his initial "foe," a publisher who didn't believe in his potential.

Writer-editor Stan Lee and artist Steve Ditko came up with the idea for this original Marvel character in 1962. The way the story usually goes (because Lee had been known to tweak details and embellish the narrative the more times he told it), Lee was brainstorming ideas for new comic book heroes they could introduce in the pages of Marvel Comics when he saw an insect crawling across a wall. In some versions of Lee's account, it's a spider. In others, it's a fly. Regardless, he adored the idea of a hero who could stick to surfaces and possibly even shoot webs. He hated the names Insect-Man, Mosquito-Man, and Fly-Man. But once he landed on Spider-Man, he ran to pitch the concept to his publisher, Martin Goodman.

To say it went poorly would be an understatement.

"My publisher said, in his ultimate wisdom, 'Stan, that is the worst idea I have ever heard,'" Lee told BBC Radio 4 in 2015. "He said, 'First of all, people hate spiders, so you can't call a book *Spider-Man*. Secondly, he can't be a teenager—teenagers can only be sidekicks. And third, he can't have personal problems if he's supposed to be a superhero. Don't you know who a superhero is?'"[10]

It goes without saying that Lee knew exactly what a superhero was. The prolific Marvel editor had already introduced the Fantastic Four and the

Incredible Hulk to readers. He would go on to create two enduring comic book super teams in the Avengers and the X-Men. Still, Lee reportedly left the Spider-Man pitch meeting with his tail between his legs. Goodman's concerns regarding Spider-Man were legitimate. The only place you found teenager comic characters at the time was in *Archie* books or *Batman* stories including Robin the Boy Wonder. Still, Lee believed in the concept and identified one last Hail Mary throw he could attempt in order to get the wall crawler in front of an audience. Marvel planned to pull the plug on its anthology comic book *Amazing Fantasy*, citing terrible sales numbers. Goodman agreed to let Lee and Ditko insert a Spider-Man story into the comic's final issue, *Amazing Fantasy* #15. The duo spun an origin for a mild-mannered high school student named Peter Parker, who gets bitten by a radioactive spider while on a class trip, instantly gaining the transformative powers of the infected insect.

By grounding Spider-Man in a recognizable reality and presenting him as an ordinary kid gifted with extraordinary powers, Lee and Ditko shattered the mold for a traditional comic-book superhero. Peter Parker wasn't an alien from Krypton or a billionaire Gotham socialite. He was an unpopular high school science whiz who would be plagued with crippling guilt after one self-ish act led to the death of his Uncle Ben, helping Peter fully understand that with great power comes great responsibility.

Lee admitted to BBC Radio 4 that he included Spider-Man in the final issue of *Amazing Fantasy* "just to get it out of my system." Months after the book was published, though, when the sales figures crossed Goodman's desk, Marvel's executives were stunned to learn that the Spider-Man issue was the company's best seller that month. Audiences loved this relatable superhero. Marvel loved the notion of selling books. A monthly Spider-Man comic book series was ordered, and an icon officially was born.

It was a massive early win for Spider-Man, but those victories would be spread out as the wall crawler scratched and clawed his way up the ladder to reach Hollywood's pinnacle.

"Quality Commerciality"

What a difference sixty years can make. Stan Lee had to fight to include a short Spider-Man story within the pages of a dying comic book in August 1962. Six decades later, the Marvel hero was the star of the highest-grossing motion picture in the world. That's how far Spider-Man has come since his debut. Even the optimistic Lee couldn't have predicted how high his creation would climb in that relatively short amount of time.

Jon Watts's 2021 hit *Spider-Man: No Way Home* is the culmination of every major step taken by Spidey on his remarkable Hollywood journey. Three live-action versions of the iconic superhero—played by Tobey Maguire, Andrew Garfield, and Tom Holland—crossed generational boundaries to unite on-screen for the first time, facing off against five classic villains from Spidey's deep rogues' gallery. Respected character actors Willem Dafoe and Alfred Molina returned to their fan-favorite roles of the Green Goblin and Doctor Octopus, respectively. Jamie Foxx, Rhys Ifans, and Thomas Haden Church reprised roles that represented alternate periods of Spidey's Hollywood history. The movie organically expanded on the current MCU by introducing the concept of the multiverse, then showcasing supporting players (like Charlie Cox's Daredevil) that are expected to return in upcoming projects. The movie was a bridge to Spider-Man's past that also honored his present while setting the character up for an exciting future.

The audience ate it up. Released at the close of 2021, *Spider-Man: No Way Home* broke through the cloud of apathy that had been hanging over the film industry since the onset of COVID-19. The promise of seeing all three Spider-Men sharing the screen helped Watts's blockbuster to lure casual moviegoers back to the multiplexes, which many had been avoiding since March 2020. It was an economic boost that theater chains desperately needed. "Needless to say, we are ever so happy to see a record-setting number of people returning to the cinema," said Adam Aron, AMC chairman and CEO, after *No Way Home* premiered. "For [the film's] opening night, we hosted some 1.1 million guests to watch *Spider-Man: No Way Home* at our U.S. theatres."[11]

Strong attendance figures helped the movie shatter numerous box office records during its theatrical run, making *No Way Home* the highest-grossing film ever released by Sony Pictures Entertainment, the highest-grossing Spider-Man film in history, the first film of the pandemic era to cross $1 billion worldwide, the third-biggest worldwide opening of all time, the second-biggest domestic debut of all time, and the biggest December opening weekend ever, knocking 2015's *Star Wars: The Force Awakens* out of that slot.

Kevin Feige, reflecting on the drawing power of *Spider-Man: No Way Home*, said, "It's a good thing when people are in a theater and they stand up and cheer. It's a good thing when people are wiping tears because they're thinking back on their last 20 years of moviegoing, and what it has meant to them. That, to me, is a very good thing."[12]

Some of the creative and financial momentum that carried *No Way Home* to the top of 2021's charts traces back to the achievements Spidey posted in 2019. In April of that year, the hero's appearance in Marvel Studios' *Avengers: Endgame* helped Joe and Anthony Russo's blockbuster become the highest-grossing feature film in Hollywood history. *Endgame*'s eventual global haul of $2.97 billion was enough to knock James Cameron's *Avatar* from the leadership position it held for nearly a decade (though a theatrical rerelease in March 2021 moved *Avatar* back atop the box office rankings). Then in June, Sony's follow-up sequel, *Spider-Man: Far from Home*, became the first solo

Spider-Man feature to sail past the $1 billion mark at the box office. Two years later, *No Way Home* would become the second.

But it wasn't just box office victories Spidey was notching, impressive as they may have been. The hero's storytelling footprint continued to expand. Confident in the character's ability to draw large audiences, Sony inked production deals in 2019 to develop a roster of live-action and animated television programs centered around Spider-Man and his world, ensuring that the character would remain in the creative mainstream for at least the next decade. Over on its film side, Sony continued to invest heavily in its Spider-Man spin-off franchises structured around the Marvel villains Venom (Tom Hardy) and Morbius (Jared Leto), while cinematic projects involving popular Spider-Man characters Kraven the Hunter (Aaron Taylor Johnson), Madam Web (Dakota Johnson), Black Cat, and Silver Sable moved into various stages of preproduction. Sony was cultivating its own Spider-Man universe of Marvel characters, one that didn't even feature Spider-Man as a main character.

Sony's situation with regard to its Marvel characters is both abnormal and groundbreaking, as no other character in comic book or pop culture history can claim to have a series of films set in his or her universe that operates independently of the character having to be involved. As a hypothetical comparison, imagine the James Bond franchise mounting expensive, stand-alone spy thrillers centered around characters like Moneypenny, Felix Leiter, or Ernst Stavro Blofeld, knowing that 007 couldn't be a part of them for legal reasons. Once again, Batman comes the closest to mirroring Spider-Man's circumstance, given that Warner Bros.' *Joker* spin-off earned $1.07 billion and two Academy Awards in 2020. But that's one experiment, which may or may not produce a sequel. Sony keeps adding movies to its connected thread of multiple Spider-Man stories, which interlock and form an independent universe.

Later in 2019, Sony and Disney's theatrical divisions strengthened their Spider-Man ties when the companies extended the existing deal to continue sharing the wall crawler between the two studios. This agreement, signed in 2015, allowed Tom Holland's Spider-Man to continue appearing in Sony's Spider-Man films, which would benefit from Kevin Feige serving as a creative liaison. The continuation of this advantageous deal inspired Feige to declare, "Spider-Man is a powerful icon and hero whose story crosses all ages and audiences around the globe. He also happens to be the only hero with the superpower to cross cinematic universes, so as Sony continues to develop their own Spidey-verse, you never know what surprises the future might hold."[13]

Box office analysts expected *Spider-Man: No Way Home* to topple records, even with the limitations created by the global pandemic. Oscar pundits, however, likely didn't anticipate that the superhero movie would generate the amount of awards talk that surfaced following the film's release. Blockbuster fare generally doesn't get recognized by the Academy of Motion Picture Arts and Sciences. Marvel's 2018 thriller *Black Panther* became the first comic book movie to earn a Best Picture nomination, but Ryan Coogler's movie is the exception that proves the Academy's unwritten rule that superhero movies—while popular—aren't considered Oscar-worthy films.

Spider-Man: No Way Home's success empowered the film's allies to champion the movie's Oscar potential and argue that the accepted definition of an "Oscar" film needs to change. Tom Rothman spoke about "quality commerciality" as he coaxed the Academy to be better about recognizing the artistry found in hit films. Both he and Feige even went so far as to compare *Spider-Man: No Way Home* to Peter Jackson's *The Lord of the Rings: The Return of the King*, which swept all eleven Oscars for which it was nominated, including Best Picture.

"In the way *The Return of the King* was sort of a celebration and culmination of all of that amazing work that had been done on that trilogy, this is a celebration both of our *Homecoming* trilogy and of the five other incarnations of Spider-Man that had happened before," Feige claimed.[14]

Support for *No Way Home* wasn't just emanating from the film's own corner, though. Variety film critic Owen Gleiberman confessed in a surprising 2021 column that while he "hated" Tom Holland's third Spider-Man movie, he believed it represented exactly the type of films the Academy membership needed to honor with more frequency if they had any hope of staying relevant and keeping their televised awards program alive.

"The Oscars are on life support, or at least they're heading there. They need mainstream cred," Gleiberman wrote. "This isn't simply about [ratings]. It's about a perception that drives the numbers. Sure, if *No Way Home* gets nominated, a swath of its vast fan base might tune into the Oscars that wouldn't have otherwise. But what I'm really talking about is the essential idea that movies are, and always have been, a populist art form. If that dimension of cinema isn't respected, something has gone wrong."[15]

Even his detractors have to admit that Spider-Man boasts the accomplishments that make him the most powerful and influential superhero during the golden age of comic book movies: sustained box office success; feature films that bridge the chasm separating critics and fans; an expanding grip on alternate storytelling methods, such as long-form television series and animation; and credible Oscar buzz, translating into the occasional win (thanks to 2019's *Spider-Man: Into the Spider-Verse*).

If Hollywood had a superhero throne, Spider-Man would be sitting on it. Yet this wasn't always the case. The web slinger's early cinematic history was riddled by uncertainty. Mediocre screenplays, endless legal battles, and suffocating studio politics stopped several filmmakers from making a Spider-Man movie until director Sam Raimi and producers Laura Ziskin, Ian Bryce, and Avi Arad finally cracked the code. Now that we know that *No Way Home* is the pinnacle of Spider-Man's Hollywood mountain, let's rewind to the first steps taken on the hero's lengthy journey.

CHAPTER TWO
TV ROOTS AND HOLLYWOOD'S FIRST SILVER SCREEN SPIDER-MAN

Spider-Man's Hollywood history doesn't begin in 2002 with Sam Raimi, and Tobey Maguire wasn't the first actor to wear the web slinger's mask. Raimi's origin film *Spider-Man* probably ranks as the first live-action Spidey story that casual fans chose to see—the blockbuster was a smash hit for Sony Pictures, banking $821.7 million worldwide. But several other storytellers took a crack at Spidey before Raimi unlocked the winning formula. After years spent establishing the print arm of its comic book universe, Marvel grew eager—creatively and financially—to license its characters out for adaptations in the late 1960s and 1970s. The company listened to every offer that reached their table, hoping to expand beyond the realm of comic book publishing and into other media avenues. These early projects represent some wild alternate paths the Spider-Man franchise flirted with on its way to the mainstream.

How wild? Hollywood producer Steve Krantz worked on the first and only season of the 1966 animated television series *Mighty Thor*, then transitioned to the 1967 animated *Spider-Man* series, which ran until 1970. He thought he understood Marvel storytelling, so he penned a letter to Stan Lee in December 1975 and pitched "a musical fantasy picture" built around the wall crawler. Krantz's dream casting for the Peter Parker role would have been either Mick Jagger or Elton John, acknowledging that these hires would lead to a stark departure from the Marvel source material because "in the comic books, Spider-Man doesn't sing or tap dance."[1] This idea never got out of the gate. Whether coincidental or intentional, Krantz didn't produce any more Marvel projects during the rest of his professional career.

Then there were Cannon Films executives Menahem Golan and Yoram Globus, Israeli cousins and B-movie provocateurs who wanted to introduce Spidey to moviegoers as part of a lower-budget horror feature helmed by *The Texas Chainsaw Massacre* director Tobe Hooper. In that proposed feature, Peter Parker literally would have mutated into an eight-armed, flesh-eating spider monster. The Israeli producers didn't grow up on comic books, so they assumed that Spider-Man worked like the Wolfman or the Fly, a teenager who literally transformed into the creature for which he was named.

Because Spider-Man ranked as one of Marvel Comics' most popular characters right out of the gate, the company fielded multiple marketing pitches that would have increased that hero's exposure to global audiences—creating a bit of a "chicken or the egg" philosophical debate raised by *Spider-Man: Into the Spider-Verse* producer Chris Miller.

"The fact that Marvel was so keen on licensing Spider-Man stuff in the Sixties, like immediately, probably contributes to his popularity," Miller said. "He was like Mickey Mouse. He was ubiquitous. [But] what comes first? Was it the popularity that led to all the licensing? Or vice versa?"[2]

Either way, the end result was enormous popularity for Spider-Man as a character. This led to another offbeat Spider-Man story that actually did get off the ground in 1978 when an international collaboration between Marvel and the Tokyo-based Toei Company led to the creation of the Japanese original television show *Spider-Man* (or *Supaidāman*, as it was known in its native land). A film and television production company known best for developing and distributing anime and live-action Manga dramas, Toei took a chance on Spider-Man at the urging of Marvel Entertainment adviser Gene Pelc, who had moved to Tokyo and recognized an untapped comic market he thought

Marvel needed to explore. Japanese audiences preferred Manga comics to Marvel, however, so Pelc and his Toei collaborators knew they'd need to implement significant changes to the Spider-Man narrative if they had any hope of attracting the adolescent audiences that turned the company's television shows into hits.

Instead of Peter Parker, Spider-Man's alter ego in the Japanese Spider-Man program was Takuya Yamashiro (Shinji Tōdō), a twenty-two-year-old motocross star seeking vengeance for the murder of his archaeologist father. Spider-Man staples such as Aunt May, the *Daily Bugle*, and the Green Goblin were replaced by genre elements Japanese audiences preferred: giant robots, bug-inspired villains, swords, Ninjas, guns, and a Spider-Man sports car that the hero drove around.

"While I was sitting here in Japan, I brought my young son with me, and he and a lot of his friends watched these shows on Japanese TV. Things like *Kamen Rider*," said Pelc. "Kids loved it, even though they didn't understand what was being said, they loved the action, they loved the music. There was a driving force behind them."[3]

By playing directly to Japanese children, the show caught on. Forty-one episodes of *Spider-Man* were produced, with one of them even being programmed as part of the Toei Manga Matsuri Film Festival on July 22, 1978. Japanese *Spider-Man* helped sell toys, of course. Toei programs essentially were commercials that peddled products to kids. Toy companies such as Popy sponsored the Toei programs, then turned around and sold the towering robots and stylish cars that were featured in the shows. But the Japanese program also helped grow Spider-Man's influence as a global brand, spreading Marvel's heroic stories to a wider audience. In a way, the show demonstrated how Spider-Man stories could succeed when creators shaped Marvel's iconic character to meet the needs of a targeted audience. The program made drastic changes to Spidey's origin, sure. But *Supaidāman* did stay true to Marvel's roots, especially when it came time to designing a comic-accurate Spider-Man suit. The Japanese costume all but mirrored the hero's comic book suit, showcasing the red and blue color combo, the expressive white eyes, and the black web patterns spread around the upper torso, culminating in a black spider logo on the chest. The most noticeable addition was a thick mechanical device worn on Takuya Yamashiro's wrist that he used to fire his webs. That technology would evolve and shrink over the years as more storytellers figured out how to visually present Spidey on-screen.

That's another realm in which Japanese *Spider-Man* broke significant ground regarding the live-action depiction of the character. The 1978 television show is one of the earliest visual projects that captured athletic superhero poses that appeared to be lifted directly from the pages of the Stan Lee and Steve Ditko comic books. Forty years after making its debut, the Japanese Spider-Man show still deserves enormous credit for delivering some of the most realistic live-action visualizations of Spider-Man that fans have seen. The program's hero looks like he swung out of a comic book panel and into our world.

"He has to be a spider. This is how Spider-Man should be done," said *Spider-Man* stunt coordinator Osamu Kaneda while reflecting on the comic-accurate physicality the show achieved during a 2020 interview for the Disney+ documentary series *Marvel 616*. "To give the impression of a spider, the action has to be spider-like, from a low center of gravity. From there, he can jump and kick, fly around and hit bad guys."[4]

Kaneda's stuntman—and the man in the costume for the Japanese *Spider-Man* action scenes—was actor Hirofumi Joga. Rigorous gymnastics training made Joga flexible enough to strike the "difficult, awkward poses" needed to bring Spider-Man to life on screen.

"It was groundbreaking, these poses," added *Supaidāman* lead actor Shinji Tōdō. "It was something totally new. It made an impact, in comparison to typical kids' shows around then."[5]

It's easy to overlook this fact because comic-accurate depictions of Marvel's superheroes are a part of our daily lives today, so we take for granted the ingenuity that's required to help flesh-and-blood actors mimic flexible animated characters. Beginning with the Raimi Spider-Man origin movie, most of these movements were completed with cutting-edge visual effects that rapidly evolved year after year. We're now at the point, technically, where Marvel directors Joe and Anthony Russo can include a sequence in *Avengers: Endgame* where Captain America (Chris Evans) throws Thor's hammer, Mjolnir, through the air so that Spider-Man (Tom Holland) can catch it and fly while holding the Infinity Gauntlet, only to get scooped up by Pepper Potts (Gwyneth Paltrow) in the Rescue Armor and passed to Valkyrie (Tessa Thompson) as she rides on a winged horse. Character interactions like this used to be limited to the pages of monthly comic books. Joga, in 1978, helped pioneer how comic book adaptations should look and specifically laid the foundation on which Spider-Man's screen legacy would be built.

Which brings us to the man who deserves proper credit for being the first actor to play Peter Parker and Spider-Man on the big screen, exactly twenty-five years before Tobey Maguire got his shot: actor Nicholas Hammond, star of the 1977 American television series *The Amazing Spider-Man*.

The First Silver Screen Spider-Man

Comic book fans in the 1960s and 1970s weren't flocking to movie theaters to see the latest adventures of their favorite superheroes. Instead, they turned to their television sets, where the major networks aired weekly stories structured around Batman (Adam West), Robin (Burt Ward), Wonder Woman (Lynda Carter), the Incredible Hulk (Bill Bixby and Lou Ferrigno), and, yes, Spider-Man (Hammond).

CBS's *The Amazing Spider-Man* was the first prime-time, live-action depiction of Marvel's beloved web slinger. The show aimed to take advantage of Spider-Man's growing popularity due, in part, to his sporadic appearances on the children's television show *The Electric Company* (where he was played by professional dancer Danny Seagren). It also filled a void left by the popular cartoon series *Spider-Man*, which went off the air in June 1970.

Show creator Alvin Boretz and producer Daniel R. Goodman did base *The Amazing Spider-Man* on Stan Lee and Steve Ditko's source materials, casting familiar roles of Aunt May (played by various actresses), J. Jonah Jameson (played by David White, then Robert F. Simon), and Robbie Robertson (Hilly Hicks). Hammond's Peter Parker even worked as a New York City–based photojournalist, masquerading as the crime-fighting Spider-Man for thirteen episodes.

And thanks to a technicality, Hammond gets credit for being the first live-action-movie Spider-Man because multiple feature-length episodes of *The Amazing Spider-Man* television program were packaged as films and released in international markets as theatrical events from 1977 to 1981.

"It's a weird kind of double life because in the U.S., it's a 1970s television series," Hammond said. "But to the whole rest of the world, these were a series of the very first superhero movies most people ever saw. . . . I've done a couple of these Comic-Cons and people turn up with these huge lobby posters that are in German, Italian, and Spanish. And they're all from the movie theaters that ran the shows. I now know how to say Spider-Man in about five different languages."[6]

This worldwide exposure for *The Amazing Spider-Man* meant that Hammond's interpretation of Peter Parker greatly influenced how numerous casual fans came to understand the character of Spider-Man, particularly those who'd never picked up an issue of Marvel Comics. And because of its status as a pioneer, *The Amazing Spider-Man* also established a number of ground rules that creatives would draw on when approaching their own Spidey stories in years to come. Hammond claims that the most important decision made by the creative team on his television show ended up becoming a building block for every Spider-Man adaptation that followed. Much like Stan Lee did in the earliest comic books, Hammond learned you have to ground Peter Parker in reality and make him a compassionate, relatable character. If audiences don't care about the man wearing the mask, your Spider-Man story likely will not achieve its intended goals.

"To their credit, the people at CBS wanted to portray Peter as a real person," Hammond recalls. "In fact, the line I remember they used was, 'We want people to forget that Peter has these powers.' We want them just to become absorbed in his story and his life and what he's going through, this young man with his job, and his allergies, and his school and all that. Where that's an interesting enough story that every now and then, you kind of get surprised when you remember, 'Oh my God, that's right. He also has this *other* persona, and these other powers that have got an influence on his life.'"

Hammond didn't work on *The Amazing Spider-Man* for very long. The show produced only thirteen episodes, and these aired sporadically on the network from 1977 to 1979. Hammond argues that the show struggled to maintain a consistent audience because CBS kept altering the program's airdates, making it incredibly difficult for even the most dedicated fans to find new episodes. (It's not like audiences back then had the ability to set their DVR and catch up with *The Amazing Spider-Man* at their leisure.) Just to give you an idea of how inconsistent CBS's programming on *The Amazing Spider-Man* was, episodes 6 and 7 of the series aired on September 5 and 12, 1978, but episode 8 didn't air until November 25, while episode 9 was held until December 30.

Still, Hammond's experiences putting the show together did teach him and the crew important lessons that would inform Hollywood's live-action interpretations of Spider-Man for the next four decades. The Spider-Man suit, for example. As the Japanese producers on *Supaidāman* would discover around the same time, comic accuracy is very important when it comes to the Spider-Man costume. However, what works on the comic page often needs to go through several stages of experimentation before it translates into reality.

Hammond, for his part, was terrified of the suit.

"It was strange, because I thought, 'Oh boy, how are we going to pull this off without the audience just, you know, wetting their pants with laughter at the sight of me walking down the street in what basically is just spandex and colored Lycra?' And again, it's because I didn't know a huge amount about the character. I'm thinking that I'm just going to look like a fool walking out there wearing this."

The opposite happened, which speaks to the power of Spider-Man and the universal acclaim for this grounded, beloved, relatable hero. Whenever Hammond and *The Amazing Spider-Man* crew had to shoot on the streets to capture scenes of Spidey in action, Hammond remembers being swarmed by fans who were thrilled to see one of their favorite Marvel characters walking around in person. Hammond's jitters washed away as waves of acceptance crashed down on him.

"It was the reaction of others that convinced me there's nothing wrong with putting that blue and red suit on," he said.

Hammond's time in the mask also taught him a very important lesson about inclusion when it comes to Spider-Man, which wouldn't become a central theme of the character and his stories until the animated Oscar winner *Spider-Man: Into the Spider-Verse* communicated that anyone could wear the Spider-Man mask.

"When I got stopped on the street by people [at the time], the demographic, interestingly enough, a very significant percentage were nonwhite. Which was very, very interesting that these fans could relate to a guy who is basically no color when he's in a suit," Hammond said. "And I thought that those little Black kids and Hispanic kids, they can see themselves in that suit because they're not looking at a white face.

"I was invited to speak at some inner city schools," he continued, "and when I saw the enormous popularity of the character, I thought, 'Oh, we're onto something here.' Because [he's] kind of like the first racially-neutral character a lot of these kids have seen on television. That was a significant thing for me."

Years after Hammond learned how Spider-Man's mask allowed just about anyone to pretend that they were him, Marvel Comics introduced Miles Morales, a Hispanic preteen who assumes the Spider-Man mantle after Peter Parker dies. (Temporarily. Heroes never stay dead in comic books.) And Morales's story eventually powered the inclusive message of *Into the Spider-Verse*, which demonstrated that anyone from a 1940s detective (Nicolas Cage) to a talking pig (John Mulaney) was capable of wearing Spider-Man's mask. It's encouraging that this important lesson traces all the way back to Hammond's trendsetting time in the suit.

Hammond confessed that he didn't comprehend at first why the show's producers wanted to cast him. In his own eyes, he was a Serious Thespian, capitalized for emphasis. Hammond played Friedrich in Robert Wise's Oscar-winning *The Sound of Music* and had television credits that included *Gunsmoke* and *Eight Is Enough*. A TV program based on a comic book shouldn't even have been on his professional radar. He recalls his agent telephoning him while he was in the midst of performing a Tom Stoppard play at the Mark Taper Forum in Los Angeles. Hammond assumed it was either a practical joke or a casting error. "I went in kind of thinking, 'Is there like a Nicholas Hamblin or something? Have they put me in by mistake?'"

It wasn't a mistake at all because, as Hammond came to learn, Spider-Man adaptations fail if they forget to focus on Peter Parker and pay too much attention to Spidey. Having a trained actor who's invested in Peter's drama is just as important as having a physically gifted stuntman in the suit for the action scenes. If either side drops the ball, the entire character rings false.

"Now *that's* interesting as a challenge, as an actor," Hammond explained. "You take a guy who has been bitten by a spider and has supernatural powers and is completely implausible, in a realistic sense. And now it's going to be my job to *make* him realistic. And I thought, 'OK, now we're talking!'"

Hammond didn't realize it at the time, but the work he was putting in on the CBS television series *The Amazing Spider-Man* was laying a foundation for future adaptations. Think of the Spider-Man franchise as a towering Manhattan skyscraper. Each planned production, whether staged on television or lingering in the script stage, adds a sturdy layer that bolsters the overall durability of the property. Eventually, we build up to the point where Sam Raimi and his team succeeded in turning Spider-Man into a viable movie screen success. Hammond believes that the main contribution of his 1977 television series *The Amazing Spider-Man* was proving how pivotal it was to cast a skilled actor as Peter.

"Especially guys like Andrew [Garfield] and Tom [Holland]," he said. "Really good actors. And that makes me feel good because they haven't just decided, 'Oh, it doesn't matter who plays Peter, because all anybody's watching this for is to see $50 million worth of special effects.' And I'm very, very pleased that that's not the way they've gone. . . . I would like to think, in some way, that we kind of set the tone for that, and that's been expanded upon and improved upon and enhanced, and everything you can do now with a movie that we weren't able to do shooting an hour show in seven days on practically no money."

Those budgetary constraints likely contributed to one creative decision on *The Amazing Spider-Man* that made sense to Hammond but reportedly bothered Stan Lee, who had sold CBS the rights to the Marvel character. The weekly television episodes didn't attempt to bring any of Spider-Man's classic villains to the screen. Instead of Doctor Octopus or the Lizard, Hammond's Spider-Man often took down petty crooks, small-scale arms dealers, and evil scientists with pedestrian schemes.

"To this day, the jury is out as to whether that decision was right or not. But to me, it made it a lot easier as an actor that all of my adversaries were real," Hammond said. "They weren't fantasy figures. They weren't monsters. They weren't Green Goblin, or something like that. Now, there are a lot of people who didn't like that. They wanted it to stay true to the comic book. Frankly, I think Stan [Lee] was one of them. But it certainly worked better for me, and I think it worked better for the show."

Hammond is right. Stan Lee wasn't a fan of the 1977 television series. Lee went on record numerous times to mildly and diplomatically criticize the show. In a 2011 interview with the Television Academy Foundation, Lee explained, "With *Spider-Man*, I felt that the people who did the live-action series left out the very elements that made the comic book popular. They left out the humor. They left out the human interest, and playing up the personality and characterizations and personal problems," Lee said. "To me, it was just a one-dimensional show. So I was disappointed in it."[7]

The show did, however, earn Nicholas Hammond at least one powerful A-lister as a fan: *Pulp Fiction* director Quentin Tarantino. The Oscar-winning filmmaker appreciates genre storytelling, absorbing exaggerated international action films, grotesque foreign horror features, and kitschy period television from his childhood. Hammond says Tarantino adored *The Amazing Spider-Man*, and he credits the show for landing him a supporting role opposite Leonardo DiCaprio in the director's 2019 drama *Once Upon a Time . . . in Hollywood*.

"When I was in *Once Upon a Time . . . in Hollywood*, Sony gave a party when we were in Cannes," Hammond said. "I was talking to the president of

Sony and I said, 'You might think you're doing the first Spider-Man movies . . .' And then Quentin Tarantino turned to him and said, '*This* is the first Spider-Man!'"

Tarantino even told Hammond that the director's collection of personal film reels includes the two-part pilot for *The Amazing Spider-Man* that was packaged and shipped to international theaters to screen as a feature film. Apparently, Tarantino discovered film canisters containing an old 35-millimeter print of *The Amazing Spider-Man* pilot in the storage closet of a movie theater in Britain. So he did what any film nut and Spider-Man fan would do.

"He got it restored," Hammond said, "and he ran it as a feature at his movie theater in Hollywood, with the Tobey Maguire movie as the second film on the double bill! So a friend of mine walked past it and took a picture of the marquee outside where it said, 'Nicholas Hammond is The Amazing Spider-Man' followed by 'Tobey Maguire as The Amazing Spider-Man.' So Quentin was the first one to honor that."

It was while Hammond was on set for *Once Upon a Time . . . in Hollywood* that the actor almost received an opportunity for which he had been waiting more than forty years. The one-time Peter Parker wanted to make peace with Stan Lee, knowing that Spider-Man's creator didn't love the decisions made by the executives running the television show. And according to Hammond, one of Lee's assistants reached out in 2018 with a message that Stan wanted to get together for lunch. It was a dream invitation, so Hammond immediately appealed to Tarantino and got it cleared to be off set for the afternoon. Hammond was heading out the door to attend this lunch when he received a devastating phone call. Lee wasn't feeling well, according to the publisher's assistant, and was heading to the hospital. The Marvel legend never left the hospital and died shortly after.

"I came that close to seeing him one final time," Hammond said. "Because I really wanted to . . . there was unfinished business there. He'd done a couple of interviews over the years where he thought the show was crap because we hadn't done what he wanted it to be. I just wanted to explain to him, like we're talking right now, [that] these are the reasons why we couldn't execute his vision the way he saw it, you know? Sure, Sony can throw $200 million at it, and they can do anything they want. They can have people come from Mars! But we just simply couldn't do that. We didn't have the money. And we didn't have . . . that wasn't what we were doing. That's all I wanted to say to him. To just say, 'It wasn't out of disrespect to you and this wonderful thing you created.'

"He had such a sense of ownership," Hammond concluded, regarding Stan Lee's intimate relationship with Spider-Man. "He always said, of all his characters, Peter was the one that was really most based on him. A guy who was a bit of a nerd growing up. A little bit of an outsider. The fantasy is, for nerdy guys, 'What if I suddenly had the power to be something other than a nerdy guy?' And I think he felt that's what he was trying to put up on the page."

That spot-on conclusion goes a long way toward explaining why Stan Lee became more involved with Spider-Man's journey to the big screen in the years that followed *The Amazing Spider-Man* television show. You can sense that Lee regretted being out of the loop on the creative decisions for the TV program, so he took a firm grip on the reins of the next chapter of Spider-Man developments to make sure that his vision of Spidey and his universe would be retained.

But it would be far more of a struggle than he probably ever imagined.

CHAPTER THREE
CANNON FODDER AND JAMES CAMERON'S BIG SWING

By the early 1980s, when Stan Lee sought collaborators to help bring Marvel's most popular comic book characters to the big screen, the roster of viable studio dance partners was slim. It's hard to remember a time when this was ever the case. In 2021, the Hollywood studios distribution calendars are clogged with superhero properties, and it's rare when you have a given calendar month that doesn't include at least one comic book–inspired blockbuster.

Not in the 1980s. Richard Donner's 1978 feature *Superman*, produced and distributed by Warner Bros., may have helped audiences believe that a man could fly. Outside of that origin story and its 1981 sequel, though, the studios weren't yet mining the pages of comic books for lucrative film franchises and wouldn't commit to that path for another fifteen years.

Because of Hollywood's lackluster appetite, this period of Spider-Man's film development ends up being marked by a series of false starts and misguided endeavors. One of the earliest attempts was producer Steve Krantz's failed bid to sell Stan Lee on a musical production that might have had either Rolling Stones lead singer Mick Jagger or "Rocket Man" singer-songwriter Elton John in the Spider-Man costume. Orion Pictures also held the theatrical rights to Spider-Man for a brief amount of time in the early 1980s and chipped away at a horror pitch with B-movie master Roger Corman. Orion's deal with Marvel allegedly fizzled because Corman and Stan Lee never saw eye to eye on a suitable budget. Although he didn't get to play with Peter

Parker, Corman eventually went on to executive produce a low-budget adaptation of Marvel's *The Fantastic Four* in 1994, which never received an official release but has since become a curiosity that superhero fans circulate using bootleg videos.

Things started to look up for Spider-Man's film potential in 1985 when Cannon Films spent $225,000 to license the rights to the Marvel character so they could develop a proper theatrical film. However, the term "proper" and "Cannon" don't really belong in the same sentence.

Since its inception in 1967, Cannon Films had developed a reputation in the industry for drastically limiting production budgets to maximize profits on mediocre films. The independent studio hit its stride, so to speak, under executives Menahem Golan and Yoram Globus, Israeli cousins who assumed control of Cannon in 1979 for the purchase price of $500,000.

Golan and Globus were infamous for investing in marketable ideas, attaching the names of major talents to their proposals, and then turning profit by preselling the international distribution rights. The productions themselves were often an afterthought.

"They didn't spend too much time nurturing projects," explained documentary filmmaker Mark Hartley, who captured the rise and fall of Cannon in his 2014 feature *Electric Boogaloo: The Wild, Untold Story of Cannon Films.* "Quantity seemed more important than quality."[1]

Proving that they knew very little about the material they were optioning, Golan and Globus's initial pitch for a Spider-Man movie was a creature feature written by Leslie Stevens (*Outer Limits*) and helmed by film director Tobe Hooper (*Poltergeist*) that would have turned Peter Parker into an actual tarantula–human hybrid. At the beginning of this story, Peter Parker gets bombarded with radiation by a mad scientist named Doctor Zork (the legendary spider bite from Spidey's origin doesn't happen). Once Parker mutates into the man–spider monstrosity, Zork tries to convince him to lead an army of creatures against humanity. Peter rejects the idea and instead battles each of Zork's creations in an escalating series of confrontations. The script's characterizations resembled "Spider-Man" in name only. Stan Lee intervened on this project, thankfully, as it might have torpedoed the web slinger's movie future if it ever got produced. Lee instead convinced Cannon to workshop a script by two writers he had come to trust: Ted Newsom and John Brancato.

"I had a meeting with Stan, and we just got along right away. We talked about pizza joints in New York. He gave me a cigar. We hung out," Brancato said, reminiscing on the early stages of their collaboration.[2]

Because Lee got along so well with Newsom and Brancato, he eventually dangled a potential Marvel assignment in front of them. Not Spider-Man, though. First came *Sergeant Fury and His Howling Commandos*. The duo quickly returned with a feature-length script that Lee loved. In his mind, he'd finally found screenwriters who could bring the authenticity that he was hoping to instill into his Marvel adaptations. "Shortly thereafter, [Lee] said, 'Well, we got this weird deal with this crappy movie company, Cannon Films. Let's see if we can do Spider-Man right,'" Brancato remembers. "And then we did."

They certainly did. The Cannon Films screenplay credited to Newsom and Brancato is the first theatrically intended script to grasp Spider-Man's core ingredients. Almost every Spider-Man script that follows it owes a debt of gratitude to the structure, characterizations, and tone captured by these fledgling screenwriters. Brancato admits that their script existed because Stan Lee hated the 1977 CBS television show and the 1978 Japanese program, which he felt "took the entirely wrong direction" with Spider-Man. This time out, the Marvel guru was adamant about shaping the screenplay he had commissioned.

Unlike the 1977 television show, Newsom and Brancato's story utilized recognizable villains from the pages of Spidey's comic books. Unlike the

Japanese series, it embraced Peter Parker's traditional origin story and all of the trappings that came with being a financially struggling student and free-lance photographer. Newsom and Brancato presented Lee with a dingy, dirty take on the Spider-Man lore, with stylized tweaks meant to appeal to a 1980s audience.

When asked which existing films they used as touchstones to set the vibe of their Spider-Man story, Brancato said, "Obviously, I love things like *Taxi Driver*. I grew up in New York, so I sort of felt like I knew how disgusting the city was back in the '70s. That was my era there. I had friends who were punks, so that whole culture was in my mind."

But this script definitely told a tried-and-true Spider-Man adventure that took its cues directly from Marvel's comics. Peter Parker attends Empire State University, where the college student pines after the pretty Liz Allen (described on the page as "the single bright spot in this otherwise drab environment"[3]) and confides in his best friend and fellow classmate, Harry Osborn. Parker lives in a one-room New York City apartment, which comes with a convenient skylight that leads to the building's roof: perfect for when the hero needs to exit quickly and web sling around the city. Given the fact that Newsom and Brancato were the first screenwriters attempting to work Spider-Man's comic book origin into a two-hour feature film, though, they also were the first storytellers to encounter some of the problems that come with that assignment. Brancato said one major challenge facing almost any Spidey adaptation lies in balancing full origin stories for both the hero and the movie's chosen villain, in this case, Dr. Otto Octavius.

"Structurally, that was always going to be awkward," he said. "The origin stories take up the first two thirds of the movie."

They solved that by having the same laboratory disaster—the explosion of a particle-acceleration device known as a cyclotron—cause both Otto's and Peter's transformations. Variations on this solution would crop back up in Marc Webb's 2012 reboot *The Amazing Spider-Man*, which went out of its way to connect Peter Parker (Andrew Garfield) to his antagonists. When Peter gets bitten by the radioactive spider in that series of films, he's attending a school field trip to Norman Osborn's Oscorp laboratories. It's Peter, in those films, who provides Dr. Curt Connors (Rhys Ifans) with the last piece of a scientific formula the doctor needs to regenerate his missing limb—turning the scientist into a sinister creature dubbed the Lizard. Later in the *Amazing Spider-Man* story, Osborn's son, Harry (Dane DeHaan), ends up becoming the Green Goblin, Spider-Man's chief antagonist.

Plotting like this can be viewed as detrimental. It makes Peter Parker's world seem small and these life-altering events too coincidental when they happen only to characters already in Peter's close-knit circle. Almost all superhero franchises wrestle with these narrative obstacles to a certain degree, though, especially when laying out the obligatory origin story.

Elsewhere, the 1985 *Spider-Man* script is steeped in colorful references that are specific to the decade. Brancato says that they envisioned actor John Cusack as their Peter Parker. By that time, Cusack had filled some awkward teenage roles, appearing alongside Anthony Michael Hall and Molly Ringwald in John Hughes's teen comedy *Sixteen Candles*. He'd also graduated to leading roles in Rob Reiner's *The Sure Thing* and Steve Holland's *Better Off Dead*, so stepping into the lead role in a Spider-Man movie wouldn't have felt like a stretch. Newsom and Brancato also include a lengthy sequence in their script where Spider-Man guest stars on *Late Night with David Letterman* after becoming an overnight sensation in New York City and impresses the studio audience by doing "Stupid Human Tricks," a trademark gimmick on the talk show.

"I had an 'in' at Letterman because I knew a bunch of the writers for the show and basically thought we could get David Letterman [to cameo]," Brancato admitted.

Finally, in the classic Spider-Man comic book sequence where Peter tests his extraordinary powers by lasting one minute in the ring with a professional wrestler, Brancato and Newsom included World Wrestling Federation superstar Hulk Hogan. That sounds like optimistic casting, but the screenwriters actually penciled "The Hulkster" into their story because Hogan was friends with Stan Lee, and they felt confident they could get him to appear on-screen.

"The power of Stan Lee was not to be underestimated. Everybody liked Stan Lee," Brancato said. "Stan was very close with Lou Ferrigno back from their days on *The Incredible Hulk*. He had an 'in' on the whole big-guy, wrestling, macho world. Which he thought was really funny, because he was a skinny kid from Brooklyn. But they all worshipped him."

Unfortunately, the *Spider-Man* screenplay that Newsom and Brancato wrote with Stan Lee's input and blessing didn't have a prayer of getting made—especially not at Cannon Films.

"One of the insane things, when I read the script [now], was how unbelievably CGI [computer graphics imagery]-driven and expensive it was, at a time when none of that stuff would have been possible," Brancato said. "It was like, 'Let's just write it the way it should be, and see what happens, or see how close they can get.'"

One of those "CGI-driven" sequences would have been the film's explosive finale. In it, one of Doctor Octopus's experiments would have lifted the entire Empire State University science center up off the ground and into the clouds, forcing Spider-Man and Doc Ock to battle in a flying building that eventually would plummet toward Central Park. Not only would this sequence have cost a fortune, but budget-conscious practical effects would have limited how realistic the set piece could look. Not that Cannon even thought that far in advance on this *Spider-Man* movie.

"Cannon never had an intention of making a good film," Brancato admitted. "For the most part, it was always 'How much can we pre-sell? How can we have the lowest possible budget, and the highest possible box office?'"

In Brancato's opinion, Cannon Films signified its mediocre expectations for *Spider-Man* when they attached *Invasion USA* director Joe Zito to their script around 1985.

Don't tell Joe Zito this, though.

Zito admits he came from humble beginnings as a filmmaker. His directorial debut, the 1975 drama *Abduction*, offered a loose retelling of the events of Patty Hearst's kidnapping. The drama worked as a calling card to land him future gigs. By 1984, Zito was improving as a filmmaker, having delivered a satisfying slasher sequel in *Friday the 13th: The Final Chapter*, a financial hit for Paramount Pictures. Cannon quickly recruited Zito to direct Chuck Norris's 1984 war thriller *Missing in Action* as well as the follow-up, 1985's *Invasion USA*. Both became significant moneymakers for Golan and Globus, elevating Zito to a "Golden Boy" status around the Cannon Films offices. So when Zito found himself riding in an elevator car with Golan one fateful morning, he took his shot. He'd recently read in the Hollywood trade papers that Cannon had acquired the rights to Spider-Man with the intention of bankrolling a comic book adaptation. Zito recalls turning to his boss and saying four fateful words: "I want Spider-Man."[4]

He didn't get it. At least, not right away. The way Zito remembers the conversation, Golan asked for twenty-four hours before making a final decision. This was strange to Zito because he said the impulsive Cannon executive was known for making deals on the spot, usually on little more than a gut instinct. Zito can't confirm, but he thinks that Golan had to run the idea of giving Spider-Man to a new director past Tobe Hooper, somehow talking the *Poltergeist* director off his in-development Spider-Man horror feature. Zito swears he wasn't trying to steal another director's project. He claims that at the time, he wasn't fully aware that Hooper even *was* attached to *Spider-Man*. Everything worked out in the end, to a certain degree, for both filmmakers. Hooper moved on to *The Texas Chainsaw Massacre 2*, while Golan gave Zito *Spider-Man* and an estimated $20 million budget. The director was off to the races.

From the very beginning, Zito wanted his Spider-Man movie to be drastically different from the films he had been making at Cannon (in other words, low-budget features that cut corners whenever possible). He wanted to inject more style into *Spider-Man*, which would match the mature vision he had for the character. To hear him describe it, Zito's picture could have been close in spirit to the *Batman* movie Tim Burton eventually made at Warner Bros. in 1989—even though Batman and Spider-Man really have nothing in common tonally.

Zito traveled to Cannon's studio spaces in London for preproduction on *Spider-Man* and immediately began assembling a high-end technical crew. The team spent weeks testing experimental ways to replicate Spider-Man's unique comic book powers in live action on-screen. They knew they needed to make the hero's wall crawling and web swinging look believable if the movie had any shot at success. Zito also had grandiose plans for his ensemble and allowed himself to think bigger than his budget would allow. He wanted Bob Hoskins, fresh off his turn in Terry Gilliam's Oscar-nominated *Brazil*, as his Otto Octavius. He hoped to cast Katherine Hepburn or Lauren Bacall as Aunt May. And Zito swears that Stan Lee consistently lobbied for the part of *Daily Bugle* publisher J. Jonah Jameson.

Zito's biggest wish? He wanted Tom Cruise to play Peter Parker. In Zito's defense, the twenty-four-year-old actor wasn't yet a blockbuster movie star. Cruise had a massive year in 1983, appearing as a troublemaking Greaser in Francis Ford Coppola's *The Outsiders*, as an ambitious high school football player in *All the Right Moves*, and as a preppy do-gooder breaking his parents' rules in *Risky Business*. What Zito didn't know was that Cruise was about to reach Hollywood's stratosphere once Tony Scott's *Top Gun* opened on May 16, 1986.

Landing Cruise for a Cannon-backed *Spider-Man* film was going to be a long shot. Zito understood this. So he had a backup plan in place in the form of Scott Leva, a stuntman and stunt coordinator whose credits included Richard Donner's *Superman* (1978), Daniel Petrie's *Fort Apache the Bronx* (1981), and Ron Howard's mermaid comedy *Splash* (1984). But it was Leva's physical stature—the former champion gymnast stood at a modest height and possessed a wiry frame—that made him a dead ringer for Spider-Man. In between movie gigs, Leva stayed busy as a professional cosplayer, getting hired out to officially appear as Spider-Man at parties and parades. Marvel Comics fans would recognize Leva for his appearance as an unmasked Peter Parker on the unique live-action cover of *The Amazing Spider-Man* issue number 262, published in 1985.

That's not even Leva's coolest Spidey-related accomplishment. His professional cosplay duties frequently included visiting sick children in New York City hospitals, hoping to distract them from their ailments. Leva tells a beautiful story about one boy he encountered who refused to believe he was really Spider-Man despite the stuntman completing backflips and performing handstands right there in the kid's hospital room. Knowing there was only one way to convince this child, Leva removed his mask, a practice that was forbidden by the company that had hired him. Leva's resemblance to Parker won the boy over. Returning to Marvel Comics' Manhattan offices, a visibly shaken Leva shared this emotional story with writer Roger Stern, who turned around and used it as inspiration for "The Kid Who Collects Spider-Man," one of the most memorable stories in *The Amazing Spider-Man* history.[5]

Leva never got the opportunity to play Spider-Man for Zito because the wheels on the director's *Spider-Man* quickly started falling off, largely because

Cannon Films didn't know how to manage its money. While Zito was deep into preproduction on his big-budget adaptation of Spider-Man, Cannon acquired two other high-profile pop culture intellectual properties (IPs): DC's Superman and Hasbro's He-Man. In an effort to divert proper funding into the studio's planned features *Superman IV: The Quest for Peace* and Dolph Lundgren's *Masters of the Universe*, Cannon slashed Zito's budget in half from $20 million to $10 million.

It was a death blow.

The director jokingly estimated that he could have made two traditional Cannon movies (translation: shlock) for that remaining $10 million budget. Typical Cannon features aimed for $5 million budgets, as ordered by Golan and Globus. But Zito also knew he couldn't do his dream version of *Spider-Man* for $10 million, which is all that Menahem Golan was offering. Heartbroken and frustrated, Zito walked away.

The director's departure didn't shut *Spider-Man* down. At least, not right away. Despite the fact that the company appeared to be bleeding cash, Cannon Films mounted several halfhearted, last-ditch efforts to keep the comic book production afloat. Rewrites were ordered so that a lower-budget *Spider-Man* could be filmed on existing movie sets that Cannon already owned. Replacement director Albert Pyun was tapped to replace Zito, while screenwriters Don Michael Paul and Ethan Wiley were hired to reimagine the story. The requested changes ended up being drastic, such as removing Doctor Octopus from the Newsom and Brancato script and replacing him with a newly created villain.

"There were a couple of things—baggage, you might say—that came with the project," Wiley told *Empire* magazine in 2017. "What I was told was that [Cannon] owned the Spider-Man character, but there was some ambiguity as to whether they owned the *other* characters from the comic. That didn't make sense to me. . . . I was instructed not to use any of the villains like Doctor Octopus. So for my script, I then invented my own Spider-Man villain, which was fun."[6]

It was all for naught. Production on *Spider-Man* ground to a halt as Cannon barreled toward bankruptcy. In 1988, Italian financier Giancarlo Parretti paid $200 million to acquire Cannon and renamed the new studio Pathe Communications. The following year, Parretti acquired 21st Century Distribution Company and appointed Golan the studio's CEO. As part of an incentive deal, Parretti let Golan keep the rights to both Captain America and Spider-Man at 21st Century. Despite his inability to shape those rights into successful movies, Golan understood the value of the Marvel IP.

What Menahem Golan didn't realize was that another high-profile savior was about to step up to the plate and take his own swing at Spider-Man, which again could have drastically altered the trajectory of old webhead's cinematic history—and Hollywood history in general.

James Cameron Wants Spider-Man, Gets a Sinking Ship

Spider-Man's journey to the big screen can best be described as a roller-coaster ride, often moving at unsafe speeds through exhilarating highs and debilitating lows. But a few years before Columbia Pictures finally secured the Spider-Man property for good in 1999, powerhouse writer-director James Cameron cobbled together a serious pitch for the character's rights, which would have altered a number of important Hollywood time lines had this dream project come together.

Cameron's obsession with Spider-Man traces back to his childhood. An avid sketcher, Cameron patterned his early artwork after Marvel artist and Spider-Man cocreator Steve Ditko. As an eighth grader, Cameron even committed to rigorous physical exercise in hopes of sculpting his body into Peter Parker's heroic frame. "I was trying to figure out how to make wrist shooters and I was doing pull-ups and stuff so that I could jump around on buildings. If parkour had been a thing back then, I would have been doing it, I'm sure," Cameron said.[7]

The director first started poking around the film rights to Spider-Man and other Marvel characters in the late 1980s after delivering back-to-back blockbusters in *Aliens* (1986) and *The Abyss* (1989). A savvy businessman as well as a visionary filmmaker, Cameron realized that the potential of Marvel's IP was being squandered in the hands of Menahem Golan and what he referred to as the "low-budget, piece-of-junk outfit"[8] known as Cannon.

Before he got his hands on the wall crawler, Cameron circled the idea of producing the first adaptation of Marvel's *X-Men* comics, which his wife at the time, *Point Break* and *Zero Dark Thirty* director Kathryn Bigelow, would have helmed. Veteran *X-Men* comics writer Chris Claremont remembers going with Stan Lee to Cameron's production offices at Lightstorm Entertainment in 1990 to pitch the blockbuster filmmaker on an X-Men treatment. The proposal had a bizarre connection to Joe Zito's failed Spider-Man production at Cannon, as Claremont also envisioned the stout Bob Hoskins in the role of Wolverine. Angela Bassett, meanwhile, was considered to step into the role of the weather-manipulating mutant Storm.

"Just think about this for a minute: James Cameron's *X-Men*. Directed by Kathryn Bigelow. That's what we were playing," Claremont told an audience at a Columbia University panel in 2012. "So we're chatting. And at one point Stan looks at Cameron and says, 'I hear you like Spider-Man.' Cameron's eyes lit up. And they start talking. And talking. And talking. About 20 minutes later, all the Lightstorm guys and I are looking at each other, and we all know the X-Men deal has just evaporated."[9]

James Cameron had fully embraced Spider-Man.

But moving ahead on a Cameron-led Spider-Man picture wasn't going to be that easy. For starters, the character's rights remained cloudy, with multiple parties claiming a piece of the hero's pie. And at Cameron's urging, a new company, Carolco, officially entered into the already complicated mix. Carolco Pictures launched in 1975 as a financier for low-budget pictures. In the 1980s, the moderately successful company earned the nickname "The House that Rambo Built" after collaborating with Sylvester Stallone on 1982's *First Blood* and its sequels. As Carolco developed, it graduated to profitable collaborations with box office draws such as Kevin Costner (*Field of Dreams*), Arnold Schwarzenegger (*Total Recall*), and Mel Gibson (*Air America*). When the company's executives were presented with the opportunity to acquire the rights to a *Terminator* sequel in 1990, Carolco jumped, putting them back in business with Cameron (who had worked on the screenplay for *Rambo: First Blood—Part II* in 1985).

Cameron's request that Carolco purchase the Spider-Man rights in 1990 cost the studio $5 million. It was a solid investment for Cameron's loyalty, and it immediately began paying indirect dividends. Cameron's *Terminator 2: Judgment Day*, released in 1991, became that year's highest-grossing film as well as the most successful film in Carolco's history.

Spider-Man's rights became available in 1990 because, surprise, 21st Century Films needed money. Menahem Golan split the wall crawler's rights between three entities as a means of generating quick cash for his struggling studio. Television rights to the character went to Viacom. Home video rights landed at Columbia. Finally, Carolco scored Spider-Man's theatrical rights. Cameron had his dream project and immediately got to work on an extensive treatment for a feature-length origin film.

Cameron's take on Spider-Man is fascinating. He largely stays loyal to the Marvel Comics origin story and adheres to the general blueprint Ted Newsom and John Brancato offered in 1985. But he also makes a few significant modifications. Cameron's Peter Parker is an outcast high school student and a science whiz with a romantic crush on his gorgeous classmate, Mary Jane

Watson. The orphaned kid lives with his Aunt May and Uncle Ben, and the latter tragically dies after Peter fails to halt a robber.[10] To this extent, Cameron's treatment follows all of the familiar story beats. It also took a page right out of Peter Parker's playbook by making the story, the characters, and the world feel as relatable and real as possible.

"I wanted to make something that had a gritty reality to it. Superheroes, in general, always came off as fanciful to me. I wanted to do something that would have been more in the vein of *Terminator* and *Aliens*," Cameron explained. "It's New York. It's now. A guy gets bitten by a spider. He turns into this kid with these powers, and he has this fantasy of being Spider-Man. [But] he makes a suit, and it's terrible, you know? And then he has to improve the suit. His biggest problem is the damn suit. Things like that. I wanted to ground it in reality and grounded in a kind of universal human experience."[11]

But Cameron wasn't afraid to detour away from the do-gooder mentality that's baked into a traditional Spider-Man story. When his Peter Parker adjusts to his new powers, for example, Cameron describes it as the teenager being beckoned by the darkness of the evening. Cameron writes in his treatment that he planned to "explore the idea that the lure of the dark replaces fear of the dark . . . that the dark becomes a comforting, nurturing place for Peter, rather than a place of uncertainty."[12]

"The whole superpower thing was, in my mind, a great metaphor for that untapped reservoir potential that people have, that they don't recognize in themselves," he said. "And it was always also, in my mind, a metaphor for puberty and all the changes to your body. Your anxieties about society, about society's expectations, your relationships with the gender of choice that you're attracted to. All those things."[13]

Naturally, this is a theme that gets explored by future Spider-Man directors Sam Raimi and Marc Webb, but Cameron gets credit for being the first to connect those coming-of-age dots in a Spider-Man origin script.

Cameron's most significant change comes in Peter's ability to create his webbing. Unlike in the comics, where the intelligent high school student invents mechanical web shooters that are worn on his wrists, Cameron suggested that the webs organically come out of "a dark shape, the size and color of a rose-thorn"[14] that emerges from Peter's skin. Cameron admits that these "spinnerets" are horrifying to Peter, and the teenager compares himself to a character in Kafka's *Metamorphosis*.

Stan Lee didn't mind. The Marvel executive befriended Cameron during this process and approved all of the changes he suggested making to the hero's signature abilities. "I wrote with Stan Lee's blessing," Cameron said. "[This] was one of his personal favorite characters, and I didn't make a move without asking him permission."[15]

Cameron didn't plunge directly into his Spider-Man adaptation, though. The director and his go-to leading man Arnold Schwarzenegger followed up *Terminator 2* with the spy thriller *True Lies*. As that shoot concluded, *Variety* ran a report on September 1, 1993, that Cameron's script for Spider-Man finally had been completed and submitted to Carolco.[16] Casting rumors immediately swirled, with Schwarzenegger's name attached to the role of Doctor Octopus and *What's Eating Gilbert Grape?* star Leonardo DiCaprio in the running for Peter Parker.

How close do we think DiCaprio came to slipping on Spidey's tights? "Not very close, but there was a screenplay," the megastar told *Empire* magazine years after the fact during a 2015 interview. "I know [Cameron] was semi-serious about doing it at some point, but I don't remember any further talks about it. We had a couple of chats. I think there was a screenplay that I read, but I don't remember. This was 20 years ago!"[17]

Cameron didn't get very far either, as the financial woes and legal issues that had stunted Spider-Man's progress for the better part of a decade suffocated any hope the *Terminator* director had of getting his production off the ground. Menahem Golan filed a lawsuit against Carolco in 1993 over his producing credits on the still-in-development *Spider-Man*, mainly because he feared that the executives were trying to squeeze him out. Meanwhile, Carolco sued Viacom and Columbia in an attempt to attain the television and home video rights for Spider-Man that Golan had sold, prompting Viacom and Columbia to countersue.

Ultimately, two major bankruptcies sealed James Cameron's fate with Spider-Man. Menahem Golan's 21st Century, facing bankruptcy, sold its film library to MGM Studios in 1995. This included all current drafts and completed versions of Spider-Man screenplays, meaning MGM now owned Spidey's rights albeit temporarily. Around the same time, Carolco filed for bankruptcy. As if that wasn't enough, the film studio 20th Century Fox, which had distributed *Aliens* (1986), *The Abyss* (1989), and *True Lies* (1994), stepped in and claimed that Cameron remained under contract as a director for the studio and that they wanted to be part of his next project—whatever that project might be.

Cameron had one last Hail Mary pass to throw. He pleaded with 20th Century Fox to make a bid on the wall crawler so he could complete his script. But Fox hesitated, unwilling to get into the tangled legal mess surrounding Spidey's rights as well as the potential bidding war that would ensue against rival studios and producers.

"Peter Chernin just wouldn't go to bat for it," Cameron said about 20th Century Fox's then chief and CEO. "He didn't want to get into a legal fight over it. And I'm like, 'Are you kidding? This thing could be worth, I don't know, a *billion* dollars!' [laughs] Ten billion dollars later . . ."[18]

It's hard to truly fathom how different James Cameron's career and the careers of several influential people in his hemisphere would have been if he'd succeeded in making a Spider-Man film around 1995. For one thing, *Spider-Man* would have delayed—and possibly prevented—Cameron from making the film he eventually transitioned over to: 1997's *Titanic*, with his preferred Peter Parker, Leonardo DiCaprio. That historical epic went on to win a record-tying eleven Academy Awards, including Best Picture and Director, crowning Cameron "the king of the world" in the process. *Titanic* catapulted DiCaprio and costar Kate Winslet to superstardom and shattered countless box office records—records Cameron held until he broke them again with his original sci-fi thriller *Avatar* in 2009. You can argue that none of this happens if 20th Century Fox takes Cameron's advice and bets on Spider-Man instead of the unsinkable ocean liner. It probably means that Columbia doesn't get the chance to grab Spidey's rights in 1999, a decision that would change the face of that studio for the foreseeable future.

Cameron, for his part, appears to have no regrets. "When I was a kid, to me, there were all the superheroes, and then there was Spider-Man," he told audience members at the 2014 Hero Complex Film Festival in Los Angeles. "So, having not gotten Spider-Man, it's not like I'm looking around for the next comic book character."[19]

He wasn't, but Columbia Pictures was. And in the next stage of development, Spider-Man was about to attain something he hadn't yet had since Stan Lee started shopping the rights to the character in the 1980s: stability.

CHAPTER FOUR

MARVEL'S ORIGINAL BIG THREE

Given what we know about the mainstream audience's appetite for Marvel Studios films and television shows, it's hard to believe there was ever a time when the biggest Hollywood movie studios would balk at the idea of collaborating with "The House That Stan Lee Built." Go back merely two decades, though, and you'll hear production horror stories that confirm that adapting a feature-length film, let alone a mega-budget blockbuster, out of a Marvel property was an uphill battle.

Hollywood wasn't suffering a shortage of comic book adaptations in the 1990s, but most of the superhero projects attempted by the major studios during that decade were experiments conducted by curious producers who were trying to figure out what worked in the genre and what didn't. DC Comics' brooding Batman dominated the decade after Michael Keaton and director Tim Burton brought the caped crusader to the big screen in Warner Bros.' 1989 blockbuster. Keaton and Burton remained with the franchise for one sequel, *Batman Returns*, in 1992 before handing the keys to the late Joel Schumacher. The director helmed two commercially successful Batman sequels in 1995 and 1997. But because they fell short of the quality bar that Burton's Batman films had established, Warner Bros. temporarily put the Caped Crusader on ice.

Meanwhile, other studios bet big on the lure of bankable celebrities playing superhero characters who weren't exactly household names. Sylvester Stallone was riding high on the momentum of back-to-back action hits in *Demolition Man* and *Cliffhanger* when he stepped into the title role of Judge Dredd for a 1995 sci-fi thriller that ended up earning $113 million at the worldwide box office—a soft hit for Buena Vista Pictures. Far fewer ticket buyers showed up to watch *Baywatch* beauty Pamela Anderson play Dark Horse comic book character Barb Wire in 1996. Yet Anderson still fared better than NBA superstar Shaquille O'Neal, who was playing center for the Los Angeles Lakers and participating on the 1996 Summer Olympics USA Basketball "Dream Team" when he agreed to star as a weapons designer who creates a suit of armor and becomes the towering crime fighter Steel. Critics and audiences largely agreed that Shaq should have stayed focused on basketball, as *Steel* received vicious reviews and earned only $1.7 million at the domestic box office.

As rival studios spent valuable resources treading water in the comic book adaptation pool, Marvel Comics finally dipped its feet into the deep end and started to make waves of its own.

Modern Marvel moviegoers likely know the name Kevin Feige and properly credit the studio president as the mastermind behind the MCU. Under Feige's leadership, Marvel Studios has constructed an expansive, multi-film and television saga that revolves around the company's vast roster of superheroes. "It was always our hope at Marvel Studios to be able to pull off, even a little bit, in a cinematic form what publishing had been able to do in the comics for 70-plus years," Feige said about the MCU. "The genius of Stan Lee, Jack Kirby, and Steve Ditko and all of the spectacular artists and writers is that they can tell, honestly, stories as big as The Big Bang and the foundation of the universe itself, and the foundation of reality, *and* tell something as small and moving as Peter Parker's origin story."[1]

Long before Feige assumed control, however, Marvel Studios belonged to famed Hollywood producer Avi Arad. And it's not an exaggeration to say that there might not *be* a "Kevin Feige" if Arad didn't precede him. Feige deserves credit for guiding Marvel Studios to its current summit. But he constructed the existing studio on a foundation that had been laid down by Arad and his partners more than a decade earlier. Arad walked through the minefield of big-budget studio comic book productions so that Feige eventually could run.

"We didn't call it 'The MCU.' But in the conversations with Kevin [at the time], we knew one day we'd be able to connect all of our characters and create the biggest franchise in history," Arad said. "And we were right. We're bigger than *Star Wars* now."[2]

Arad is the one who picked up the proverbial pieces of a disorganized Marvel Entertainment Group in 1993 and placed them under the singular banner Marvel Films, where he served as the company's initial president and CEO. Avi wasn't the first person to push the concept of Marvel Comics characters in major theatrical productions. Stan Lee had been singing that tune for decades. But Arad gets the lion's share of the credit for the company's sizable early successes because he aggressively pursued licensing deals at the major film studios, believing that Marvel's IP was strong enough to carry proper movie adaptations. It was Arad who argued with financiers during Marvel's prolonged and painful bankruptcy filings in 1997, convincing the executives in charge of the purse strings that "Spider-Man alone is a billion-dollar entity,"[3] so the rights to the company's full roster of characters should not be sold for anything less. Also, preliminary deals struck by Arad at the major studios in the late 1990s led to the production of big-budget comic book features, such as Bryan Singer's *X-Men* (2000), Mark Steven Johnson's *Daredevil* (2003), its spin-off feature *Elektra* (2005), Ang Lee's *Hulk* (2003), and, of course, Sam Raimi's *Spider-Man* in 2002.

Not to mention the fact that it was Arad who hired Feige at Marvel Studios in the first place.

"Kevin Feige was my right hand, and left hand, man," Arad said about the ace Marvel executive, who, at the time they met, was working as an assistant for uber-producer Lauren Shuler Donner on the first *X-Men* movie. "I got to know him. I fell in love with him. I begged [the Donners] to let me have him after that movie. And thanks go to Dick Donner, who said, 'He's a good boy. Sure. Take him.' The rest is history."[4]

The specific details of Arad's start at Marvel—which at the time was known as Marvel Entertainment Group—could fill another book. For the benefit of Spider-Man's story, you only need to understand a few key details about Arad, for he was the wall crawler's loudest supporter and most passionate champion in the filmmaking community, a "true believer," as Stan Lee often called him.

Arad was born in Poland in 1948 but raised in Israel by his mother and father, two Holocaust survivors. As a teenager, Arad served in the Israeli Defense Forces and fought in that country's Six-Day War in 1967, sustaining a devastating injury that shortened his military service and left him hospitalized for fifteen months. Having moved to the United States in 1970, Arad studied industrial management at New York's Hofstra University, paying his way through school with an assortment of odd jobs. His life drastically changed for the better, though, when Arad partnered with fellow Israeli business tycoon Isaac "Ike" Perlmutter in the toy manufacturing business Toy Biz beginning in 1993. This decision placed Arad on the eventual path to Hollywood stardom, as he and Perlmutter would come to be two of the most influential figures in the early days of Marvel's moviemaking efforts.

Perlmutter knew nothing of comics when he and Arad started working together. Instead, his best idea for the duo involved noted sex therapist Dr. Ruth Westheimer.

"My partner Ike made his fortune in [corporate] closeouts. Overproduction. Things like that," Arad revealed. "Friends of mine wanted me to visit him. He wanted to show me something. He showed me the [board game] for *Dr. Ruth's Game of Good Sex*."

Arad still chuckles at that scenario, remembering how skeptical he was of his partner's pitch. Perlmutter insisted that everyone loved Dr. Ruth, telling

Arad that the game was a sound investment. Ike apparently did an outstanding impersonation of Westheimer, which made Arad laugh, but it wasn't enough to sway the man's opinion and get him to invest.

Instead, Arad picked up a catalog that was sitting on Perlmutter's desk for the existing company Toy Biz, which Perlmutter had purchased in 1990 after the company filed for bankruptcy. Arad was intrigued. He grew up loving comic books and had spent time designing toys for Hasbro, Mattel, and Tyco earlier in his career. Perlmutter's immediate plan was to liquidate Toy Biz, which made Arad bristle, primarily because the company produced action figures based on Marvel Entertainment's many characters. Avi's toy-designing instincts kicked in. He recognized a golden goose and begged Ike not to slaughter it.

"I showed Ike the [catalog] page with the X-Men. I said, 'Do you know who they are?' He said, 'No.' These are the X-Men. In my opinion, these are the strongest properties after Spider-Man," Arad explained. "Ike said, 'What do you do with this?' Uhh, you make a television show! Because all toys were sold on syndicated shows in the great days of TV syndication for children."

Arad pleaded with Perlmutter not to liquidate, based only on Toy Biz's Marvel partnership. Perlmutter reportedly replied, "What's Marvel?" But he was willing to listen. Perlmutter was a shrewd businessman who also identified a debilitating problem facing toy manufacturers. Small companies lost a significant amount of their profits because they were forced to pay licensing and royalty fees to larger companies such as Marvel or Disney for the right to include the likeness of recognizable characters on merchandise. So Toy Biz approached Marvel with a new deal in 1993. They would hand over 46 percent of the toy company to Marvel. This gave the perpetually cash-strapped comics company an instant influx of funds. In exchange, Marvel granted Toy Biz an exclusive, no-fee license to make as many toys, action figures, games, and merchandise that they wanted. Marvel Entertainment and Toy Biz were now joined at the hip. Ike was thrilled because Toy Biz no longer had to pay inflated royalties to make Marvel products, thereby increasing his profits. Avi was thrilled that Toy Biz's deal opened the door to more creative opportunities with the recognizable Marvel properties.

Little did either man know that this deal was just the beginning of a long and lucrative marriage.

Trying to Ice-Skate Uphill

Arad believed that the brightest future for Marvel's assorted characters waited for them in Hollywood. Successful superhero movies produced by high-powered studios essentially would serve as widely seen commercials for Marvel toys and merchandise, and Toy Biz owned the rights to produce endless Marvel products without having to pay the royalty fees. Hell-bent on setting up multiple production deals at the top Hollywood studios, Arad began commuting to California from the East Coast in 1993, taking as many meetings as possible.

Unfortunately for Arad, the superhero movie boom hadn't yet begun. DC Comics' top two heroes, Superman and Batman, had established winning franchises at Warner Bros. But the comic book genre produced far more duds than hits, and bombs like *Howard the Duck*, *Dick Tracy*, and *Darkman* made studio decision makers leery.

"They would ask, 'Who is this new guy coming in? Who needs Marvel? Kids don't read Marvel. Adults don't like comic book movies.' . . . It was all a negative vibe," Arad said. "There was no culture of comic books. So it was a fight all the way."

Arad envisioned a scenario where Marvel Films would produce its own movies, thereby maintaining full creative control while also reaping the majority of the profits. In these early stages, however, the financially challenged Marvel needed a studio partner's influence (and deep pockets), so Arad recruited three valuable allies who would provide Marvel with that important foot in the door of the insular film community.

Ask a Marvel fan to name the film studio's "Big Three," and they'd likely rattle off the same names: Iron Man (Robert Downey Jr.), Thor (Chris Hemsworth), and Captain America (Chris Evans). This trio of superheroes each received their own stand-alone feature films between 2008 and 2011, helping to lay the sturdy foundation on which the rest of the MCU was built. The MCU's legacy, no matter how it expands, will always trace back to the early, pivotal successes enjoyed by these three characters in their debut films.

Twenty years prior to the MCU's Big Three, however, Marvel Studios— then known as Marvel Films—had an alternate "Big Three," one that helped a fledgling company figure out how best to convert its valuable superhero properties into viable blockbuster movie franchises. They were Blade (Wesley Snipes), the X-Men, and Spider-Man (Tobey Maguire).

As the head of Marvel Films, Arad was the one shopping these movie deals (and many others) around Los Angeles. One of Avi's first stops was to New Line Cinema, where President of Production Michael DeLuca bet big on *Blade*, becoming one of the earliest believers in the potential of a Marvel film. DeLuca grew up on comics and loved all shades of genre storytelling. His own writing credits included *In the Mouth of Madness* for horror master John Carpenter and Stallone's previously mentioned *Judge Dredd*, based on the comics series created by John Wagner and Carlos Ezquerra. DeLuca and Arad also flirted with an adaptation of Marvel's *Ghost Rider* that never came to pass, though the duo remained friendly and collaborative. Avi, though, brought a secret weapon to his pitch meeting with DeLuca. He had invited along a young screenwriter named David S. Goyer, who already had a bit of a comic book reputation thanks to his adaptation of James O'Barr's supernatural graphic novel *The Crow: City of Angels* for Dimension Films. Goyer also took a stab at a feature-film screenplay for Marvel's Nick Fury character that went on to become rewritten as a 1998 television movie starring David Hasselhoff. Goyer pitched Arad an intriguing idea about how to make a Marvel horror movie based on the character of the vampire hunter Blade, an idea that Arad turned around and took to New Line.

DeLuca snatched it up.

Blade is a human–vampire hybrid, a "daywalker" who frequently popped up in Marvel anthology comics like *The Tomb of Dracula* or *Vampire Tales*. Blade probably was considered an unusual character to choose when kick-starting Marvel's movie experiment because he didn't have a popular comic of his own and wasn't starring in an animated program that would have lured kids and families to the theater. Also, the *Blade* movie took full advantage of its R rating, delivering stylish but unapologetically gory horror kills. This content fit well at New Line, which was enjoying successes in its *Nightmare on Elm Street* series while at the same time developing a strong urban audience thanks to 1990's comedy *House Party* and the more grounded *Menace II Society*. The studio liked Goyer's story pitch enough to take a gamble on *Blade* in 1998. The studio hired first-time director Stephen Norrington to helm *Blade*, then cast *White Men Can't Jump* and *Demolition Man* star Wesley Snipes in the title role. The reviews were decent, the film grossed $131.2 million globally against a reported $55 million production budget, and two sequels followed in 2002 and 2004. As a result, the film industry started to sit up and take notice of Marvel's potential.

"Once *Blade* came out, and was successful, then Hollywood realized there was a lot of gold in those hills," Goyer said. "There was this epiphany with Hollywood that, 'Oh, we don't have to just adapt Spider-Man or Superman. We can adapt something like Blade and it can become a big franchise.' There was this gold rush where all the studios were clamoring for any Marvel or DC property without even knowing what they were. There was probably a ten-year period where a lot of executives just had no idea what they were doing, and would profess to be comic book fans without having read a comic book in their lives."[5]

Blade also helped Marvel break into an underutilized ancillary market: DVDs. As the home video experience evolved from VHS tapes to DVDs in the mid-1990s, studios scrambled for fresh content to package in the improved format. Arad said *Blade* DVDs were a major seller for Marvel following its theatrical run. The impact of home video sales will become an important factor as we approach Spider-Man's introduction to this expanding film landscape.

After decades of trying to break into the film industry with its characters, Marvel finally had its first franchise thanks to *Blade*. Instead of resting on its laurels, the studio immediately worked to expand its footprint. While New Line was figuring out how to bring *Blade* to the big screen, Arad struck a deal at 20th Century Fox in 1994, this time selling the license to produce a live-action movie based on the Marvel mutant superhero team the X-Men. The project was deeply personal to Avi, as he'd been executive producing a popular animated X-Men cartoon on Fox Kids Network since 1992.

"What I loved about *X-Men* is that I felt that it contained such a big message for kids all over the world. In that, we are *all* mutants, in our own way," Arad said. "The show was incredibly successful, so I decided to make a movie out of it, because I loved this property."[6]

Stan Lee and Jack Kirby first introduced the X-Men in 1963, inventing a team of characters who were "mutants," or humans born with a genetic enhancement that produced unique abilities. Unlike their Marvel Comics counterparts, the X-Men often are feared by the general public and ostracized because of their genetic differences, and the stories written for the X-Men over the years used this anti-mutant paranoia and hostility to explore cultural, social, and political issues readers of the comics often were facing.

Arad claims he brought X-Men to Sony first but received no bites on his offer, which was par for the course when he was selling Marvel stories back in those days. His next stop was Fox, where 20th Century Fox Film Group had just promoted Tom Rothman, the former president of Fox Searchlight, to its head position. Rothman was literally setting up his new desk the day he met with Arad.

"The office was still smelling from this fresh, new white paint," Arad remembers. "That's what they did whenever a new president came in."

Avi launched right into his pitch. He showed Rothman several X-Men comic books and raved about the number of X-Men action figures that Toy Biz was moving off the shelves.

"To give you an idea," Arad explained, "when X-Men started on TV, we sold 7,000 figures, which was nothing for action figures. The next year, when it became a hit, [we sold] 200,000 figures. Which is huge!"

With Rothman as a captive audience, Avi hammered home the success of the animated program. He told the studio executive, "College kids wake up in the morning, the first thing that they do is they throw a shoe at the television so that they can watch the X-Men!" Arad was convinced that the interest in the animated versions of these characters, as well as the success that Marvel writer Chris Claremont was having on *The Uncanny X-Men* comic book series at the time, would translate into significant box office numbers for a live-action X-Men movie.

For Arad, though, the appeal of an X-Men movie went beyond film profits. He saw the way that readers from around the world were connecting with Marvel's mutants, from the heroic Charles Xavier to the misunderstood villain Magneto. "Kids fell in love with the powers, and with the fact that they used them to do the right thing," Arad said. "It's all the revolution that is happening [in the streets] right now. We did it in 1994, when we did *X-Men*."

Rothman takes great pride in being one of the earlier supporters of the potential of Marvel's characters as blockbuster fodder. "We were a small group of believers at that time," he said. "It's great when you believe in something against all the doubters, and those few of us at Fox in those days did."[7]

But Fox definitely took "a huge gamble," in Arad's estimation, when it bankrolled an *X-Men* origin movie in 2000. "They were scared shitless," Arad says with a smile.[8] He can laugh now, in hindsight, because thanks to some brilliant casting choices—including newcomer Hugh Jackman in his now signature role of Wolverine; Sir Ian McKellan as the powerful manipulator of metals, Magneto; and Sir Patrick Stewart as X-Men team leader Charles Xavier—and by staying faithful to the comic book source material, Bryan Singer's *X-Men* generated critical raves and posted tremendous box office numbers. The $54.5 million gross that *X-Men* earned in its opening weekend in the United States set a new record for a superhero movie at the time (topping the $52.7 million opening for Joel Schumacher's *Batman Forever* in 1995). *X-Men* went on to gross $296 million worldwide, making it the ninth-highest-grossing film of the year.

Arad's production deals meant that Marvel Films finally was experiencing success in the film industry (though the frugal Ike Perlmutter would frequently complain to his partner about their deals, arguing that he wasn't making nearly as much profit as he believed he should have pocketed). The screenplays were adhering to the source materials, and the studio was learning how best to translate comic books to the big screen. But even the most loyal Marvel Comics readers would have to admit that neither Blade nor the X-Men would be considered the crown jewels in Marvel's stable of characters, and those movies were only helping to make second-tier comic heroes into household names. But the fledgling film studio was on the precipice of an explosion, a marriage of pop culture celebrity and moviemaking know-how that would change the company's course. Marvel Films was about to release its first Spider-Man movie.

Along Came a Spider-Man

While Avi Arad shopped Marvel's characters around Hollywood, Sony Pictures was working on its own deal to secure a large slice of the Marvel pie. But if history has taught us anything, it's that nothing comes easy when adapting Marvel's comic book characters to the big screen.

Throughout the 1980s, Spider-Man's film rights had been passed from one potential suitor to the next, with previously discussed production companies like Orion, Cannon, and Carolco trying but failing to mount a proper Spider-Man movie. After nearly a decade spent mismanaging Spider-Man's rights, producer Menahem Golen divided the valuable asset among three companies in 1990 in order to generate cash flow for his struggling spin-off venture, 21st Century Films. As mentioned, the home video rights landed at Columbia/Sony, which gave the studio a significant foot in the wall crawler's door. In 1996, Sony Pictures Entertainment President and CEO John Calley tried to capitalize and kick that door in.

Marvel was suffering through yet another debilitating bankruptcy that year. The publishing arm of the comic book corporation had been taking significant financial hits for years, and the movies—which Arad saw as Marvel's lifeboat—hadn't yet pulled away from the dock. Arad constantly argued with his bosses that blockbuster comic book movies were the only solution to Marvel's financial woes. He even began to suspect that some executives above him at the company were sabotaging his efforts to produce Marvel films because they preferred that Arad pursue lower-risk projects, such as television shows and animated series.

"The hardest thing for us to do was getting movies made, because every time I'd get close to making a movie, something would happen," Arad said. "We got to the point where I said to them, 'You're going to go bankrupt if we don't make movies. Movies will drive the brand. It will be the best way to build the brand!' Movie companies that will make the movies will have to promote Marvel. The movie opens with the Marvel [logo]. After two or three movies, Marvel becomes a household name."⁹

In 1996, however, a court-appointed trustee was ordered to field purchase offers for Marvel, and multiple entertainment companies circled the wagons on the debt-ridden brand. Sony's team assembling a bid to acquire Marvel included upstart entrepreneur Yair Landau, who wrote up a proposed partnership between the studio and the toy manufacturer Hasbro, generating an offer to buy the nearly bankrupt Marvel for $500 million.⁹ Hasbro would assume the role that Toy Biz was enjoying, producing endless toys based off the recognizable Marvel Comics characters. Landau, meanwhile, had convinced Sony that he could easily acquire the rights to the majority of Marvel's character roster, some of which already belonged to Universal (Hulk) and 20th Century Fox (the X-Men), allowing the studio to be the singular home for the on-screen Marvel Universe.

Sony's deal never came to pass. In fact, no other outside proposals to take over Marvel crossed the finish line. Marvel's bankruptcy hearings lasted three years, with numerous companies arguing that they were the right stewards to lead Marvel to financial solvency. And in the end, it was Perlmutter and Arad who convinced Marvel's lenders to invest in them and permit the Toy Biz honchos to assume full control of Marvel.

"The king of bankruptcy is Ike," Arad joked. "Also, they voted to go with us because I explained to them there's value in these characters. And when I said 'a billion,' I thought I was exaggerating. Well, I was wrong. It's a lot more than that.

"For me, it was a mission," Arad continued. "I was not going to let someone else close this art form, to destroy these characters, to sell them individually like Yoran Globus and his cousin [Menahem Golan] did. . . . We had one thing, though, that we knew that if we get that, someone will buy it. And that one thing was Spider-Man."[10]

Once Arad and Perlmutter took full control of Marvel in 1998, Avi immediately considered his options for a studio partner on Spider-Man. Paramount and Sony were in the mix. Arad also took what he calls "a secret meeting" with Tom Rothman at 20th Century Fox, who already was producing Marvel's *X-Men* movie. But Avi's suitors were hesitant to close any deal because of the complicated litigation that would be required to untangle Spider-Man's rights from Viacom, Sony, and MGM, which had acquired Carolco's portion at James Cameron's urging.

Again, Yair Landau and Sony saw their opportunity. They knew that the home video rights they held were a valuable negotiating chip and that without those rights, Marvel Films would lose out on a significant revenue stream that came from VHS sales of hit movies. Landau approached Perlmutter and Arad with a pitch: sell Spider-Man to Sony.

To Landau's shock, Perlmutter and Arad offered him a lot more than that.

"We needed money out of the bankruptcy," Arad admitted. So the newly branded Marvel Studios offered Sony Pictures *all* of their available characters for a grand total of $25 million. This would have included every significant character who currently is holding down a franchise in the MCU, from Captain America, Thor, and Ant-Man to Black Panther, the Guardians of the Galaxy, and Spider-Man. The only ones not included in the deal were the Fantastic Four, the X-Men, and the Hulk because they had been sold to competing studios.

But John Calley, speaking on behalf of a team of Sony executives, said no to Perlmutter and Arad's offer. He didn't think any of the Marvel characters outside of Spider-Man had measurable value. Landau pleaded, knowing (as Arad had been saying) that Spider-Man alone would have been worth a billion dollars in revenue—and actually has earned far more than that since 2002—so $25 million for the entire roster was a steal. But his arguments fell on deaf ears.

"[Landau] fought like a lion," Arad said. "His bosses told him, 'We don't need this. There's nothing here!'"

Sony's alleged belief that there was "nothing here" cost them significantly in the historical spectrum of superhero blockbusters. But they didn't walk away empty-handed. Calley sent Landau back to Arad and Perlmutter with the order to secure a deal for Spider-Man—and Spider-Man only. Marvel kept shopping the package deal around town but got no takers. Eventually, they circled back to Sony and sold Spider-Man for $10 million. As part of the deal, the two sides struck an agreement on merchandising that benefited both Marvel and the studio.

After years of wandering through a wasteland of cinematic uncertainty, Spider-Man finally had a Hollywood home. "Amy [Pascal] believed in it," Arad said. "I think she felt that the potential was great. I'll never forget, she said to me when we agreed to do it, 'You know, I'm a Chick-Flick girl. Make me into a Man-Movie maker.'"

Arad promised that if Pascal did her homework on Spider-Man, it would all work out. For the most part, it did.

CHAPTER FIVE
SAM RAIMI'S SPIDER-MAN

Good follows bad.

It's not nearly as recognizable of a Spider-Man mantra as, "With great power comes great responsibility." Nevertheless, the belief that things often have to get very bad before they can reverse course and improve applies to most if not all of Spider-Man's most memorable adventures. Peter Parker is the perennial underdog who tends to suffer more, both physically and emotionally, than his Marvel counterparts. But Spider-Man's strength, internal grit, and unwavering perseverance motivate him to never quit until the cause of his pain has been vanquished and the hero has emerged victorious on the other side of the conflict.

Good follows bad.

Those words also propel *Spider-Man: Blue*, a heartfelt, six-issue Spider-Man story credited to award-winning collaborators Jeph Loeb and Tim Sale that was released in 2002—coincidentally, the same year that Sony Pictures Entertainment delivered the industry's first official Spider-Man movie. Loeb and Sale's tender anthology finds Peter Parker speaking into a tape recorder late one evening, documenting the tumultuous story of his courtship with Gwen Stacy. In the process, *Blue* also pits Spider-Man against the full array of his deadliest antagonists, introduces Peter's eventual spouse Mary Jane Watson, and dives into the personal sacrifices this man makes because of his superhero calling. It's a beautiful miniseries, offering a sentimental ode to Parker's rocky romantic relationships, which are integral to the formation of his character. And in the text of the *Spider-Man: Blue* series, Loeb captures a quintessential observation about Spidey that happens to apply to the web slinger's film career.

Good follows bad.

Spider-Man endured decades of false starts and failed endeavors in the early years of his on-screen development. But those struggles needed to happen before the character finally was able to soar under the guidance of director Sam Raimi in the 2002 origin story *Spider-Man*. The Spider-Man film franchise had to endure the "bad" ideas involving tarantula–human hybrids as well as the stifling budget constraints of the Golan–Globus production cycle so that when the time came to properly mount a successful adaptation of Marvel's Spidey comic books, the mistakes of the past could be acknowledged and overcome.

Comic book movies have several masters they need to serve. Fans who have been raised on the source material, for example, demand to see accurate portrayals of the heroes they've grown to idolize. Studio executives, on the other hand, want healthy returns on the monies invested to kick-start what they hope will be a lucrative franchise. Multiple boxes need to be checked on an invisible checklist in order for a superhero movie to be deemed a victory.

Raimi's 2002 *Spider-Man* remains the most pure and accurate on-screen representation of Stan Lee and Steve Ditko's iconic creation. It is the "good" movie (arguably a great movie) that followed the multiple bad attempts at getting a proper Spidey series off the ground.

"There was no reason why *Spider-Man* should have worked," Loeb said. "I'm sure that Sony was terrified. The Batman franchise had flamed out. The Superman franchise had flamed out before that. Was the world ready to see a guy wearing a mask?"[1]

Raimi's 2002 film excels because it seamlessly adapts Spidey's origin story from the pages of *Amazing Fantasy* issue number 15 while adhering to the building blocks of the web spinner's universe. Loeb bestowed his blessing on the film, crediting Raimi for getting as close to the tone and spirit of the comics as possible. *New York Daily News* film critic Jack Mathews echoed this in his opening-weekend review when he summarized, "*Spider-Man* is an almost-perfect extension of the experience of reading comic-book adventures."[2]

Raimi and his screenwriter, David Koepp, embraced all of the core elements that Stan Lee's comic book editor infamously told him would lead to the character's failure. *Spider-Man* presents a story about an outcast, blue-collar New York teenager wrestling with real-world, recognizable problems. Peter Parker (Tobey Maguire) gets picked on by bullies, can't catch the eye of his dream-girl neighbor Mary Jane Watson (Kirsten Dunst), and commits an egregiously selfish mistake that leads to the death of his father figure, Uncle Ben (Cliff Robertson). *Spider-Man* doesn't tweak the hero's arachnid-focused origin and takes its time to visualize every necessary step in the Marvel hero's well-known creation story. Raimi even doubles down on the comically down-trodden aspects that make Parker awkward yet relatable. For these reasons, Raimi's *Spider-Man* frequently ranks alongside Richard Donner's *Superman*, Tim Burton's *Batman*, Bryan Singer's initial *X-Men*, and Christopher Nolan's *Batman Begins* as exemplary comic book origin stories.

"In many ways, Sam Raimi's 2002 take on Spider-Man ushered in the blockbuster era of superhero movies in which we now live," wrote Matt Miller in a 2021 *Esquire* magazine column ranking the nine existing Spider-Man films at that time. "[That film] set the bright color palette and slick visuals that later defined the MCU. It revitalized the character, along with the genre, setting the course for all the Spider-Men and superheroes that came after it."[3]

No one knew this at the time, but Raimi's work on *Spider-Man* also had a life-altering influence on an up-and-coming producer who found himself in an enviable position that allowed him to observe and absorb as much as possible during this unique "Big Bang" moment for the comic book genre: Kevin Feige. The eventual architect of the MCU points at his experiences working under Raimi's tutelage as the guidance he needed to shape Marvel's philosophy to this day.

"I was there mainly watching and learning on those early Sam Raimi Spider-Man movies. And I watched and learned from a group of people who were trying to exceed expectations, and trying to fulfill their own childhood dreams and the childhood dreams of fans of the characters," Feige said. "And that's what we've done on every single film and TV series [at Marvel] since then."[4]

It's easy to look back on the decisions that led to 2002's *Spider-Man* and conclude, "Of course they made a great Spider-Man movie! All of the necessary ingredients were at their fingertips." Superhero blockbusters of this scope and scale were still extremely new in the marketplace, however. And Marvel characters, specifically, had just begun to prove their worth in Hollywood.

"There was no playbook," recalls Matt Tolmach, president of Columbia Pictures when the studio took a chance on the web slinger. Even he recognizes that it's "almost hard to get your head around that [now]"[5] given the overwhelming popularity of the comic book blockbuster genre and Spider-Man's success individually. But at the time, no Hollywood executive could have predicted how a live-action Spider-Man would appeal to a mainstream audience. Also, cutting-edge visual effects were improving year to year, but even the most skilled technicians hadn't yet tested whether the fluid motions attributed to Spider-Man could be realized in live action on-screen. Christopher Reeve's Superman convinced audiences that a man could fly, but Sony's Spider-Man faced an uphill battle to prove that a man can credibly swing through New York City while holding a pencil-thin strand of webbing.

"I had to figure out how to do things that weren't real, but were close enough to real so that people would not be aware of the cheat," said John Dykstra, the two-time Oscar-winning visual effects supervisor who collaborated on *Spider-Man* and its 2004 sequel, *Spider-Man 2*.[6]

Almost everyone who worked on *Spider-Man* will tell you that the main reason that movie worked as well as it did was because Sony hired Raimi to direct.

"The key is Sam. There's no question about it," Dykstra said.

"Sam was able to tell a story that people wanted to see, and put some heart into it," added Don Burgess, director of photography on Raimi's first *Spider-Man*. "I've been fortunate to have been involved with several films in my career that just seemed to happen at the right time, with the right people. That's when the magic happens, and it connects with an audience. It's great to be a part of it."[7]

Raimi's involvement in the picture essentially convinced a reluctant Burgess to interview for the DP gig. Burgess had become Robert Zemeckis's go-to cinematographer, having shot the critically acclaimed *Forrest Gump* (which got him an Oscar nomination), the sci-fi thriller *Contact* with Jodie Foster, and the Academy Award–nominated *Cast Away*. Comic book movies weren't anywhere near his to-do list, but Burgess agreed to take a meeting because he admired Raimi as a director. In turn, it was Raimi who sold the cinematographer on Spider-Man's potential.

"Sam had a really good handle on Peter Parker, what that character was about and where he was from," Burgess said. "I really enjoyed [Sam's] enthusiasm, and his take on what he wanted to do. It just felt like he was the right guy to make this movie."

Raimi's résumé might not have positioned him as the perfect choice to direct a big-budget superhero movie. But anyone who dug deeper into his personal and professional history would recognize Raimi as a lifelong comic book fan with an unquenchable passion for the material. The Michigan native first landed on Hollywood's radar in 1981 when he directed the ultra-low-budget horror film *The Evil Dead*—a picture he essentially remade with frequent collaborator Bruce Campbell six years later. The effortlessly cool Campbell would go on to become a staple of Raimi's three Spider-Man films, playing small supporting roles in each installment. His most pivotal part has to be that of the overzealous ringmaster presiding over the wrestling match in *Spider-Man* who changes Peter's stage name from "The Human Spider" to "The Amazing Spider-Man," handing the hero his legendary nickname.

Raimi's reputation may have been shaped by the unapologetically over-the-top *Evil Dead* franchise, but that pulls focus away from his other directorial accomplishments. By 2000, when he began interviewing for the Spider-Man gig, Raimi had created his own gruesomely exhilarating superhero story in 1990's *Darkman* and had been maturing as a filmmaker by exploring several alternate film genres in films, such as the revisionist western *The Quick and the Dead* (1995), the intricately plotted crime thriller *A Simple Plan* (1998), and a nostalgic baseball vehicle for leading man Kevin Costner titled *For the Love of the Game* (1999).

None of those movies got Raimi the Spider-Man gig, however. That distinction goes to *Indian Summer*, a 1993 comedy-drama written and directed by Mike Binder. Don't feel bad if you've never heard of the film. Very few have despite it boasting an impressive ensemble that includes Alan Arkin, Diane Lane, Bill Paxton, Elizabeth Perkins, Kevin Pollak, and Kimberly Williams, fresh off her 1991 smash hit, *Father of the Bride*. Raimi had a small supporting role in *Indian Summer*, basically agreeing to appear in the ensemble because he and Binder were childhood friends. The film barely made a blip at the box office that year, taking in just over $14 million in total domestically. But it made a lasting impression on producer Avi Arad, who loved Raimi in the film, and mentally added the director's name to a short list of talents with whom he wanted to collaborate.

Fast-forward to 1999, when Arad and fellow producer Laura Ziskin are meeting up-and-coming filmmakers in New York City in hopes of finding the ideal storyteller for *Spider-Man*. Arad, by that point, had reapproached *Titanic* helmer James Cameron because of the A-list director's previous interest in shepherding a Spider-Man blockbuster. Sadly, the Cameron ship had sailed. Experienced directors Ang Lee, Roland Emmerich, M. Night Shyamalan, Chris Columbus, and the late Tony Scott all were in contention at the studio. *Fight Club* filmmaker David Fincher allegedly lost the gig because he asked for too much control over the project. Even *Batman* director Tim Burton agreed to meet with the team but ruined his chances when he told them he was more of a DC Comics guy.

Sam Raimi arrived to the meeting draped in a long coat and projecting an attitude that suggested he didn't expect an offer. The more he talked, however, the quicker he sold the producers on his deep understanding of this beloved character. It turns out that Raimi personally connected with Spider-Man's stories of self-sacrifice and admired how far the hero would go to protect innocent people. He confessed that Peter Parker and Spider-Man acted as role model characters during his formative teenage years and closed the interview with a true story about how, when he was a child, his parents hired a local artist to paint a Spider-Man mural on his bedroom wall as a birthday gift.

"I knew Sam loved Spider-Man. He always loved him," Arad said. "But I said to him, 'Yeah, I could see your love of it in *Indian Summer*.' And he cringed! He hated his role! [laughs] Lucky for him, and for me, no one saw it. And that was it. He came on board, and the rest is history. Literally."[8]

Arad uses that phrase often when telling a story. He'll punctuate a charming but rambling anecdote with the exclamation, "And the rest is history." Usually, it's an embellishment. When Arad is recounting Spider-Man's rise at Sony and the nascent development of Marvel Films in Hollywood, it is not. History was being made.

The Clothes That Make the Spider-Man

At Sony Pictures Entertainment, Spider-Man received something that the character never got from Cannon, Carolco, MGM, or the other companies that took halfhearted shots at adapting his adventures: full support from every aspect of the studio. Tolmach went so far as to describe the vibe around Sony in 2001 as a "universal euphoria" that was felt by virtually all of the employees working for the studio at the time.

"Here's the word I would use. It was ownership. Everyone felt that Spider-Man was theirs at the studio," Tolmach said. "There were some of us who loved Spider-Man before we had the rights, and dreamed about getting it. We knew it's value. I think part of the ownership was a testament to the people who made the movie. It was allowed to be a shared thing that everybody at the studio [enjoyed]. We often had 'Spider-Man Day' at the studio! Everybody on the lot got to come out and partake in a celebration of this thing. It didn't matter where you worked on the lot. Spider-Man was sort of yours."[9]

That doesn't mean there weren't significant battles waged along the way on *Spider-Man*. Precious few big-budget studio pictures are immune to conflict. "Nothing about it was easy," Burgess said. "In the prep of that movie, there were a lot of streets we went down that didn't work. We had to try a lot of different things when it came to, in essence . . . all of the things that play in a comic book, but how do you make them work in a movie?"

Arad, meanwhile, continued to argue with his investors back on the East Coast so that the first batch of movies being made by Marvel Studios stayed faithful to the source materials. The board of executives Marvel had to answer to at the time—the ones who determined how tightly they needed to tie the purse strings on their investments—consisted of garment executives, toy-manufacturing executives, and suits that had no real interest in making comic-accurate movies. They'd cut any corner of the developmental process if it meant increasing their profit.

Arad's willingness to push back against the financiers and maintain the integrity of the property was both recognized and appreciated by Dykstra as they collaborated on the first *Spider-Man*. "For many people who do that kind of thing, they don't really care about the product. They only care about how much money they make. He wasn't that way," Dykstra said of Arad. "He seemed to be very protective of his characters. At that point, they weren't big franchises. But his vision put him in a position to say, 'I've got to be careful with these characters because they have futures beyond anything that any of us could have ever imagined.'"

Finally, when it came down to casting on his own film, Raimi had to fight to land Maguire as his Peter Parker. Not that Sony doubted Maguire's acting abilities. His turns in *Pleasantville*, *Wonder Boys*, and *The Cider House Rules* generated critical raves, with *Cider House* being the film Raimi often cites when explaining why Tobey was his only choice to play Peter Parker. It was Maguire's lean physical makeup that gave casting agents at the studio pause. Although twenty-six years old at the time of shooting, the soft-spoken Maguire certainly appeared young enough to play a high school–aged Parker. But anonymous execs let it be known to the trades that Maguire's name wasn't the first that leapt to mind when an audience member was picturing "adrenaline-pumping, tail-kicking titans."[10] This kept competing actors Chris Klein, Scott Speedman, and Joe Manganiello (who'd eventually get cast as the bully Flash Thompson) in contention for months while studio heads waffled.

Stan Lee even had a strong opinion about Maguire's potential casting at the time. And who knew more about the creation of Spider-Man than the man who actually created Spider-Man?

"If somebody said to me, in the beginning, 'Who should play Spider-Man?' I don't think Tobey Maguire would have been one of the first guys I would mention," Lee told the *Orlando Sentinel* in 2002.[11]

Maguire, at the time, probably would have agreed. He has admitted to being reluctant about transitioning from director-driven dramas such as Ang Lee's *The Ice Storm* or Curtis Hanson's *Wonder Boys* into the soulless, studio-driven machinery of a superhero blockbuster. A conversation with Raimi swayed the wary actor and opened him up to the possibilities.

"I went and talked to Sam, and he just talked about it from the stand-point of character," Maguire said. "A coming-of-age story about this ordinary kid who becomes a superhero, and who is struggling with the big questions in life along with the regular, personal stuff. I really liked that approach, and I thought it would be interesting to bring my sensibility, together with Sam's, for this kind of movie."[12]

Maguire eventually earned the part because Pascal—who's had her hand in the casting of all three Spider-Men—knew that the actor cast in the role had to be able to convincingly portray Peter first and Spidey second.

"It's about the authenticness of the character. It's about the innocence of the character. It's about the, without getting too pretentious, the *Hamlet* of the 'to be, or not to be' of the character," Pascal says. "He has to be a normal kid that anybody can identify with."[13]

And Lee admitted that the relatability found in Maguire's performance instantly won him over.

"One minute into the movie, when I saw him on the screen, I said, 'That is Peter Parker!' [Maguire is] a very natural actor, and he looked like he might be a bookworm," Lee said. "He played the shy, introverted guy perfectly."[14]

The casting department's indecisiveness, however, was causing serious delays in the costume department for *Spider-Man*, where three-time Academy Award–winning costume designer James Acheson (*Dangerous Liaisons* and *The Last Emperor*) was busy solving problems associated with bringing a practical version of Spidey to the screen. For example, whomever ended up earning the part would have his entire face covered by a mask.

"I don't think that they realized that Spider-Man hasn't got a mouth until they started shooting," Acheson said.[15]

With Pascal, Arad, and Raimi focused on finding their perfect Peter Parker, Acheson concentrated on what the hero would look like once he donned his signature red and blue suit. In his mind, Acheson pictured athletes and gymnasts, body types that resembled Spider-Man from the comics but maybe didn't mirror the actors being considered for the part. Costume designers pored over countless sketches of potential suit concepts, including one piece submitted by Eisner and Harvey award winner Alex Ross, a giant in the comic art field. Meanwhile, major corporate brands lobbied the studio to have their equipment be part of Spider-Man's costume. Nike wanted to contribute material and designs for the hero's boots. Oakley sunglasses hoped their lenses could be used for Spidey's mask.

Not that Acheson and his team were reaping any noticeable fringe benefits from all of this high-profile attention.

"We built the first Spider-Man suit, or did the sculpting for it, in a little space just off of Santa Monica Boulevard which turned out to be an ex–pornographic film studio called The G-Spot," Acheson recalls with a laugh.

Still, the team was feeling immense pressure to get the very first live-action Spider-Man costume right. One cause for Acheson's concern might have been the criticism leveled at the costumes worn by the mutants in Marvel's first *X-Men* movie. A major hit for 20th Century Fox in 2000, *X-Men* cast actors who delivered impressively accurate live-action portrayals of Wolverine (Hugh Jackman), Professor Charles Xavier (Patrick Stewart), and Storm (Halle Berry). But while the casting department went above and beyond, the costume staff on *X-Men* misfired. Vibrant colors worn by Marvel's mutant warriors in their comics were ditched for monochrome black leather suits on every character. This choice actually gets made fun of in the movie when team leader Cyclops (James Marsden) asks a disgruntled Wolverine, "What would you prefer? Yellow spandex?"

With those criticisms in mind, Acheson focused on creating a Spider-Man costume that respected the expectations of the fans. But casting hadn't pulled the trigger on Maguire yet, and time was running out if the *Spider-Man* costume department had any prayer of staying on deadline. Acheson's team needed to begin constructing the suit, which included musculatures (or padding) that could be adjusted in the arms, legs, chest, and shoulders depending on which stuntperson was wearing it for the scene of the day.

"Because Spidey's been bitten," Acheson explained. "He suddenly stops being the nerdy boy. He's got a *body*."

But Acheson didn't have a "body" to focus on. Drastic times called for drastic measures, so the costume designer recalls filling a room with twenty men of all shapes and sizes, wearing nothing but thongs and Speedos. He invited Raimi to the costume department and demanded that the filmmaker choose his preferred Spider-Man body type.

"I've never seen such an embarrassed director," Acheson said. "And he chose one guy—I still remember him. He was a really beautiful looking man, but he was about six-foot-two, and built like a shithouse door! And then [Sam] chose Tobey Maguire!"

Acheson's design team was scrambling in those early stages because they were starting from scratch, not being able to carry over any costume design concepts from either Nicholas Hammond's live-action network television show or the Japanese series *Supaidāman*. And each step forward on Raimi's vision for his suit seemed to produce a new obstacle.

"Like the webbing. Which is a three-dimensional webbing. How do you stick a three-dimensional webbing onto a suit that's got 16 parts? Do you glue the webbing on in the stretch position? Or do you do it in the contracted [position]?" Acheson said. "Because Spidey's suit looks kind of like a used condom when it's hanging up on a rail."

But nothing progressed quickly in these departments at that time because every craftsperson contributing to *Spider-Man* was figuring out the practicality of the movie as he or she went. Acheson recalls a visual trick for the Spidey suit that he borrowed from 1960s pop art, where British painter Bridget Riley used specific linear patterns to create the optical illusion of dimensionality on flat surfaces. Acheson wanted to replicate that process by painting shadows onto his costume to better create defined muscle structures.

"I remember a wonderful, mad woman who told us it would take her three weeks to work out that process," Acheson said. "Six months later, we were still waiting for them."

This goes a long way toward explaining why costume designers Kym Barrett (*The Amazing Spider-Man*) and Deborah L. Scott (*The Amazing Spider-Man 2*) abandoned the elevated webbing patterns that were signatures of the Raimi suits when they got their own shot at designing a practical Spider-Man costume for their respective film assignments.

These early costume design conversations also raised two issues other Spider-Man projects hadn't tackled to that point: how does an actor deliver a screen-worthy performance when his facial features are hidden, and how can a stuntman endure long production days if his mouth and eyes are obstructed by a mask? As he sought proper solutions, Acheson suggested an innovative visual design that would have allowed Raimi to show Maguire's face while it was inside of the Spider-Man mask (similar to the technique *Iron Man* director Jon Favreau eventually used so audiences could see Robert Downey Jr. once he was inside the Iron Man suit). Acheson must have been ahead of his time, however, because his idea was misunderstood by his superiors and immediately shot down. Additionally, Acheson figured out that he had to physically construct an "inner mask" that fit inside of the Spider-Man mask and that was also big enough to fit every stuntman. This way, no matter which performer was wearing the costume in a particular scene, Spider-Man would always maintain the same facial profile.

These were small-scale issues, though, when compared to the health and safety of the men wearing the Spider-Man mask during the lengthy film shoot because, as Acheson came to learn, "Once you put somebody in a full mask, you forget about them. You don't realize that they're suffering in there because you can't see their eyes. And so I realized that if we could make something that people could breathe out of, and that we could take the eyes out, we could put a man in a Spider-Man costume for eight hours, and he'd be fine."

Acheson's herculean efforts paid off. Even if you personally prefer one of Spider-Man's later costume designs (Spidey fandom expresses a lot of love for Scott's *The Amazing Spider-Man 2* suit), there's no denying that Parker's suit in *Spider-Man* and its sequel perfectly replicates the Silver Age style drawn by Steve Ditko and John Romita Sr. in the hero's earliest years. The webbing and spider symbols on the chest and back are comic accurate, as are the angles and shapes of the character's recognizable eyes. There's a reason CinemaBlend writer Jason Wiese placed the Raimi suit at number one on a ranked list of on-screen Spider-Man costumes, calling it "a game changer for costume design in comic book movies" and referring to the suit as "a true original that has never been duplicated."[16]

Creating a practical look for Spider-Man's on-screen costume was only half of the production team's battle, though. Across the Sony lot, Dykstra's visual effects artists were encountering their own unique challenges as they raced to invent a visual vocabulary for a superhero who needed to crawl across walls, fight a sinister antagonist who rides a flying glider, and credibly swing on a sticky web through the vast canyons created by New York City's immense skyscrapers.

"Unlike Anything You've Ever Seen!"

You get only one shot to make a great first impression. That's why Spider-Man fans should feel lucky their hero's first opportunity for a proper Hollywood adaptation repeatedly got dismantled for a grueling period of eighteen years before Sony got its chance "because the technology didn't really exist to have Spider-Man do the things that the fans would expect him to do," producer Laura Ziskin astutely concluded while recording the commentary track on the 2002 *Spider-Man* DVD.[17]

If the frugal Cannon Group managed to force one of its lower-budget Spider-Man features into the marketplace, then poor reception for an inferior product could have tainted the property and prevented the launch of a superior franchise, perhaps permanently. There's a good chance VFX pioneer James Cameron would have applied the time, money, and ingenuity needed to transition Spider-Man from the page to the screen. But in reality, any version of *Spider-Man* heading into production prior to 1999 would have appeared inferior because Hollywood refined and improved its visual effects processes annually, and using practical effects to mimic Spidey's specific movements wasn't a viable option.

"There was no way to make *Spider-Man* without visual effects," Arad said. "You can not fly. You can not fight in the air. You can not do 3D. There are too many things you can not do. . . . It's impossible."[18]

Spider-Man went into production as the film industry gradually transitioned away from stunt performers and into computer-generated characters. Visual effects artists working on comic book movies realized it was impractical to replicate the outlandish actions and movements of a superhero with a human, so the studios financing blockbusters in this genre continued to invest in animation and CGI.

"There was a way to do it," Dykstra confirmed, "but the physics of it are pretty phenomenal."[19]

Prior to joining Raimi's *Spider-Man*, Dykstra experimented with superhero CGI when he created a digitally animated Batman figure for stunt sequences in Joel Schumacher's *Batman Forever* (1995) and *Batman & Robin* (1997). In a way, Batman "learned" how to soar over Gotham City so that Spider-Man could eventually swing from the rooftops of Manhattan's tallest skyscrapers.

"It's a learning process. And the beauty of working in visual effects is that you get to earn while you learn," Dykstra said. "When we set about doing *Spider-Man*, obviously a huge portion of Spider-Man's vocabulary is his prowess at moving in all fashions, whether it's fighting or traveling through the city. So it was a great opportunity to explore the limits and push everything as hard as it would be pushed to try and get that character to happen.

"A favorite line of script writers in those days, and probably in these days as well, was 'Unlike anything you've ever seen before,'" Dykstra continued. "So we were always in the business of building a prototype. Because nobody wanted the tried-and-true version. They wanted something new and different."

That meant testing, testing, and more testing. Dykstra's team started with stuntmen wearing motion-capture suits, who then jumped from high risers onto soft landing pads. The results suggested that motion capture's limitations didn't account for physics and basic human anatomical structure, so that method couldn't be used. Next came the creation of a completely CGI Spider-Man character using a technique called keyframe animation. This is a frame-by-frame animation process that creates motion in a character. It's time consuming, but it allows for more fluidity in your action, and Dykstra sought to prove to studio executives (and also to himself) that an animated Spider-Man could maintain a realistic look when projected onto a massive theater screen.

As part of his CGI test, Dykstra filmed an actual stuntman crawling up the side of a building, then built an animated version of Spider-Man doing the exact same movements.

"We showed [the executives] both pieces without telling them which was which," Dykstra said. "And they went, 'We don't know which one is which!' They were pretty much indistinguishable from one another. And so that gave us the greenlight to go ahead with Spider-Man."

The visual effects team received one lucky break, which gave them a bit of a head start. Because Spider-Man is covered from head to toe in a skintight suit, he's an easier character to animate versus a lifelike character requiring massive amounts of hair or exposed skin.

At the same time, Raimi and his director of photography Don Burgess were running their own trials to decipher what level of practical effects could be blended into their shoot to capture Spider-Man's distinct movements. In Burgess's opinion, he and Raimi did "as much as humanly possible to make it look unhuman."[20] This meant some use of stuntpeople on cables and high-speed winches in order to, as Burgess put it, "take gravity out of the equation." But it was Raimi's request that the stunt teams and the VFX artists figure out how to collaborate together to achieve Spider-Man's fluidity through the right combination of practical and digital.

The minute that wires were introduced into the process, Acheson knew exactly where the team needed to go: Cirque du Soleil in Las Vegas. The costume and VFX teams shared a plane to Sin City, eventually arriving at a garage on the outskirts of the gambling mecca that served as the headquarters of Climbing Sutra, a manufacturer of state-of-the-art theatrical harnesses.

It was Climbing Sutra founder Todd Rentchler who had mastered the art of harnessing performers for high-flying stunt and wire work. Rentchler was a devoted rock climber and hiker who invented his own unique gear, which has been utilized by everything from Las Vegas stage shows to big-budget

Hollywood productions. Climbing Sutra has contributed to the *Bourne* series, the *Fast & Furious* saga, *The Hunger Games*, Christopher Nolan's Batman trilogy, and all five *Pirates of the Caribbean* films.

"If anybody knew how to disguise a harness, it was this man," said Acheson. "It was everything. The buckles, the weight, the fitness, the comfort—he'd been there. He'd worked it all out."[21]

And he succeeded in helping Raimi's creative team figure it out as well.

"It was just Sam's personal taste, at the end of the day, of what was 'Spidey,' shall we say, and what the stuntmen were capable of doing," Burgess said. "So it was a cross between the two worlds, of finding that rhythm of what looked right to Sam, as far as what looked like Spider-Man, and how he was portrayed in the film. And I think that ultimately, we ended up taking it in a direction that has become how superhero movies are filmed to this day."

Not-So-Subtle Spider-Man Changes

The *Spider-Man* production team strove for comic book accuracy in almost every aspect, but that doesn't mean Raimi opposed all changes to the hero's origin story. *Spider-Man* presents an extremely faithful adaptation of the web slinger's earliest days, documenting such touchstones as the spider bite, the death of Peter's Uncle Ben, and the existence of the *Daily Bugle*, with its cantankerous publisher J. Jonah Jameson (played to perfection by character actor J. K. Simmons). But the movie tweaks a few of Spider-Man's core foundations, and some of these alterations would be addressed—and even reversed—in subsequent Spider-Man movies.

Raimi's decision to give Peter Parker organic web shooters has to be considered the most significant alteration to the traditional origin. In the comics, the high school science whiz constructs mechanical web shooters that he wears on his wrists. He also invents his signature web fluid, which he stores in refillable cartridges that are worn on his belt. Stan Lee loved that aspect of Spidey's reality because sometimes his web fluid would run out in the heat of battle, forcing the now vulnerable hero to rely on his wits to defeat a powerful foe. This discrepancy also led to an amusing conversation between the three on-screen Spider-Men in the spectacular team-up *Spider-Man: No Way Home* as Tom Holland and Andrew Garfield peppered Tobey Maguire with questions about his unusual but admittedly convenient source of web fluid.

"So you, like, make your own web fluid in your body?" a fascinated Garfield asks.

"We can't do that," Holland explains, "so naturally we're curious as to how your web situation works."

"I have to make my own in a lab, and it's a hassle compared to what you got," Garfield's Peter Parker concludes.[22]

Raimi borrowed this idea from James Cameron's early treatment for his Spider-Man adaptation, which planned to make Peter's webbing an organic by-product of his spider bite. Raimi's decision wasn't meant to downplay Peter's scientific intelligence. Rather, he believed that a teenager having the wherewithal to invent something as complicated as webbing would "distance him from a real human being, and distance him from the average kid in high school."[23]

"So we felt that the best thing to do was, since he's bitten by this spider and takes on the powers of the spider—crawling walls, the ability to leap like some leaping spiders have, the great proportionate strength of a spider, relative to his size—we felt it was a logical progression to let him also spin his own webs," Raimi said. "And in that way, keep him a complete human being that we could identify with, and being consistent with, 'Well, once he's bitten by the spider and takes on all of the powers, why just take on four of the five? Why not take on all five?'"

Raimi believed this choice pushed the narrative that his Peter Parker was "cursed" with these powers. A vocal subset of Spider-Man fandom still disagrees with this decision, but Stan Lee eventually gave his blessings. Sort of.

"Having seen the movie, it looks so good the way they did it. I have no problem with it," Lee decreed in 2002. "But had I done it, I probably still would have tried to have used the web shooters."[24]

Another complicated decision facing the *Spider-Man* crew was the choice of antagonist for the hero's big-screen debut. Spidey's colorful rogues' gallery offered a wealth of options, though the obvious selection would be Norman Osborn, aka the Green Goblin. Osborn is Spider-Man's true archnemesis, the father of Peter's best friend as well as a scientific mentor who eventually goes insane due to his lust for power. He's the equivalent of the Joker for Batman or Lex Luthor for Superman. But Matt Tolmach admits that the Goblin wasn't the first choice when Sony was batting around ideas.

Multiple early drafts of Spider-Man screenplays settled for Doctor Octopus, who would be both visually spectacular and an intelligent nemesis who shares Parker's passion for scientific exploration. But by the time Sony got around to mounting its first Spider-Man adaptation, Tolmach clarified, "No, we weren't flirting with Ock. [And] it wasn't always Goblin. There was a Sandman moment in the original. Electro was in the first one. And then we came around to Goblin. And Norman, in the lexicon of villains, is a gateway to so many things. He's a great character, with his obvious relationship to his son, *and* his relationship to Peter, makes it ripe for soap opera, which is great. And also Oscorp being the hub of where bad things get created, it just made sense to start there."[25]

Once the team settled on Goblin and long before Willem Dafoe landed the part, Acheson was handed what he refers to as a "disaster"—namely the hard-shell Green Goblin mask design that would appear in the finished feature. The costume designer passes the buck of blame on that creation, noting that by the time he'd been hired on *Spider-Man*, an outside company landed the contract to complete the Goblin head.

"I hated what they were up to," Acheson said. "I hated the sculpt. They weren't interested in talking to me. I was 'the English kid' who was new off the block, and they knew what they were doing. Plus, they had the support (of the studio)."[26]

This didn't stop Acheson from repeatedly appealing to Ziskin for a better solution. He confirms that the team working on Green Goblin did experiment with a rubbery mask for the villain, something akin to what the character wears in the comics. And he admits, "It was much better, I thought, than what they came up with. But that [also] looked really cheesy. That really looked like Halloween time. I loved the idea of going somewhere else, because where they'd gone seemed to be rather pedestrian. But I didn't have the clout to say, 'Look, I think we can do better than this.'"

Acheson singled out one scene from the script that legitimately terrified him because he knew it would require the Goblin to do something that the hard-shell mask would never allow. After Norman knocks Spider-Man unconscious with gas, the villain carries our hero from J. Jonah Jameson's *Daily Bugle* office to a nearby rooftop for, of all things, a conversation. During the scene, the eye shields on the Goblin's mask retract, permitting Dafoe to partially emote. But the mask's frozen mouth can't move, creating an uncomfortable sensation that Acheson remembers cringing and laughing at when he finally saw it play out in theaters. For the amount of time spent creating a near-perfect Spider-Man suit, the Goblin's costume design, at least in the eyes of the film's costume designer, left a lot of room for improvement.

The villain was a complicated choice. The film's love interest choice was not, even if eventual star Kirsten Dunst believed she would be playing someone different than Mary Jane Watson.

"I'd seen more of Gwen Stacy, for some odd reason," Dunst said. "When I first met Sam, I was just flipping through the comics. I saw her, and I was like, 'Oh, alright, I'm blonde. It makes sense.' I really didn't know a lot about Mary Jane and Peter's relationship. But of course, I did lots of research after I got the role."[27]

What further confuses the Gwen–for–Mary Jane swap is the fact that *Spider-Man* includes one of the most iconic sequences from Spider-Man's history, "The Night Gwen Stacy Died," in the movie's third act, but makes crucial changes to the expected outcome. In the comics, Green Goblin figures out Spider-Man's true identity. In an effort to punish his enemy, Goblin kidnaps Parker's love, Gwen Stacy, and strands her atop the Brooklyn Bridge. (Stan Lee had to admit, years after the fact, that he mistakenly labeled the bridge in the scene as the George Washington Bridge, even though *The Amazing Spider-Man* penciler Gil Kane clearly had sketched the Brooklyn Bridge. The location was properly sourced in later editions.) During a fight between Spider-Man and Goblin, Gwen is knocked from one of the bridge's 278-foot-tall suspension towers, and even though Parker snags her with his webbing before she hits the ground, Stacy's neck snaps, killing her instantly.

"It was totally unexpected, the death of Gwen Stacy," Arad said about the two-arc comic book run that Marvel published in 1973. "The whole world was in love with her. . . . Gwen was his real first love. His biggest love."[28]

According to Arad, they did consider starting with Gwen in the first *Spider-Man* movie but ultimately shifted to Mary Jane because they liked the drama caused by the fact that Mary Jane loved Spider-Man without knowing that he's also Peter, the nerdy kid who lives next door to her.

"If we went with Gwen, it would have been a smaller story, in a way," Arad said.

Possibly. But I'll also argue that forcing Mary Jane into a facsimile of the "Death of Gwen Stacy" story does a disservice to that historic narrative.

Also, when Stacy finally does surface as a supporting character in *Spider-Man 3* (played by the capable Bryce Dallas Howard), Raimi and screenwriter Alvin Sargent are unsure how best to even use her. She has limited ties to Peter, starts as a love interest for Eddie Brock (Topher Grace), and gets used by Parker (Maguire) to make Mary Jane jealous after he's possessed by the symbiote. By opting not to feature Gwen in *Spider-Man*, it damaged the character's chances of having any real impact in the Raimi franchise overall. Then again, Mary Jane's prominence in Raimi's trilogy meant that Sony turned to Gwen in the eventual Spider-Man reboot, and we got Emma Stone's pitch-perfect portrayal for two feature-length adventures. That has to be considered a win.

September 11 and Its Impact on *Spider-Man*

The aforementioned changes, from organic web shooters to the design of Green Goblin's mask, could be controlled and managed by the *Spider-Man* filmmakers. Some changes could not. Spider-Man is a New York City native, and on September 11, 2001, the hero's home city was attacked. Two commercial airliners were flown into the North and South towers of the World Trade Center in Lower Manhattan, and the world looked on in horror as the buildings burned and eventually fell.

There's hardly any aspect of our day-to-day lives that was not affected by the terrorist attacks on September 11. This included something as frivolous as the marketing campaign for a superhero blockbuster that planned to rely heavily on Spider-Man's identity as the quintessential New York hero. Raimi had completed principal photography on *Spider-Man* before the attacks, and the studio maintained the movie's May 2002 release date. But following the tragedy, the studio promptly—and wisely—decided to remove all references to the World Trade Center in the film and its marketing materials. This included a theatrical poster featuring a profile shot of Spider-Man's mask, with the Twin Towers reflected in his eyepiece. And it also led to the pulling of a Spider-Man trailer that has since become relatively famous due to the controversial reasons for its removal.

"That was a piece specifically made for the trailer," Burgess remembered. "It was not in the story that we were making at the time. It was shot at the same time. We put another unit together just to do that. So instead of a trailer being cut out of the movie to make, it was a trailer cut out of footage that was specifically for the trailer. That's the first time I've ever experienced that, and I haven't experienced it since."[29]

The clip runs for two minutes and sixteen seconds and focuses on a team of bank robbers who pull off a job, then attempt to flee the scene in a helicopter. Only, before they are able to clear Manhattan's airspace, they're captured by Spider-Man and left dangling on a massive web he has spun between the North and South towers of the World Trade Center. It's a remarkable image that instantly identifies the location of the movie and the home of the hero.

"We were trying to be super ambitious," said Josh Goldstine, who served as the senior executive vice president of marketing at Sony Pictures during this era.[30] His team planned this original theatrical short film as a "rug pull" or a "misdirect" to keep audience members off the scent. "That bank robbery teaser was all about thinking that you're in . . . a Michael Bay action movie or something like that, and then realizing you're in this kind of classic bank robbery. And then the last thing you expect is that element of surprise. That was a classic piece of 'surprise and delight,' because it was a misdirect. But at the core, that was really an announcement of a title, or an announcement of a character."

The trailer matches the eventual tone of Raimi's movie because it was shot by the team that was making the actual film. Burgess's camera operators and Dykstra's visual effects creators all contributed to that piece of marketing, helping it feel like a scene that had been removed from the finished movie, even though it was scripted and shot independently of the actual feature.

"I remember it was a super bold swing," Tolmach said. "This notion of a singular postcard for the movie that is not borrowing, like traditional marketing, from the movie, but is its own little short. It was a giant swing. . . . This whole [marketing campaign] was about invention."[31]

Spider-Man removed references to the Twin Towers out of respect, but the movie didn't ignore the hero's New York heritage. If anything, the movie leaned harder into the strong sense of New York pride that enveloped the five boroughs in the months that followed September 11. *Spider-Man* embraced the Big Apple in the run-up to the film's premiere.

"I've always associated Spider-Man with that moment, that healing, cathartic experience," said director Jon Watts, who was a twenty-year-old student at New York University when Raimi's movie opened.[32]

"There was just a feeling that Spider-Man was kind of a unifying figure, and someone who spoke for hope and optimism at a time where those things were desperately needed," Tolmach said.

Like a true hero does.

Spider-Man's Very First Opening Weekend

When Don Burgess met with Sam Raimi to trade ideas about Spider-Man and feel each other out as potential collaborators, the director of photography said he eventually walked away with a job offer in his hands and two questions on his mind. "You kind of have to ask yourself, 'First of all, would I go see this movie?' And then second of all, you've got to ask yourself, 'Would anybody *else* want to go see this movie?'" Burgess said.[33]

As it turns out, millions of other people wanted to see *Spider-Man*. The film opened in U.S. theaters on Friday, May 3, 2002, and the shock wave generated by the film's debut reached Sony's executive team in Los Angeles by Friday evening. Amy Pascal, Avi Arad, Matt Tolmach, Laura Ziskin, and screenwriter Alvin Sargent had just accompanied Raimi and Maguire on a promotional trip to the trendy Los Angeles shopping center The Grove, where they surprised a packed theater of *Spider-Man* audience members. That visit was Pascal's first indication that they'd tapped into something remarkable.

"No one knew who Tobey was at the beginning [of the movie], and everyone knew who he was at the end," Pascal said. "At the time, it was the complete highlight of my life, career wise."[34]

Now the team was toasting the film's success while gathered around a table at the famous (and now shuttered) Morton's steakhouse in Los Angeles. Pascal was "completely terrified" waiting for the reactions and preliminary box office figures to start arriving from the East Coast. Initial predictions called for a $20 million Friday night, though Sony's head of marketing and distribution, Jeff Blake, almost immediately started bumping up the estimate to $22 million. Then $27 million. And then $30 million.

"We were in uncharted territory," Tolmach said. "That was the moment where you were like, 'Oh my God, we touched something insane.' That was the Friday night of that weekend. That was the beginning of the whole thing."[35]

Sam Raimi's *Spider-Man* eventually set a box office record for single-day ticket sales by taking in $39.4 million. That same weekend, *Spider-Man* became the fastest movie in Hollywood history to cross $100 million domestically (it took only three days) as well as the first movie to earn more than $100 million in its opening frame (the movie had raked in $114.8 million by Sunday, May 5). By the time *Spider-Man* had finished its box office run, the movie's $403.7 million domestic haul made it the highest-grossing comic book adaptation of all time.

Josh Goldstine attributes a portion of Spider-Man's box office victories to Sony's marketing approach, which he said looked beyond the stereotypical nerdy image of a comic shop denizen and targeted mainstream crowds who could identify with the humanistic elements of Peter Parker's story.

"There was always going to be that core fan base that loved Spider-Man," he said. "But at the time, this was perceived as potentially the stuff of little kids or, you know, 'This is the movie about a guy running around and climbing walls in his underoos.'"[36]

So Goldstine and his team countered that perception by crafting "a campaign that had a fun quality to it, but that also spoke to the ideas in literature and the things in storytelling that really mattered to me. I believed that Spider-Man was a truly great character, [so] I wanted to make a campaign that would get me to see the movie. And I figured if I could convince me, as a customer, to see the movie, then I could get everyone on the planet to see the movie."

Spider-Man wasn't seen by every person on the planet. But the marketing playbook created by Goldstine's team has helped the Spider-Man movies that followed Raimi's find increasingly larger audiences. Writing for the *Washington Post* in 2014, comic book culture columnist David Betancourt tracked the formation of the superhero movie universe in which Hollywood currently lives. Betancourt labeled the launch of the first trailer for 2002's *Spider-Man* as the "Big Bang" moment that birthed the landscape in which so much of the film industry's blockbuster strategy now lies. As for *Spider-Man*'s historic box office run, Betancourt echoed Goldstine's findings when he surmised, "One movie truly made [it] clear that comic-book movies weren't just for fanboys—that they could be 100-million-dollar opening-weekend blockbusters that produce billion-dollar movie franchises."[37]

Twenty years after Tobey Maguire brought Spider-Man to life on the big screen, the actor returned to the franchise opposite Andrew Garfield and Tom Holland in *Spider-Man: No Way Home*. The character's enormous popularity in the years following his debut powered *No Way Home* to a $260.1 million domestic opening in its first weekend. Twelve days later, *No Way Home* had earned $1 billion at the worldwide box office. Betancourt was right. Spidey was producing a billion-dollar franchise. It just took longer than the columnist predicted.

CHAPTER SIX
THE OVERWHELMING CHALLENGES OF SEQUELS

Five days after *Spider-Man* opened in cinemas, Sony announced its plans for *Spider-Man 2*. The sequel even received a tentative release date, giving Sam Raimi a target at which to aim.

The news hardly surprised the industry. Tobey Maguire and Kirsten Dunst already were under contract to reprise their leading roles for not one but two sequels. "That's a nervous thing to do," Maguire admitted, "to sign on to scripts you haven't even seen."[1] The actors also were figuring out how to deal with the overnight success that came with having a hit film.

"I'd been making movies for a while, so I had experienced some attention," said Maguire. "But then, all of a sudden, the Sunday after [*Spider-Man*] was released, I remember I went to lunch with my little brothers and there were all these people outside, and photographers. It was a lot more attention than what I was used to."[2]

Raimi, meanwhile, transitioned directly from the first film into its follow-up with no break whatsoever. Sony intended to strike while the iron was hot, and *Spider-Man*'s $114.8 million opening weekend gross provided all the motivation the studio needed to get the sequel's wheels spinning.

In theory, the wind should have been at the creative team's backs. They'd spent years teaching themselves how to produce a winning Spider-Man adaptation, which fans around the world had embraced. Doing it again should have been a walk in the park.

Think again.

"It was very tough to get the second movie together," said Matt Tolmach.[3]

Right off the bat, *Spider-Man 2* faced an obstacle that *Spider-Man* didn't have to consider: audience expectation. Raimi's initial film was such a sensation that it established fan loyalty and a devotion to his interpretation. But with that acceptance comes an assumption from fans that the next film will deliver something superior to what they just watched.

"I think you got away with a lot more in the early days because people had never seen [Spider-Man] before, so they were just grateful," Tolmach said. "And then when people become more experienced, and they've seen it, they're going to be more demanding."

Sequels struggle whenever "bigger" triumphs over "better." Studio executives make commercial decisions instead of creative ones, and a once-promising franchise veers away from the elements that initially won audiences over.

Sony, to its credit, avoided such mistakes on *Spider-Man 2*. By maintaining the bulk of its core creative team and keeping Raimi at the helm, *Spider-Man 2* upheld the tone of its predecessor while fine-tuning its visual effects and expanding on Peter Parker's recognizable world. The action and fight sequences in Raimi's sequel are frenetic but fluid in their design. They're also superior to the set pieces in its predecessor, which John Dykstra attributes to a loose translation of Moore's law, a decades-old technology theory associated with microchips. In 1965, Intel cofounder Gordon Moore theorized that the number of transistors found on a microchip would double every year but that the cost of computers would be cut in half. Or, in Dykstra's superhero blockbuster terms, "The exponential increase in speed and capacity of digital devices over the course of time quadruples every two months, or some ridiculous thing. And we were in the heart of that curve. The increase in quality [of visual effects] had a lot to do with rendering things at higher resolution, which is always much better. And then, computational capacity meant that you could make more complex models, more complex textures, and you could use ray-tracing instead of a more conventional light source rendering. So a huge portion of the improvement of the image [in *Spider-Man 2*] came as a result of technology improving vastly over the course of the time between the completion of the first one and the execution of the second one."[4]

Put more simply, Dykstra says, "Because we'd done one before, we'd already made a lot of the mistakes. So we were able to make new, more complex mistakes, which resulted in a more sophisticated execution."

An example Dykstra points at would be the movie's exceptional third-act fight sequence between Spidey and Doctor Octopus (Alfred Molina), which begins atop a New York skyscraper but eventually transitions to the roof of a rapidly moving commuter train. The choreographed action sends our hero over, under, and through the vehicle as he tries to slow Doc Ock's attack while also pausing to rescue passengers that the villain has tossed toward the streets. Ask Spider-Man fans to name their favorite action set piece from any of the character's movies, and the train fight in *Spider-Man 2* should come out on top the majority of the time.

Dykstra seems surprised to hear that because, as he remembers it, "We had no idea how we were going to do it."

Due to the sequel's ferocious time constraints, Dykstra and his team started filming the footage they would need to construct the train fight long before they possessed the final assets for the sequence. That process may sound backward, but that's common on effects-heavy blockbusters that need as much production time as possible to refine their creations. The visual effects artists set up shop in Chicago in the dead of winter, braving frigid conditions because they'd secured access to a section of elevated track and two train cars.

"We'd taken all the windows and doors out of the train car," Dykstra remembered. "We were freezing our asses off. It was so cold, especially when the train was moving."

Dykstra circled the Windy City for several days photographing everything that he thought they needed to create the complicated sequence. Yet, even with weeks of preplanning, Dykstra claims they made up the bulk of the fight as they went along.

"Most of it panned out," he said with a laugh, adding, "I've been fortunate in that, a lot of films I've worked on—I'd like to think it was because I'm incredibly insightful, but there's probably a great deal of luck involved—you basically make a bet that something's going to work, even though you can't be certain about it. You build a structure that executes the visual effects for the movie from the ground up. The key is that the stuff that's at the ground level has to be pretty reliable, and pretty robust. And then the higher you get up the pyramid, the more prototypical and more out-of-the-box you can get. I've been really fortunate that we've had a lot of 'pyramids' that mostly ended up with a final product that was successful.

"You've got to take those kinds of risks, though," Dykstra summarized. "If you don't, then you end up with pedestrian stuff."

That penchant for VFX risk taking helped *Spider-Man 2* surpass Raimi's initial film, at least on a technical level. But it's Raimi's storytelling skills that elevated the human conflicts contained in his second Spider-Man movie, delivering a well-rounded superhero installment that *Esquire* film journalist Brady Langmann called a "piece of art that will live on generations from now."[5]

Spider-Man 2 also feels more "Raimi" than the first movie, embracing the director's kinetic action as well as his passion for the horror genre. Raimi likely went into the sequel with more confidence now that a global audience had bought into his vision. For example, the director doesn't hesitate to linger inside of an awkward physical comedy bit that has Peter Parker (Maguire) catching mops and brooms as they fall out of a closet or to milk Bruce Campbell's comedic timing as he prevents Peter from entering Mary Jane's stage show. Raimi's also brave enough to employ his trademark horror tactics in a visceral and over-the-top hospital sequence where the mechanical arms of Dr. Otto Octavius come to "life." And because *Spider-Man* had established the underdog nature of Parker's persona, Raimi was free to enlarge the dark cloud that hovers over our hero, leaning into his money problems, his academic issues, and the will-they/won't-they status of Peter and Mary Jane's relationship.

"It felt right to us that the next movie be about, 'OK, now he's accepted the mantle. He's been on that road for a while. And there are positives and negatives,'" said Laura Ziskin.[6]

Several screenwriters took a stab at *Spider-Man 2* before Raimi discovered the mix of story components and character developments that best inspired him. The secret weapon in this creative consortium? Two-time Academy Award–winning screenwriter Alvin Sargent (*Ordinary People* and *Paper Moon*). Sargent didn't contribute to the first *Spider-Man* and had no comic book experience on his résumé. But the acclaimed writer reached out to Tolmach and Ziskin—whom he'd eventually marry in 2010—during a crucial stage of the sequel's script development.

"The person who really, I think, broke the spine of what the movie needed to be about was Alvin Sargent," Tolmach said.[7]

The *Spider-Man 2* team was kicking around the idea of stripping Peter of his powers but couldn't find a credible way into that story. Sargent pointed them toward a very famous comic book panel located inside of *The Amazing Spider-Man* issue number 50, titled "Spider-Man No More!" It shows Peter rejecting his crime-fighting persona, fed up with the toll his heroism inflicts on his personal life. In the frame, Peter has thrown his costume into a trash can, though portions of the suit remain visible as a dejected Parker slinks away. Raimi loved this imagery so much that he basically re-created the live-action version of the scene in *Spider-Man 2*.

"What was brilliant about it, and what Alvin and Sam really got about it—and embraced, and loved about it—was that it was emotional," Tolmach said. "It wasn't like, 'Oh, someone took my powers.' That would have been someone else's version of it. 'Someone did a sinister thing and took my powers!' In the hands of Alvin Sargent and Sam Raimi, it was emotional. It was, 'What happens when you're a boy, and you just want to be a boy?' And you just don't want to deal with the stress, the accountability, the responsibility of being a grownup. Which is what Peter was always having to do. And *that's* why you lost your powers. And so it was, again, pivoting to character. Not plot. Character. That's what I think was so extraordinary about all of Sam's movies. It always came from emotion.

"And so that was the thing that broke the spine of what (*Spider-Man 2*) became," Tolmach continued. "All of it came from that one panel, and Alvin understanding what it meant."

Raimi's love of and faithfulness to the Marvel Comics source materials helps his Spider-Man movies stand apart from other entries in the superhero genre, many of which play fast and loose with the comic stories on which they are based. *Spider-Man 2* directly referencing Stan Lee's 1967 story "Spider-Man No More!" was a welcome visual homage to a beloved comic. And it's just one sample of the multiple times Raimi weaved pivotal moments from the Marvel books into his films. Norman Osborn's death by glider at the end of *Spider-Man*, for example, is a carbon copy of the villain's demise in the 1973 story "The Goblin's Last Stand." And Peter Parker's use of a deafening church bell to separate himself from an alien symbiote in *Spider-Man 3* seamlessly re-creates the same sequence found at the end of a 1985 *Web of Spider-Man* comic, "Til Death Do Us Part."

"You cannot make a better story than what Stan Lee wrote," said Avi Arad when explaining why the better Spider-Man movies pull directly from the comics. "You start with source materials. The comic book is a storyboard. And the story has moral value."[8]

For reasons unknown, Marc Webb avoided this practice when he took over directing duties on the two *The Amazing Spider-Man* movies that followed Raimi's run. Very few scenes in Webb's films, if any at all, directly mimic a frame or sequence from a Spider-Man comic. But it's worth noting that director Jon Watts returned to the art of comic book replication when he was constructing 2017's *Spider-Man: Homecoming*, the first solo Spider-Man movie that was part of the MCU. Watts drew up a scene that references one of the most famous and beloved story lines in Spider-Man lore: 1963's *The Amazing Spider-Man* number 33, titled "The Final Chapter." At a pivotal moment in that comic, an exhausted Spider-Man finds himself pinned under tons of iron as he's fighting to retrieve a rare serum that can cure his ailing Aunt May. Watts didn't recycle those exact story beats, but he did come up with a reason to bury Tom Holland under a mountain of rubble so he could capture a chill-inducing moment of fortitude that undoubtedly made Spider-Man comics readers cheer. Future Spider-Man movies might be better served by finding memorable Marvel Comics moments that fit into their stories.

In 2004, Raimi's emotional embrace of his characters, as well as the industry's rapid technical advancements, helped *Spider-Man 2* become a global sensation. The commercially successful sequel banked $788 million in worldwide grosses, and critics lavished the film with praise. The late Roger Ebert of the *Chicago Sun-Times* went so far as to call *Spider-Man 2* "the best superhero movie since the modern genre was launched with *Superman*."[9]

But Sony, believe it or not, came dangerously close to missing the sweet spot with *Spider-Man 2*. One or two decisions made during this stage of the webhead's cinematic development could have derailed the franchise and cheated the fan base out of what's frequently labeled the best Spider-Man movie. As mentioned, numerous screenwriters from Alfred Gough and Miles Millar to Michael Chabon took a swing at a script for this anticipated sequel. And one draft from *Spider-Man* screenwriter David Koepp highlights some drastic detours that could have affected Raimi's second film if he'd chosen to remain loyal to his original collaborator.

David Koepp's *The Amazing Spider-Man*

Raise your hand if this plot sounds familiar. Richard and Mary Parker, noted pioneers in the science community, are also covert government agents who hide dangerous secrets from their closest family members. When those long-ignored skeletons threaten to burst from the duo's proverbial closet, the Parkers flee, leaving their adolescent son Peter in the hands of Ben and May Parker. Decades pass, with Peter believing his birth parents have died in a plane crash. Now a teenager, Peter obtains a nondescript item that once belonged to his mysterious mother and father. And within that item, Peter unlocks a major clue to Richard and Mary's true identities. Unsure of whom to trust, Peter turns the coveted information over to the only living scientist who worked with the Parkers prior to their disappearance, inadvertently providing that character with sinister motivations that will lead to the birth of a maniacal supervillain.

That's essentially the framework for Marc Webb's first Spider-Man movie, 2012's *The Amazing Spider-Man*. The reboot literally opens with Richard (Campbell Scott) and Mary Parker (Embeth Davidtz) hurriedly scooping up file folders filled with their research and dashing off into a rain-soaked evening. The item that their son, Peter (Andrew Garfield), discovers down the line is a leather briefcase that once belonged to his dad. And the crucial information Peter unearths is a scientific algorithm that completes the research of Dr. Curt Connors (Rhys Ifans), turning him into the Lizard.

Here's what's interesting, though. Almost a decade before Webb and his screenwriters weaved those plot elements into their first Spider-Man story, they were introduced in a script David Koepp turned in for consideration as the basis for Sam Raimi's *Spider-Man 2*. There were subtle differences. In Koepp's draft, ironically titled *Amazing Spider-Man*, Peter doesn't discover a leather briefcase but instead is handed a faded manila envelope that Aunt May promised to give to the boy on his twenty-first birthday. Inside the envelope is a letter, some photographs, and a shiny silver key that leads Peter to a safety deposit box holding a device that Koepp called "The Image Refractor."

Also, the scientist with deep connections to Richard and Mary Parker that Peter eventually hands the Refractor over to isn't Curt Connors. It's Dr. Otto Octavius, the man who'll become corrupted by his lust for power and eventually morph into Doctor Octopus.

It's shocking how many elements from Koepp's 2002 script found their way into Webb's 2012 film of the same name, enough so that Koepp probably deserved a "Story By" credit alongside *The Amazing Spider-Man*'s screenwriters James Vanderbilt, Steve Kloves, and the franchise's adopted lucky charm, Alvin Sargent. Aside from the emphasis on Peter's mysterious parents and the plot development of making Peter responsible for the creation of his main antagonist, Koepp introduces Gwen Stacy to the ensemble, making her one leg of a love triangle involving Parker and a jealous Mary Jane Watson. Gwen's father, Captain George Stacy, also plays a significant role in Koepp's story (as he did in Webb's film, played by comedian Denis Leary). In fact, a dinner-table sequence penned by Koepp where Peter and George argue over the legality of Spider-Man's vigilantism appears, almost word for word, in Webb's eventual movie.

If Raimi had adapted Koepp's script as it was submitted, he might have ended up producing a movie that more resembles Webb's *The Amazing Spider-Man* than his own *Spider-Man 2*. That's a strange possibility to consider.

Koepp's original plan mapped out a trilogy of Spider-Man movies, one that would have told the saga of Peter and Gwen's tragic relationship as well as Harry Osborn's Green Goblin legacy following the death of his father, Norman, in the debut film. "The first [Spider-Man] movie was the structure I intended," Koepp said. "The second two movies, I would have moved heavily into Gwen Stacy, with the death of Captain Stacy in the second movie."[10]

Captain Stacy's death is yet another plot point that resurfaces in Webb's *The Amazing Spider-Man* movie, though Koepp's script faithfully adapts the sequence from 1970's *The Amazing Spider-Man* comic, issue number 90, titled "And Death Shall Come," which has Stacy dying while saving a child from falling debris. Webb, meanwhile, chose to have Stacy die on the roof of Oscorp tower after helping Spider-Man defeat the Lizard.

Some elements from Koepp's 2002 sequel script did make their way into Raimi's *Spider-Man 2*. Although the director sifted through multiple drafts submitted by Gough, Millar, Chabon, and Sargent, he kept several ideas suggested by Koepp in this treatment. Raimi clearly appreciated Koepp's decision to have Peter organically lose his powers, though Koepp came up with a stronger scientific reason for our hero's disappearing abilities. On page 45 of the *Amazing Spider-Man* script, Curt Connors explains "recidivism" to Parker, which is the gradual erosion of the enhanced physical powers found in Connors's genetically engineered spiders.

"Their abilities turned sporadic, random, came and went for no reason," Connors said. "Eventually, the spiders reverted to rather unspectacular arachnids."[11]

This, to me, is a preferred explanation to the one that ultimately appears in *Spider-Man 2*, where Peter's loss of powers is more psychological, driven by internal doubt he feels regarding his commitment to the responsibility that comes with being Spider-Man. Or, as Tobey Maguire calls it in 2021's *Spider-Man: No Way Home*, "Existential crisis stuff."

Raimi cherry-picked additional plot developments and action sequences he liked from Koepp's script. This 2002 screenplay begins with Harry Osborn hating Spider-Man because of his alleged role in Norman Osborn's death. Eventually, Koepp had the young Osborn communicating with visions of his dead father and collaborating with Octavius so he could learn Spidey's secret identity (much the same way it plays out in 2004's *Spider-Man 2*). Also, the spectacular stunt where Peter saves Mary Jane from a car that Doc Ock throws through a restaurant window takes up pages 67 to 70 of Koepp's work.

But Koepp's *Amazing Spider-Man* script isn't completely represented by either Raimi's *Spider-Man 2* or Webb's first *Amazing* film. This screenplay takes a few exciting risks both directors ignored, though they would have rapidly expanded Parker's on-screen universe and implemented key changes to the direction Raimi took the franchise. Koepp, for example, introduced Eddie Brock in this sequel, establishing him as a rival photographer competing with Peter for assignments at the *Daily Bugle*. He also wrote Octavius as the man who murdered Richard and Mary Parker, giving the blood rivalry between Spider-Man and Doctor Octopus more dramatic weight. Koepp laid the groundwork for the birth of the Lizard by having Curt Connors get his arm crushed during a final battle at Harry Osborn's wedding. And Koepp would have ended his second movie with Peter emotionally torn between his love of both Gwen and Mary Jane, setting up a devastating conclusion in the trilogy capper in his head.

"My *Spider-Man* conclusion was a set up," Koepp said. "That was why, in the third movie, Harry was going to kill Gwen on the same bridge. I was going to have 'the Gwen Stacy scene,' so I used it in the first movie as a set up, which I never got to pay off."[12]

In the end, Raimi didn't rely too heavily on Koepp's treatment. "A lot of different people brought things to the story," Raimi said. "It was really [about] finding our way through these different ideas to the ones that reverberated with me. We found our way, [but] there was no real formula."[13]

And even though the *Spider-Man* screenwriter didn't fully guide Raimi's sequel, Koepp remained incredibly busy in the years following this attempt. He continued to collaborate with his *Jurassic Park* partner Steven Spielberg, adapting the H. G. Wells novel *War of the Worlds* in 2005, then almost helped dismantle the Indiana Jones franchise with the off-key *Kingdom of the Crystal Skull* in 2008. He also continued to direct feature films, helming a Stephen King adaptation with Johnny Depp called *Secret Window*, as well as 2020's horror thriller *You Should Have Left* with Kevin Bacon and Amanda Seyfried. But Koepp's *Amazing Spider-Man* script serves as a fun alternate peek at what could have been a possible Raimi sequel as well as a reminder of how easy it is for a franchise to drive down unexpected roads during the chaotic preproduction period.

Spider-Man 3 "Just Didn't Work Very Well"

Quit while you're ahead. It's excellent advice, though it often goes unheeded in Hollywood. Think how many film franchises have overstayed their welcome, petering out (no pun intended) after one or two strong films, then lingering long enough to sully the reputation of the series. And why? Usually because boardroom executives greenlight meager sequels in pursuit of easy box office dollars. Brand recognition helps draw large audiences, so studios are reluctant to close the door on a popular series no matter the creative droughts experienced by directors and writers behind the scenes. *Alien*, *The Terminator*, *Superman*, *X-Men*, *Beverly Hills Cop*, and even Francis Ford Coppola's *The Godfather* are just a few of the many notable film franchises that can boast one spectacular sequel and one or more disappointing entries. Sometimes those misfires lead to the end of the series. Other times, they trigger severe narrative pivots in hopes of restoring audience interest.

Raimi's *Spider-Man* series earns a spot on that undesirable list. After launching the web slinger's film franchise, then topping said accomplishment with a rousing follow-up, Raimi and his series came crashing back down to Earth with 2007's trilogy capper *Spider-Man 3*. The film and its script lack focus despite the return of Raimi, Sargent, the entire core cast, and the bulk of the crew. Bloated and unwieldy, *Spider-Man 3* succumbs to the common sequel issue of having too many cooks in the production kitchen, wrestling the vision away from a proven director.

"It was hard to recapture the magic [for *Spider-Man 3*]. Life happens. People become successful," Tolmach said. "Everybody has a feeling about why something worked. They're all right, in their own ways, but . . . gone was the innocence of it."[14]

In an effort to top the spectacle of *Spider-Man 2*, Raimi crammed three villains into his follow-up, introduced another potential love interest for Peter in Gwen Stacy (Bryce Dallas Howard), rewrote the story of Uncle Ben's murder to gin up the dramatic stakes, turned Peter Parker into a self-serving jerk, saddled Harry Osborn (James Franco) with a corny bout of amnesia, and attempted to squeeze in the character of Venom, who had become increasingly popular with Spider-Man fans thanks to story lines in the comics and on the animated Spider-Man series. Where *Spider-Man 2* created a superhero-sequel template that many filmmakers tried to replicate, *Spider-Man 3* became a cautionary tale, a warning not to overstuff one movie at the expense of story and character development.

But don't take my word for it. Listen to Raimi, who candidly described the film as "awful" while appearing as a guest on the Nerdist podcast in 2015.

"It's a movie that just didn't work very well," Raimi said. "I think [raising the stakes after *Spider-Man 2*] was the thinking going into it, and I think that's what doomed us. I should've just stuck with the characters and the relationships and progressed them to the next step, and not tried to top the bar. I think that was my mistake."[15]

Tolmach agrees with Raimi's assessment. Trying to top what the team had accomplished in *Spider-Man 2* ended up being too difficult a task.

"*Spider-Man 2* was that thing where a group of people are suddenly firing on all cylinders," he said. "That was that moment. It was better than it was before, and it was better than it was afterwards. And that sometimes happens."[16]

The way Tolmach describes it, Sony treated *Spider-Man* and *Spider-Man 2* as traditional movies that operated independently of each other. The focus during the production of the first two *Spider-Man* installments remained on the films in question and nowhere else. By the time Sony and Raimi were moving ahead with preproduction on *Spider-Man 3*, however, the series had become a "Franchise" with a capital "F." And franchises serve multiple masters, often forgetting to focus on the film in question.

"There was, I think, a real ambition to do more," Tolmach said. "Then you start seeing the international [numbers], and you're feeding it in a different way. All for good reason. But it isn't always the best thing for the creative integrity [of the movie]. And I think there was a fairly tangible strain on the creation of that one."

The bulk of that strain was caused by Raimi's disinterest in the Venom character, whom producer Avi Arad pushed to include as one of the chief *Spider-Man 3* villains. As Raimi told the Nerdist hosts, "I tried to make [*Spider-Man 3*] work, but I didn't really believe in all the characters, so that couldn't be hidden from people who loved Spider-Man. If the director doesn't love something, it's wrong of them to make it when so many other people love it."

Raimi, in that quote, was talking about Venom. The villain made his comic book debut via a cameo appearance in *The Amazing Spider-Man* issue number 299 and came with a complicated origin. Venom exists because a sentient symbiote that Spider-Man acquired on an alien planet separated itself from Peter Parker. Then, in a fit of rage, the symbiote bonded with Eddie Brock, a rival photographer who jealously blamed Parker for his professional hardships. Fitting that into the first act of an already busy superhero sequel would have been difficult. Also, even a watered-down version of this alien origin story would have felt out of place, tonally, in the recognizable neighborhood atmosphere that Raimi worked so hard to establish over the course of two films.

Still, Arad loved Venom. The lethal and borderline-psychotic villain was the producer's second-favorite Marvel character after Spider-Man. Arad paid close attention to how popular Venom had become not only in the animated series and the comics but also through retail sales of Venom-related toys at Toy Biz.

"I saw what the kids were gravitating to," Arad said. "Of course, they loved Spider-Man. They loved Iron Man. And they absolutely loved Venom. Young kids usually don't like villains. But they loved him."[17]

In Avi's eyes, Venom's overwhelming popularity on the toy market would translate into increased tickets being sold for *Spider-Man 3*. And in the end, he was right. Raimi's *Spider-Man 3* was a box office juggernaut. Released on May 4, 2007, the sequel posted $151.1 million domestically in its opening weekend. It eventually earned $336 million at the U.S. box office, making it the highest-grossing domestic film released that year. The $894 million worldwide gross for *Spider-Man 3* also made it the highest earner in the Raimi series. To date, only two other Spider-Man movies, *Spider-Man: Far from Home* and *Spider-Man: No Way Home*, have earned more money at the global box office than *Spider-Man 3*. Financially speaking, Raimi's third movie was a tremendous success for Sony Pictures.

Creatively, though, it broke the director and hastened his early exit from the lucrative franchise. Costume designer James Acheson, an integral collaborator on the first two Spider-Man movies, recalls the struggles Raimi and his team endured while working the symbiote and the requisite black suit into *Spider-Man 3*.

"It was a nightmare," Acheson said, adding that he believed the "extraordinary" Venom suit should have been the responsibility of the visual effects department instead of the costumers. "I just didn't think we could do it. We did all sorts of sculpts and everything. We failed. Terribly. But we also had a director who didn't want to know anyway, because he hated Venom and didn't want to do it."[18]

"It wasn't something Sam ever embraced," Tolmach said. "It's a very different character than 'a Sam Raimi character.' . . . It's an old, silly cliche, but directors either make movies about themselves, or they find themselves in their movies. And I don't think Sam ever found Venom in his life. It didn't resonate for him."[19]

Raimi made it clear he preferred classic Spider-Man antagonists from the earlier comic story lines, ones that were more in line with Willem Dafoe's Green Goblin or Molina's Doc Ock. Months after *Spider-Man 2* opened in theaters, Raimi's brother Ivan went so far as to draft a treatment for *Spider-Man 3* that would have concluded Harry Osborn's Goblin arc while also introducing recognizable Silver Age foes Sandman and Vulture. Sir Ben Kingsley reportedly was circling the latter role before that character was cut during rewrites.

The prevailing thought regarding *Spider-Man 3*, at least in the Spider-Man fandom, is that Arad forced Venom on Raimi and thereby ruined the director's chance at sticking the landing on a perfect Spider-Man trilogy. But Tolmach claims that assumption is both unfair and inaccurate.

"More has been made out of, 'Avi was jamming it. . . . ' Those things don't happen that way," Tolmach said. "People talk about that stuff, but it's like, 'No, nobody was jamming.' We had creative meetings. Avi's a powerful voice, and always has been. And also, he was passionate about it. We all went down that road, and anybody who says they didn't is not entirely embracing the truth."

Arad, however, remembers it a little differently. He admits to being "disappointed" in the way that *Spider-Man 3* turned out and acknowledges that Raimi hated Venom. He also admits to pushing Venom on the director while also pointing out that the decision saved the movie at the box office.

"Sam Raimi never liked Venom. And he said it. 'I never liked him. Avi made me do it.' [laughs] You know, he's very naive this way," Arad said. "So, I got calls. And I said, 'Yeah, I made him do it.' Because without [Venom], the movie wouldn't have done the number it did. There were other problems in the movie. And it's true! And [Raimi] admitted it. He said, 'You're right. I should have listened to you and done it right.' He wasn't interested in this character."[20]

Dedicated fans continue to debate the merits of the *Spider-Man 3* they received. Those who like the film appreciate Thomas Haden Church's casting as Flint Marko, aka Sandman, and praise the visual effects used to bring the granular villain to life. Raimi purists argue that the director's stylish approach to an unquestionably messy script helps *Spider-Man 3* stand apart from Webb's heartfelt but undercooked *Amazing Spider-Man* movies or the Marvel-approved safety of Jon Watts's three features.

Just don't tell Raimi that anyone likes his third Spider-Man movie because he's unlikely to believe you.

"I messed up plenty [with] the third Spider-Man," Raimi said. "So people hated me for years. They still hate me."[21]

That's an exaggeration. Most fans just would have preferred a scenario where Raimi got to exit the franchise he created on his own terms, with a Spider-Man movie that was purely his vision and free from studio interference.

That scenario almost came true.

Spider-Man 4

Under normal circumstances, a franchise film that generates nearly $900 million in global ticket sales immediately receives a sequel—whether justified or not. Studios, as discussed, have no interest in turning off the spigot when consumer cash is flowing. But things were far from normal following *Spider-Man 3*, leading to a period of confusion that froze Sony in its tracks.

Despite the commercial success enjoyed by *Spider-Man 3*, Sony could sense that the cultural winds surrounding the franchise suddenly blew hot and cold. Critics no longer stood in Spider-Man's corner. National Public Radio's Bob Mondello called *Spider-Man 3* "seriously overextended."[22] Respected *New York Times* scribe Manohla Dargis criticized that the sequel "shoots high, swings low, and every so often hits the sweet spot, but mostly just plods and plods along."[23]

Denver Post film critic Michael Booth hit the nail on the head when he surmised, "All in all, the fun has simply gone out of it."[24]

"Fun" wasn't the only thing that drained away. Raimi's heart also had gone out of the franchise by the time he'd wrapped on *Spider-Man 3*. Perhaps it was the battles he had to wage over Venom that drained his enthusiasm. Maybe it was the fact that Raimi had worked on nothing but Spider-Man since 2000 and needed to shift gears away from blockbuster superhero storytelling to revitalize his filmmaking passion.

Whatever the reason, Raimi's reluctance prevented Sony from immediately announcing plans for a sequel to the enormously successful *Spider-Man 3*. That made the studio nervous.

"There was a time where we thought about making three and four together, because we saw this coming," said Tolmach. "I don't know if I've ever told anybody that. But I pushed for that hard. 'What if we did two together?' Because you began to feel like getting the band back together was [going to be] harder and harder. It's more expensive. People have other ambitions and aspirations. All that natural stuff."[25]

This plan of filming *Spider-Man 3* and *4* back-to-back got far enough down the pipeline that Sony had calendared out the dates needed for production and filming. Logistics and strategies were tentatively mapped. Basically, the idea was entertained until it became too complicated on almost every level.

"It would have meant having two great scripts. We were struggling to have one for that movie," Tolmach said.

Spider-Man fans tend to have two lingering questions when it comes to Raimi's mythical *Spider-Man 4*: "How close did we come to getting it?" And "What would it have been about?" The first one is easy. We didn't get as close as most would've liked. The reasons why, though, are complicated.

Sony officially secured Raimi and Maguire for a fourth Spider-Man movie in September 2008, sixteen long months after *Spider-Man 3* opened to record-setting amounts. Rumors swirled in the Hollywood trade papers that a fifth movie would be filmed simultaneously, but nothing developed on that front. Curiosity kept the production under a microscope of scrutiny, as fans and industry followers wondered if Raimi could reclaim the creative heights of *Spider-Man 2*.

News on *Spider-Man 4* was scarce during development, and any time an item surfaced, it suggested problems. Sources leaked rumors that Raimi couldn't resolve major script issues. The studio reportedly was pushing for Raimi to film the sequel in 3D even though he'd never worked in that format before (and had no real interest to start). Raimi ended up having to field countless questions regarding his return for *Spider-Man 4* while doing press for his 2009 throwback horror thriller *Drag Me to Hell*. His answers were politely vague and inconsequential, as when he told On Demand Entertainment that, in an effort to make *Spider-Man 4* "the best of the bunch," he'd aim for a "more intimate" sequel that would "find the heart of what made Spider-Man great, originally, in the comic books."[26] Maguire, meanwhile, opened up to film journalist David Poland in an interview that aired on January 11, 2010—mere days before Raimi's movie was officially canceled. In that sit-down, Maguire praised his and Raimi's working relationship and said the duo was constantly asking themselves, "How do we press this? How do we make it more exciting, more fun? How do we evolve the character and make it a rich story?"[27] Maguire also emphasized that he wanted to keep Spider-Man interesting for himself if he was about to plunge back into the overwhelming grind of a studio blockbuster.

He and Raimi never get the chance though not from a lack of effort on the studio's part.

"We *begged* him to do it," Tolmach said about Sony's negotiating tactics with Raimi to stay on board for *Spider-Man 4*. "We begged Tobey to do it. We were the studio! Spider-Man was what you woke up and worried about. It was everything that we could do to get number four to happen. . . . It's always on us, the suits—and I loved being one at the time, I stopped loving it later—but [our] job is to get Sam to do another one. You *have* to! And so Amy [Pascal] and I threw everything we possibly could in terms of our most convincing, begging-and-pleading at him. And it just wasn't meant to be."[28]

Pascal confirms that as much as she wanted the creative core to return and make a fourth Spider-Man movie for Sony, the decision came down to Raimi and Raimi alone. While it remains Pascal's opinion that the end of the Raimi Spider-Man era was "foisted" on her, she believes she needed to respect her filmmaker's wishes.

"At the time, Tobey wanted to make a certain kind of movie. And Sam wanted to make a different kind of movie," she said. "And we kept trying to make it work and fit. In the end, it all starts and ends with the director. He just didn't feel that there was a movie there that he wanted to make at that time. And that's how that happened."[29]

Almost every person working behind the scenes on *Spider-Man 4* confirms that the story and script never came together in any way that satisfied Raimi. James Acheson knew the Vulture would have been the sequel's primary villain, and his team spent roughly six months crafting models off which costume designers and visual effects artists would have worked.

"We did a lot of work. And it was so sad," he recalled. "Sam's heart didn't really seem to be in it."[30]

That brings us to that second lingering question. "What would Raimi's *Spider-Man 4* have been about?" Fans searching for sequel details have been able to unearth plot points and visuals on different news outlets over the years. And a great many of them were provided by storyboard artist Jeffrey Henderson.

Henderson is a Los Angeles–based actor and musician whose day job is to storyboard scenes for popular movies and television shows. His credits vary from Amazon's sadistic superhero drama *The Boys* and M. Night Shyamalan's sci-fi two-hander *After Earth* to Marc Forster's gentle Disney feature *Christopher Robin*. And for a span of time, Henderson found himself working for a director he admired and adored when he was hired as one of the artists assigned to sketch sequences for Raimi's *Spider-Man 4*.

"My experience on *Spider-Man 4* was wonderful. Sam was wonderful. And just to have the experience of working with him on a Spider-Man movie is a professional and creative high point," Henderson said. "And the fact that he was so sweet, and he was so earnest, and so collaborative just made it that much better."[31]

Twenty-seven storyboards for Raimi's unrealized sequel live on Planet Henderson, the artist's official website. They tease Spider-Man fans with their potential, plastering action set pieces and high-flying fights that we know we'll never see. Most involve the Vulture, one of Spider-Man's earliest villains, who was introduced in the second issue of *The Amazing Spider-Man* comic.

Raimi planned to modernize the Vulture and make him more ruthless than comic book readers might have remembered. The feathers on the wings of Vulture's costume were designed to flip out like razor-sharp blades, which the villain would use to stab his enemies. Raimi and his artists also conceived a fight scene for the film's first act where an army of goons are sent to a library to take the Vulture down. Henderson said the sequence would have matched the "birth of Doctor Octopus" scene from *Spider-Man 2*, tapping into Raimi's horror roots and solidifying the Vulture's raw power.

"He was essentially a guy that did a lot of ugly stuff for the government, did a lot of ugly stuff as a private contractor," Henderson said of the updated take conceived for *Spider-Man 4*. "I thought a clever thing to do would be to say that part of the reason they called him The Vulture was because when he was done, he didn't leave anything but bones behind."

Raimi told his storyboard artists that he also wanted the fourth Spider-Man to get back to the tone and texture presented by 1960s and early 1970s Marvel artists, such as Steve Ditko, who introduced the Vulture in May 1963. The director made it clear to Henderson that he viewed *Spider-Man 3* as "a missed opportunity," and he very much wanted to redeem this character that he loved with this fourth and, for him, final film.

"If he was going to do a 'last' Spider-Man movie, he wanted to go out on a high note. He wanted to do it his way. No compromise. No last minute [orders to] 'change this, change that,'" Henderson said. "That was the studio's pitch to bring him back. And unfortunately, I just don't think it worked out that way."

Several pieces of concept art for the Vulture used the likeness of Oscar nominee John Malkovich (*In the Line of Fire* and *Burn after Reading*) because that's who the sketchers were told was in negotiations to play the *Spider-Man 4* villain. Raimi likely was remembering how effective Willem Dafoe and Alfred Molina were as his early *Spider-Man* villains and hoped to recapture some of that character-actor magic.

The storyboard artists working on *Spider-Man 4* were divided up into groups that worked on action set pieces, even though the script was still being finalized. One would have been set in the New York City subway tunnels, an underground battle that eventually would emerge from beneath the city and soar up into the skies.

Henderson's primary assignment involved an aerial battle between Spider-Man and the Vulture, which would have taken place at the top of the T-shaped Citicorp Center on Lexington Avenue in Midtown Manhattan. In mapping out this anticipated fight, Henderson said, "They were going to have a big brawl-for-it-all, where Vulture almost kills Spider-Man. And then Spider-Man at the last minute—he's really wounded, he's bleeding really badly, he's in real trouble—Peter finally, almost as a reaction, forces The Vulture off. When he does, it snaps some of the stuff from the wings, so he ends up just tumbling into the ether, off the top of the Citicorp building. That's what does him in."

These were possibilities for *Spider-Man 4*, sequences that were being designed by Raimi's team as he plotted with his screenwriters where the movie might go. A lot of it could have and would have changed before cameras started to roll on the sequel. *Spider-Man 4*'s scripters contemplated a B-plot involving the Vulture's daughter, who was an accomplished executive representing a venture capital firm that was trying to buy the *Daily Bugle*. Felicia Hardy, a comic book villain known as the Black Cat, almost appeared as a love interest for Peter. Casting rumors placed Anne Hathaway in contention for the role. And Henderson also recalls Raimi's plans for what sounds like an incredible opening sequence, which is realized in the storyboards on the artist's website.

"We were going to open the movie with this montage of all the villains we knew that Sam would never be able to use in Spider-Man movies," he said. "Because Peter, now that MJ [Mary Jane] has gone, he has finally made peace, and he loves being Spider-Man. He's actually enjoying it. So we were going to try to do The Shocker, Mysterio, The Stilt Man, and that kind of stuff."

As part of that montage, Raimi would have become the first Spider-Man director to feature Mysterio, the master of illusion (who Jake Gyllenhaal eventually went on to play in 2019's *Spider-Man: Far from Home*). Bruce Campbell, Raimi's longtime collaborator and a staple of the Spider-Man franchise, likely would have assumed this villainous role.

Malkovich and Hathaway weren't the only big names considered for this sequel. Henderson recalls a plan to have the Vulture be the primary villain of *Spider-Man 4* only until that aforementioned scene where Spider-Man sends him tumbling from the roof of the Citicorp building. After that shocking death, the movie would have passed the Vulture mantle to the criminal's daughter, turning her into the Vultress. The name attached to this pivotal role for a short amount of time was Angelina Jolie.

No matter how hard the team tried to get *Spider-Man 4* off the ground, giving Raimi the chance to exit the franchise on that proverbial high note, obstacles in the script department continuously cropped up until Raimi finally told Sony he couldn't move forward. His historic run on Sony's Spider-Man franchise came to an official end on January 11, 2010.

"Sam had said what he had needed to say," Tolmach reflected. "I really mean that. I have so much respect for him in that way. Sam gave us three Spider-Man movies that set the tone for a generation, and beyond, of filmmakers and filmmaking."[32]

Raimi's influence on the Spider-Man film franchise and on the superhero genre as a whole can still be felt to this day. He blazed the trail for storytellers seeking more character development in effects-heavy blockbusters. Thanks to

Raimi, audiences invested just as much emotional stock into Peter Parker's everyday woes as they did to the physical danger he encountered in the Spidey suit. Raimi oversaw the visual artists who broke down Spider-Man's unique physical movements and learned how to translate them to the big screen. Their work inspired and educated craftspeople who continue to perfect live-action comic book adaptations. And more than anything else, Raimi's Spider-Man movies legitimized Marvel as a source material, opening the floodgates for a tsunami of superhero movies that still crowd movie theaters decades later.

Raimi might have been done, but Sony had no intention of hopping off the Spider-Man train. The studio decided to reimagine the franchise, recast the role, and reintroduce Spider-Man to a new generation. They thanked Raimi for his contributions, then did everything they could to escape the enormous shadow he cast over the entire series moving forward.

CHAPTER SEVEN
ANDREW GARFIELD GOES TO COMIC-CON

A ndrew Garfield had an idea. It ultimately would produce what he lovingly refers to as "one of the most magical moments I've ever had."[1] Yet it almost didn't happen because it made the executives at Sony Pictures very nervous.

The accomplished British actor was riding high in 2010, enjoying what had to be considered the hottest streak of his still-young career. Critical groups from around the globe bestowed nominations on Garfield for his mesmerizing turns in Mark Romanek's sci-fi drama *Never Let Me Go* and David Fincher's *The Social Network*, the latter of which earned him Best Supporting Actor nominations at the BAFTAs, the Critics' Choice Awards, and the Golden Globes. Garfield was ready to capitalize on that momentum and graduate to blockbuster storytelling, which is how he found himself standing next to producers Laura Ziskin and Avi Arad on a small stage in Cancun, Mexico, during a splashy international media presentation on July 1, 2010.

"To be Peter Parker is a huge responsibility. And it takes a lot of power, too. So we found an amazing, amazing young man," Arad told the gathered journalists.[2] Ziskin then invited director Marc Webb onstage to formally introduce the twenty-six-year-old actor the team had chosen to be Hollywood's next on-screen Spider-Man. Garfield emerged from behind a curtain looking shell shocked, probably due to a combination of the incessant camera flashes popping off in his face and the fact that Ziskin had only just informed the young man that he'd won the coveted role thirty minutes prior to his standing on that stage before the global press corps.

Garfield has a cheeseburger to thank for this life-altering role. Webb, who directed the quirky romantic comedy *(500) Days of Summer*, says he realized Garfield was the right actor to portray both Peter Parker and Spider-Man during an audition scene where Peter was talking with love interest Gwen Stacy and trying to calm her down while the two of them ate. Garfield decided to improvise with the burger he had been holding, and something about the way he conducted himself with this specific food item caught Webb's eye and held his attention.

"The way he ate this food—it was such a dumb task, such a dumb independent activity that you give to an actor to do, and he did it," Webb said. "I can't explain exactly [why] I felt like it worked, but that was it."[3]

Convincing Webb and the suits at Sony that he was right for the role was only half the battle for Garfield—and what a battle it was. The Spider-Man audition process was every bit as arduous as one might imagine, with Garfield eventually beating out Josh Hutcherson (*The Hunger Games*), Logan Lerman (the Percy Jackson film series), Michael Angarano (*Sky High*), and Jamie Bell (*Billy Elliot*) for the iconic part. Matt Tolmach remembers Garfield's presence as being "extraordinary" during the numerous Spider-Man audition sessions.[4] And Tolmach had good reason to be heavily invested in the actor selected to lead Webb's *The Amazing Spider-Man*. By 2010, Tolmach had resigned his position as copresident of Columbia Pictures and had transitioned into a full-time producer's role on these new Spider-Man films. Industry insiders viewed Tolmach's Sony exit as unusual. Even he told the trade website Deadline at the time of his departure, "These jobs are great and it's hard for people to imagine anyone leaving voluntarily. We've been saying to each other all morning, 'Nobody does this.' But I like that."[5]

His previous position at the studio allowed Tolmach to be an influential voice when Sony hit its original home run by casting Tobey Maguire in the first Spider-Man trilogy. Now he was asking lightning to strike the same spot a second time.

"The goal was clear. You have to find someone who *is* Peter Parker. Which is that every man, that still touches on the massive humanity and selflessness and a degree of innocence [in the character]," Tolmach said. "We fell in love with Garfield."

Not that he needed it, but Garfield also received an important blessing when Maguire gave the casting his seal of approval. "When it was coming together, I was particularly excited at two moments," the original Spider-Man said. "One was when Marc Webb got involved. I think he's an interesting and cool choice. And then I was certainly curious as to who was going to play Peter Parker. When I heard it was [Andrew], I was literally like, 'Fucking perfect!'"[6]

It was Garfield's parents who introduced him to Spider-Man at a young age, first through the multiple animated series featuring the hero and then through the comics. He remembers being three years old when his mother, Lynn, first stitched a homemade Spidey costume out of felt so he could wear it on Halloween. Andrew's immediate love of the character propelled him on weekend excursions to a comic book shop in the English town of Sutton, where he'd snatch up issues and absorb as many Spidey stories as possible.

"I was just hungry for it. I needed it in my life. I needed to have a relationship with him, and it grew," Garfield said. "And as I grew, the relationship deepened. I started to understand more and more what he stood for, and what he was. It just continued to mean the world to me."[7]

Garfield was nineteen by the time he saw Sam Raimi's *Spider-Man*. He viewed it on a pirated DVD he'd snagged in North London with his friend Terry McGuiness, and the two watched the entire feature two times in a row before turning to face a mirror to practice reciting Maguire's final line in the film: "Whatever life holds in store for me, I will never forget these words. With great power comes great responsibility. This is my gift, my curse. Who am I? I'm Spider-Man."

"Terry has this thick accent, and every time I would recite that line, he would laugh this very distinct laugh and say, 'No, man, you could never be fucking Spider-Man. You'll never be fucking Spider-Man!'" Garfield remembers. "I was so humiliated and upset."[8]

Because he'd grown up idolizing the character, Garfield knew that the real challenge to being Sony's new Spider-Man lay with winning over the countless fans who viewed the studio's reboot with healthy amounts of skepticism. Fan loyalty to Raimi's signature vision for Spider-Man remained rock solid, even after the uneven results of the director's 2007 sequel *Spider-Man 3*. So Webb's pending interpretation frequently met a defiant attitude of "prove yourself worthy of our affection" from the Spider-Man community, which was understandable. Webb's first Spider-Man movie had something Raimi's first movie did not: a predecessor that had established an extremely high bar of expectation. Heading into the production of the 2012 reboot *The Amazing Spider-Man*, the producers acknowledged that they were cursed, for lack of a better term, by the success of the Raimi films that came before it.

"It was iconic. Tobey was iconic. Tobey *was* Spider-Man," Tolmach said. "So how do you say to the world, 'Well, wait a minute. Spider-Man is this *other* guy now.' It was always something we were aware of, that we needed to do."[9]

That's where Garfield's idea came in. The actor has made it abundantly clear in the years that followed his two-film stint as Sony's web slinger that the role never completely belonged to him, and all he actually did was borrow it for a short amount of time. It's a healthy approach to a daunting task that, in theory, should have kept the actor at a safe distance from the enormous scrutiny that accompanies the gig.

"The suit is what people love. Whatever body is in that suit doesn't really matter," Garfield has been quoted as saying, humbly. "That's what I find wonderful about this character is that he is everyone's, and he *is* everyone."[10]

So Garfield told Sony he wanted to make a bold proclamation aimed directly at the fan base telling them that he understood each fan's passion for the character because he himself possessed that same devotion, which is why he wanted to deliver a message of Spider-Man unity directly to the fans at the mecca of pop culture geekdom: the annual San Diego Comic-Con convention.

"He Saved My Life"

The team responsible for *The Amazing Spider-Man* believed they had found the perfect actor to play the next Peter Parker. It was time to sell their choice to the global Spider-Man fan base.

The studio chose a Hall H panel at San Diego Comic-Con as the ideal way to introduce Garfield to a curious crowd. Hall H footage presentations and fan question-and-answer sessions frequently serve as the marketing launchpad for comic book blockbusters. And Sony enjoyed a favorable history with the hall, bringing both *Spider-Man 2* and *Spider-Man 3* to San Diego for star-studded presentations that helped the sequels earn fan approval. "Comic-Con creates buzz that, in the world of these kinds of movies, is really, really important. What the dedicated fans have to say can really impact your franchise," said Tolmach. "Then you have to go out in the world and make a whole bunch of *other* people happy. But it's a great way to start the conversation."

Yet the film's creative core also recognized that a swing and a miss in San Diego could have damaged their whole *Amazing Spider-Man* endeavor before it even lifted off the ground.

"The fans who tend to show up in Comic–Con are the really dedicated, devoted people who care a ton about the movies and the quality of these movies," Tolmach said. "They are comic book readers, they are book readers, they're television-show watchers. They come with tremendous investment in the character, and in the IP that we are turning into a movie franchise. And so you want their blessing, because they matter. They talk to each other. They can have a tremendous amount of sway over the sentiment towards a franchise. And so you *want* their buy-in."

That's exactly what the *Amazing Spider-Man* team got the moment Garfield stood in the middle of 6,500 Hall H patrons on July 22, 2011, and revealed his true colors as a die-hard, lifelong Spider-Man fan. The speech he delivered to the anxious crowd that day was so authentic and so genuine and beautiful that it gives me goose bumps every time I revisit it (which happens roughly twice a year). Garfield's panel surprise came off as spontaneous, despite the fact it was planned as thoroughly as an unpredictable live event like Comic-Con will allow. In hindsight, this tender marketing stunt was the best possible first step for *The Amazing Spider-Man* franchise. It's understandable why Garfield considers this moment to be the highlight of his entire tenure as Spider-Man.

"That was one of the most magical moments I've ever had, being able to speak from my heart to a room full of people that I felt a part of, and I always have," Garfield said.[11]

No one in Hall H expected anything like this when the San Diego Comic-Con panel for *The Amazing Spider-Man* began. Host Ralph Garman was barely able to welcome the movie's cast and crew to the stage before he was interrupted by a man in a store-bought Spider-Man costume standing at the microphone that had been set up in the audience to field fan questions.

"Hey! Hey, I'm sorry," this visibly nervous person stammered into the mic. Garman tried to inform the guy that the question-and-answer portion of the panel would occur later, but this stranger plowed through.

"Yeah, I know, I'm sorry. Do you mind if I just quickly . . . I'm sorry. *Hey everybody!* I'm sorry, do you mind if I just say one thing? I think this might be the most incredible day of my life. I've always wanted to be at Comic-Con in Hall H as Spider-Man with all of you guys. It's always been a dream of mine."

The costume this person was wearing looked baggy and cheap. The mask he sported was comically oversized, and the lenses had very visible holes poked in the middle to allow the person inside to see. But none of that mattered once the mask was pulled off to reveal that the man at the microphone was Garfield, Hollywood's new wall crawler.

"So thanks for having me," the actor stated as the Hall H crowd erupted. Garfield turned to the audience and pounded his chest, signifying the love flowing from him to the gathered masses. It was genuine. It was heartfelt. And the words that followed conveyed the young man's passion for Spider-Man to this crowd.

"You have no idea how much this means to me. I've always wanted to come here as a fan. And this is my first time. So here I am, as a fan," Garfield said.

His smile was radiant. He paused for a second, letting the growing levels of crowd adoration soak in before he turned to a prepared statement he'd scrawled on a sheet of paper.

"Stan Lee says that the reason why Spidey is so popular is because all of us can relate to him, and I agree. I *needed* Spidey in my life when I was a kid, and he gave me hope. In every comic I read, he was living out mine and every skinny boy's fantasy of being stronger. Of being free of the body I was born into, and that swinging sensation of flight. And upon receiving his power, unlike most who become corrupted, he used it for good. And I think we all wish that we had the courage to stick up for ourselves or to stick up for a loved one, or even a stranger who you see being mistreated. Peter Parker has inspired me to feel stronger. He made me, Andrew, braver. He reassured me that by doing the right thing, it's worth it. It's worth the struggle. It's worth the pain. It's worth even the tears, the bruises, and the blood. And I wouldn't be able to stand here in front of you guys right now without feeling that Spider-Man was here with me, with his reassuring hand on my shoulder, making sure I don't fall over and concuss myself.

"He has inspired countless people—girls, boys, men, women, all of us," Garfield continued. "And he has saved lives. And he saved my life. And I owe Webhead a lot. And I owe Stan 'The Man' a lot. And I'm humbled to be here, like you do not know, to share the work that we've done with all of you. And this is my first Comic-Con. This is definitely the coolest moment of my life, and thank you for being here and sharing it with me."

Those raw, emotional sentiments carried an immeasurable amount of weight that day. Garfield's Comic-Con speech did so much more than win over a protective fan base. It proved to attendees and those tuning in from around the world that the role was about to be occupied by someone just like them: a fan. Spider-Man was as important to Garfield as he was to everyone watching him introduce that *The Amazing Spider-Man* panel. "He wasn't interested in the big, grand entrance of a movie star, so to speak," Tolmach said. "The idea he pitched was, 'I feel like the excitement belongs to the people. And I want them to know that this, to me, is about . . . *we* are all Spider-Man. Spider-Man is one of the people. He's one of the fans. Everyone is Spider-Man.'"[12]

This attitude immediately set Garfield apart from his predecessor. Maguire didn't have the same deep-rooted attachment to Spider-Man when he first assumed the role. Garfield's casting as Spider-Man, in fact, reminds us of just how rare it is to see a genuine fan land a coveted role in a superhero movie instead of the part going to a flavor-of-the-month star who happens to have box office draw. Ryan Reynolds connected with the sarcastic attitude of the mercenary Deadpool as an example and still had to fight an uphill battle against studio opposition just for the chance to bring the foulmouthed Marvel character to the big screen. His passion propelled two unconventional but enormously successful R-rated comic book adaptations. But casting stories like that are few and far between.

Because Garfield placed Spider-Man on a pedestal long before he was in contention for a movie, he considered it a genuine honor to get to bring his interpretation of the character to life. Regardless of your thoughts on Webb's *The Amazing Spider-Man*, it's hard to deny Garfield's reverence for the characters of both Peter Parker and Spidey and the sincerity he injects into virtually every scene. "Stories are the things that remind us of who we are as human beings, and we actually have an opportunity to provide deep wisdom and medicine and guidance," Garfield said about his time in the Spider-Man suit. "So for me, it was like: How do I help to infuse this with as much soul and universality as possible, knowing that millions of young people are going to be watching? So it's not an exercise in selling t-shirts and mugs and Happy Meals. But it's giving young people the opportunity to feel their own extraordinariness, and their own ordinariness, and seeing someone who's just like them struggle with those two things living inside of themselves."[12]

As for Garfield's emotional Comic-Con speech, Tolmach summarized, "He wanted to make a statement. Which is, 'We're with you. And I'm one of you. And Spider-Man is one of you. And I'm like every other guy in here with a Spider-Man suit.' That was his idea."[13]

And the funny part is that this iconic moment might never have happened if Garfield hadn't begged the studio to let him risk everything and give it a shot.

Living Up to a Legacy

The Comic-Con speech, according to Tolmach, was born out of necessity because the *Amazing Spider-Man* sizzle reel the studio meant to bring to San Diego was solid but not spectacular. Primarily, it lacked eye-popping stunt work, and Garfield recognized they were going to need to offer something additional in order to win the audience.

In hindsight, his speech was brilliant because it helped to temporarily ease fan concerns over the reboot and was a huge part of the reason why *The Hollywood Reporter* referred to Sony's *The Amazing Spider-Man* presentation at the 2011 Comic-Con as the convention's most "should-have-been-there panel."[14]

"There was a feeling of, 'This is a big deal,'" Tolmach said. "We're launching a new Spider-Man. There had only been one. And this is a giant moment. How we come out of the gate, and how we define who this guy is—who is now going to be the face of this beloved character for however long—is *so* important."

But at the time, Tolmach confessed that certain Sony executives reacted to Garfield's pitch of a Comic-Con publicity stunt with equal parts "enthusiasm and terror."

"Because," he elaborated, "anytime you're not in control of a narrative, it's scary for people in Hollywood. Who knows what's going to happen? Is it going to play? Are they going to know who he is? Is it going to land? Is it goofy? Is it great? But Andrew was super passionate about it. And it was blessed, on the highest level."

That's exactly how Garfield remembers the moment as well. He's never watched any video capture from the event, claiming that he "just wanted the pure experience to remain. Because it was one of the most pure experiences I've ever had, in terms of connecting with a group of people that I felt connected to."[15] In an interview conducted years after his franchise had ended,

Garfield elaborated even further on why the surprise he pulled off in San Diego stands out as the highlight of his whole experience playing Spider-Man.

"Because it felt like just me. Vulnerable. And terrified," he said. "And that could've really failed. That whole idea could have failed. And everyone told me it was going to. Emma [Stone] told me it was not a good idea. The studio said, 'What the fuck are you thinking?!' And I was, 'Just let me do one thing! Just one thing!' And to their credit, they allowed it, and they saw that it worked. They trusted me a lot more after that, to their credit."[16]

The San Diego Comic-Con panel surprise wasn't Garfield's first time in a Spider-Man suit. But it was the first time he wore one in front of so many Spider-Man fans. Despite the intense publicity of the stunt, it still had to feel less intimidating, less dysfunctional than the hours he spent in the infamous red and blue bodysuit during his multiple rounds of auditions alongside virtually every young actor in Hollywood who was hoping to land the coveted role.

Garfield told Maguire during a May 2012 conversation that he and fellow contender Jamie Bell grabbed dinner immediately following their auditions to swap notes and compare their experiences. "[We] thought it would be a nice idea to get everyone together and kind of interview each other about how messed up the process is, being against each other, and remember that we're all in it together," he said. "Knowing that when you take off that bodysuit, someone else is going to be stepping into your sweat immediately after. It's a weird kind of cattle call."[17]

That realization likely helped Garfield form the mind-set we've discussed, that the role of Spider-Man never really felt like it fully belonged to him. Garfield might have emerged from the cattle call as the chosen one for *The Amazing Spider-Man*. But he was stepping into large shoes already worn by Tobey Maguire, and he'd one day pass the mantle to Tom Holland, who no doubt will see another person playing Spider-Man on-screen in the distant future. Spider-Man belongs to everyone, and he belongs to no one.

The Amazing Spider-Man tried its best to honor the legacy of what had come before it by leaving it alone. Marc Webb actively chose to do as many things different from the three Raimi films as possible, going so far as to demand that no one who worked on that franchise (at least in a technical capacity) be allowed to contribute to *The Amazing Spider-Man.*

"Marc was a little dogmatic about this in the beginning. He was basically like, 'Don't do anything from the original Spider-Man [films],'" said Jerome Chen, the visual effects supervisor on Webb's two *Amazing Spider-Man* films. "We couldn't even use the webbing system created for the *old* Spider-Man movies, the Raimi Spider-Man movies, because we wanted our webs to look different. We spent months on webbing design. It was probably one of the hardest things to figure out."[18]

Webb approached the material with a fresh vision, a new cast, an expected case of the jitters, but also the full support of the studio to carry its franchise to greener pastures. Whether the movie succeeded is still up for debate in the Spider-Man fan community.

"No One Suffers As Beautifully As Andrew"

Looking back, it's appropriate that *The Amazing Spider-Man* kicked off its public-facing publicity cycle with a potentially disastrous stunt that felt like a gamble because several creative decisions Webb made when bringing his unique interpretation of Spider-Man to the big screen could also be described as gambles. These choices produced an uneven combination of moderate wins and glaring mistakes for the origin story and its sequel, 2014's *The Amazing Spider-Man 2*—some of which later informed studio executives how to and how not to reboot a popular comic book franchise.

Sony also allowed Garfield to step out in front of its pivotal marketing campaign and attempt his San Diego Comic-Con stunt because, deep down, the *Amazing Spider-Man* brain trust of Amy Pascal, Avi Arad, Matt Tolmach, and Laura Ziskin knew that their leading man and his passion for their Marvel character was the wild card this reboot needed to have any real shot at success. Casting makes or breaks a Spider-Man film. Even the most ferocious critics of Webb's *Amazing Spider-Man* films can't deny Garfield's authentic relatability in the role of Peter Parker. Garfield's acting choices help Peter come across more as an outsider who's uncomfortable in his own teenage skin versus the socially awkward bookworm Maguire presented.

"No one suffers as beautifully as Andrew," noted Lin-Manuel Miranda, the Pulitzer Prize–winning force behind Broadway's *Hamilton* who also directed Garfield in the 2021 musical *Tick, Tick . . . Boom*.[19]

Garfield's Parker isn't Maguire's Parker at all. He stands up for bullied classmates. He rides a skateboard around Queens. He even has enough self-confidence to flirt with his high school crush, Gwen Stacy.

Ah yes, Gwen Stacy, played by the charming, intelligent, and effervescent girl next door, Emma Stone. She and Garfield shared an explosive on-screen chemistry, which, in turn, led to an off-screen, tabloid-fueling romance. Thanks in large part to their performances, the tender, tragic relationship between Peter and Gwen serves as the big, beating heart pumping blood through Webb's Spider-Man franchise.

"Andrew was a fantastic Peter Parker. And I think Marc Webb did a wonderful job, too," Pascal commented. "[But] I think particularly what works so beautifully about the *Amazing* movies is the relationship between Peter and Gwen."[20]

When Webb's vision for Spider-Man works, it's devastatingly good. When it misses, it frustrates. Webb wanted his audience to believe that his action took place in our recognizable world. Since Raimi, John Dykstra, and Don Burgess achieved hyperrealism for their Spider-Man, Webb deliberately countered with a gritty, street-level take on this classic Marvel mythology. He exchanged Maguire's organic webs for mechanical web shooters, believing that they emphasized Peter's scientific intelligence. He had elaborate but practical New York City sets constructed on a vast studio back lot so that stuntmen could physically complete the movie's action set pieces and not rely on computer-generated stand-ins. *Amazing Spider-Man* costume designer Kym Barrett made sure that Garfield's Spidey suit felt like a do-it-yourself costume any teenager could make, implementing over-the-counter sunglass lenses into her hero's mask and using tennis shoes with the bottoms cut off to complete Spidey's boots. Even when visual effects were necessary, Webb made it clear that they should exist to help the action feel as real and grounded as possible.

Webb referred to *The Amazing Spider-Man* as a palette cleanse. In his mind, the world they built and Garfield's performance in it differed so drastically from Raimi's three films that they justified the existence of this reboot, even though it was arriving only five years after the enormously successful *Spider-Man 3*.

"I felt like Spider-Man is a perennial character, and he's somebody that belongs on screen," Webb said. "And I thought there was enough worthwhile material that justified rediscovering this character."[21]

He's right. The Spider-Man character should be strong enough to survive different adaptations of his story. New creative teams have been retelling Spidey stories in the comics for decades. The same logic should carry over to film. Webb's hiring ensured that *The Amazing Spider-Man* would offer a grounded tone, strong emotional through lines, and an emphasis on the development of human characters. Sony didn't tap Webb for his visual effects expertise or his vast experience in blockbuster entertainment. *The Amazing Spider-Man* was only his second feature film. The studio instead appreciated the angsty pathos and light comedic touch that elevated Webb's relatable *(500) Days of*

The first ever appearance of Spider-Man in *Amazing Fantasy #15* in the Marvel Comics exhibit at Museum of Pop Culture MoPOP in Seattle. © Emily743 | Dreamstime.com

Above: Stan Lee attends the world premiere for *Spider-Man: Homecoming* at the TCL Chinese Theatre in Los Angeles, June 28, 2017. © Featureflash | Dreamstime.com

Left: Avi Arad at the *Spider-Man Far From Home* Premiere at the TCL Chinese Theater IMAX on June 26, 2019 in Los Angeles. © Hutchinsphoto | Dreamstime.com

Amy Pascal at the Los Angeles premiere of *Spider-Man: No Way Home* held at the Regency Village Theatre on December 13, 2021. © Starstock | Dreamstime.com

A recreation of concept art from Sam Raimi's unproduced *Spider-Man 4*, which would have featured The Vulture as the primary villain. Jeffrey Henderson

The Amazing Spider-Man 2 star Andrew Garfield poses with P.J. O'Connell following a press junket interview in New York City in 2014. Author's photo

Above: A large statue located near Harbour City, Hong Kong promotes *The Amazing Spider-Man 2*, and demonstrates the hero's global appeal. © Pindiyath100 | Dreamstime.com

Left: Marvel Studios President Kevin Feige poses with the author in London during press events for *Spider-Man: Far From Home*, June 2019.

The author joins film journalists on the Staten Island Ferry set from *Spider-Man: Homecoming* in Atlanta, Georgia. Author's photo

The author on the London-based "Venice" set of *Spider-Man: Far From Home*. Author's photo

Left: *Avengers: Endgame* co-directors Joe and Anthony Russo conducted the first all-spoilers interview with ReelBlend cohosts Sean O'Connell and Kevin McCarthy in 2019. Author's photo

Below: The author poses with Spider-Man in front of London's Tower Bridge, the location of the *Spider-Man: Far From Home* finale, in 2019. Author's photo

Summer. They hoped he could inject those elements into a big-budget super-hero property, in essence delivering a $220 million indie film that happened to be about Spider-Man.

And he did.

Chen remembers the first thing Webb showed him to explain his intended approach to *The Amazing Spider-Man* was the movie's elaborate crane scene, believing the sequence would demonstrate the grit and determination that live in this underdog hero. In the film's third act, a wounded Spider-Man needs to swing across Manhattan to Oscorp Tower to prevent the Lizard (Rhys Ifans) from infecting the city's population with a dangerous chemical formula. Sensing that the web slinger needs an assist, a crane operator who Spider-Man helped earlier in the film (played by C. Thomas Howell) orders his colleagues to turn their machines so that they extend over the streets, giving Spidey a clear swinging path through the concrete jungle.

"It was a touchstone for what the movie was supposed to feel like," Chen said.[22]

During the pitch process, Webb also wrote an e-mail that he sent to Tolmach, describing a scene he'd imagined to illustrate the scale of this teenager protecting one of the world's largest cities. He laid out the point of view of the shot, which would show dirty Converse sneakers that were standing up several stories high as Spider-Man perched on a ledge. The cartoon polish of Raimi's eye was being buffed out for a street-level access point. "There was just a different tone to the character because, again, every director finds his or her voice and self in that character," Tolmach surmised. "So this was where Marc found purchase."[23]

Webb's team couldn't ignore the Raimi films completely. To do so would be foolish. "So much work was done in studying how a person would move as he's webslinging," said Chen.

But being the next franchise meant that *The Amazing Spider-Man* could recognize where its predecessors had stepped out of line and attempt to correct course.

"What's interesting is that we found that with Sam's movies, in the earlier movies, he obeyed physics a little bit more in terms of how Spider-Man would move," Chen continued. "But by the third movie, you could tell he just needed to get Spider-Man to the action as quickly as possible. So he would just do very quick moves to get through the shot. And then the editor would speed it up just so he could get to the action. The animation supervisor for *Amazing Spider-Man* was named Dave Schaub. He was pivotal in really making sure that gravity felt its presence with Spidey. He was instrumental with that. We spent a long, long, long time basically making sure that the physics felt right."

Easily, the most drastic change implemented by Webb and his *Amazing* screenwriters was a plot point borrowed from David Koepp's unused *Amazing Spider-Man* script from 2002: an emphasis on Peter Parker's parents, Mary (Embeth Davidtz) and Richard (Campbell Scott). The film literally opens with an adolescent Peter (Max Charles) playing hide-and-go-seek with his dad, though the game is interrupted when Parker's parents are forced to hastily flee because they've learned of a looming threat. Mary and Richard leave their son with his Aunt May (Sally Field) and Uncle Ben (Martin Sheen), and their absence provides Peter with the motivation he needs to learn more about them, complete his father's scientific research, and fill a void that's consuming this emotionally stymied orphan.

The Parker parent plotline signifies Webb's boldest swing at being different. It was never a part of the Raimi stories. It directly contributes to the creation of the Lizard, Peter's antagonist in *The Amazing Spider-Man*, and it's a dominant thread tying together significant chunks of Webb's sequel, *The Amazing Spider-Man 2*. But it's also the franchise addition that detractors routinely single out as the weakest part of Webb's movies, a convoluted mystery assigned enormous weight in Peter's universe that's completely lacking any form of resolution.

The Amazing Spider-Man also did something no other previous Spider-Man movie dared to do: it assumed it would receive a sequel. Raimi's 2002 *Spider-Man* included one scene hinting at conflict on the horizon between our hero and his best friend, Harry Osborn (James Franco), over the death of the Osborn patriarch, Norman (Willem Dafoe). *The Amazing Spider-Man* doubles down on its teases for a follow-up story, all but ensuring the next chapter, audience acceptance be damned.

These scenes also manage to be the two moments that deviate the most from the overall tone of Webb's story and feel tacked on. In one, Peter sits behind Gwen as their teacher delivers a monologue about making promises one can't keep. "Those are the best kind," Peter whispers, causing Gwen to smile. But that smug defiance instantly negates the gut-wrenching challenge Peter accepted only minutes before, when he ensured a dying Captain Stacy (Denis Leary) he'd leave Gwen out of his heroic lifestyle. With one line of dialogue, audiences were assured that Peter and Gwen's conflicts would be resolved before the sequel, when a downbeat ending and an uncertain future would have been more character appropriate for Peter Parker.

Second, and perhaps more brazenly, *The Amazing Spider-Man* teased its place in a much larger story by including what had become the norm for superhero movies thanks to Marvel Studios: a mid-credits stinger. Usually these sequences were meant to set up the action for a follow-up film, and in Webb's scene, he has Curt Connors (Ifans) being visited by a mysterious man in a trench coat and hat who claims he has bigger plans for Parker.

Who is that guy?

Webb suggests that they initially considered making him Electro, which is why there's a bolt of lightning seen outside Connors's cell window right

before the man appears. The more he spoke with screenwriter James Vanderbilt, however, the more the guy's true identity morphed.

"It was a little bit of a bunch of people," Tolmach confessed, "and a little
bit of just a tease that it would *become* someone significant. The Man In The
Shadows we called him. There were conversations about Norman [Osborn].
We honestly just wanted to create a mysterious figure who we would figure
out—because here's what you realize. There are so many people that want to
kill Spider-Man. And there are so many people that want to *use* Spider-Man,
and control him, and own him. He sort of represented all of them . . . and
none of them. That's the truth. And it was a little bit of a cinematic game
we were playing based on a few different characters who were mysterious in
the Spider-Man universe. Had we been around long enough, that character
would have been realized, but we never got to it."

It's fitting that Tolmach laments the amount of time the *Amazing Spider-
Man* movies got in the public forum because time is the reason those films
receive an unusual amount of scrutiny. Hindsight suggests that not enough
time had passed between the end of the Raimi franchise and the start of this
rebooted world, meaning that no matter how hard Webb tried to differentiate
his work on-screen, comparisons between the two were unavoidable. While
not an apples-to-apples comparison, Warner Bros. allowed eight years to pass
between 1997's disastrous Batman sequel *Batman & Robin* and Christopher
Nolan's complete reconfiguration, 2005's *Batman Begins*. That's one of the
reasons Nolan's stripped-down masterpiece doesn't invite direct comparisons
to Joel Schumacher's garish, overstuffed franchise killer. DC fans collectively
believed it was time for a new Batman movie.

On the flip side, mainstream audiences seemed to believe that it wasn't
yet time for another Spider-Man origin story when *The Amazing Spider-Man*
was released in 2012. Some criticized the reboot for its redundant plot elements, from the classic spider bite that gives Peter his powers to the tragic

murder of Uncle Ben, played here with the right amount of warmth and compassion by the versatile Sheen. There's no question that apathetic fan reaction to Webb's recycled origin story prompted Marvel Studios to forgo these scenes when they finally got their hands on Spider-Man in 2015. "People had seen it before, at least twice," said *Captain America: Civil War* co-screenwriter Christopher Markus.[24]

The Amazing Spider-Man got caught between a rock and a hard place with the Spider-Man fandom. It strayed from the Raimi template but also followed core elements of the character's origin. It took risks but somehow felt safe. It was brand new yet strangely familiar. Plenty of Spider-Man fans embrace Webb's tender vision. But the majority of mainstream movie theater patrons met the relaunch with indifference, which explains why, when the *Amazing Spider-Man* creative team got a crack at a sequel, they weren't going to make those mistakes again. They were going to make completely different ones.

CHAPTER EIGHT
"THINK BIGGER"

The Saturday morning after *The Amazing Spider-Man* opened in theaters, Amy Pascal reached out to Matt Tolmach with an emotionally packed three-word message: "We did it." Their reboot had earned more than $95 million at the domestic box office by that point. Tears were shed by both executives, and congratulations were tossed back and forth. Pascal expressed sincere thanks to her longtime partner for successfully relaunching their beloved Spider-Man and getting a new series off the ground. For Tolmach, Pascal's praise carried more emotional weight than usual. It's not often that a character, superhero or otherwise, is asked to reinvent themselves on-screen. The entire team felt a tremendous burden during the production of *The Amazing Spider-Man* to get the movie right, so Pascal and Tolmach breathed a sigh of relief. For the most part, everyone's efforts paid off.

No sooner had Tolmach cast off that encumbrance that he immediately assumed another: producing a worthy sequel that would continue Andrew Garfield's run. Adding to the pressure was the reality that Sony had an existing *Spider-Man 2* to measure up against, and Tolmach understood how much fans adored that sequel. He himself shared their passion.

"The second *Spider-Man* with Raimi was the best one," Tolmach said. "And so it was like, 'Let's do something special here.'"[1]

Development on *The Amazing Spider-Man 2* got under way almost immediately, and a release date of May 2, 2014, was circled on Sony's calendar. Webb remained in the director's chair for the sequel. James Vanderbilt agreed to return for screenwriting duties, though *Star Trek* and *Star Trek into Darkness* twosome Alex Kurtzman and Roberto Orci eventually stepped in to rewrite his treatment. By the end of 2012, the casting wheel on *The Amazing Spider-Man 2* was rapidly spinning. Garfield and Emma Stone would reprise their lead roles. Oscar winner Jamie Foxx (*Ray*) signed on to play Electro, the film's primary antagonist. Dane DeHaan joined the sequel's cast shortly after in the part of Harry Osborn, Peter Parker's childhood friend. Before production officially got under way, the cast swelled even larger—and increased its pedigree—as Webb hired Oscar nominee Paul Giamatti (*Cinderella Man*), eventual Oscar nominee Felicity Jones (*The Theory of Everything*), B. J. Novak, and Oscar winner Chris Cooper (*Adaptation*) to play the Rhino, Felicia Hardy (aka the Black Cat), Alistair Smythe, and Norman Osborn, respectively.

The sequel's overflowing roster, specifically the presence of six potential villains in *The Amazing Spider-Man 2*, caused a noticeable murmur in the Spider-Man fan community during preproduction. The harshest criticism leveled at Sam Raimi's final Spider-Man film attacked its reliance on three villains, which detractors deemed as too many. Upset fans complained in online chat rooms that Sony appeared ready to make the same mistake on just its second Garfield Spider-Man film. Some even began posting petitions on websites such as Change.org, arguing that Sony should surrender Spider-Man to Marvel Studios, where they assumed he'd thrive alongside Iron Man, Thor, and Captain America as a member of the MCU.

But a new approach to large-scale storytelling mesmerized the top executives at Hollywood's major studios by the time Sony embarked on 2012's *The Amazing Spider-Man* and its 2014 sequel, and it potentially influenced decisions made by Sony's brain trust. Marvel Studios helped introduce the concept of a cinematic universe to audiences, inspiring producers, directors, and screenwriters to seed characters and plot threads across separate feature films, then connect them under the umbrella of one ongoing story arc. The greatest example of this long-range moviemaking would be the MCU. Jon Favreau's 2008 origin story *Iron Man* launched this experiment, which fed directly into Louis Leterrier's *The Incredible Hulk*. Next, Favreau's 2010 sequel *Iron Man 2* included a post-credit scene where S.H.I.E.L.D. agent Phil Coulson (Clark Gregg) encountered a mythical hammer in the desert, directly setting up Kenneth Branagh's *Thor*. And by the end of Joe Johnston's *Captain America: The First Avenger*, Steve Rogers (Chris Evans) had been defrosted and introduced to Nick Fury (Samuel L. Jackson), establishing the foundation for the genre-changing superhero team-up movie, *Marvel's The Avengers*.

Marvel Studios President Kevin Feige traces the idea for the cinematic universe to a 2006 panel the company held at San Diego Comic-Con. Marvel wasn't yet commanding the spotlight of a Hall H panel, instead filling a 2,000-seat auditorium where Favreau, Leterrier, and original *Ant-Man* director Edgar Wright discussed their upcoming MCU films with fans. Someone in the crowd asked Feige if the characters would ever get a chance to cross over and if these team-ups could produce an Avengers film.

"And I said, 'Who knows? This is a big new experiment for Marvel. But it's no coincidence that we have the rights to Iron Man, Hulk, Thor, Cap . . .' and the whole audience started cheering," Feige remembers. "That was one of the moments where I went, 'Boy, if only. If only we could actually pull this all together.'"[2]

In the wake of Marvel Studios' success at world building, almost every rival studio executive looked around at their assets and IP and thought, "Why not us?" Fans showed a hunger for this level of elaborate storytelling, and creators tried their best to satiate the masses. Film producer Lorenzo di Bonaventura spent years contemplating a crossover event between his live-action *Transformers* movies and the *G.I. Joe* films he was making for Paramount Pictures. Ultimately, di Bonaventura concluded that the franchises still had more than enough juice individually, so mashing them together for the benefit of a marketing bump made little sense.

Warner Bros. and its content partner DC Comics, meanwhile, paid very close attention to the Marvel model and made several moves behind the scenes to try to replicate it. The DC Extended Universe began when *The Dark Knight* director Christopher Nolan handpicked *300* helmer Zack Snyder to direct *Man of Steel*, a 2013 origin story for Superman (Henry Cavill) that launched a universe of connected DC Comics films focused on Justice League heroes Batman (Ben Affleck), Wonder Woman (Gal Gadot), Aquaman (Jason Momoa), and the Flash (Ezra Miller).

Sony didn't have a deep comic book roster in its IP stable. They had only Spider-Man. So they doubled down hard on Webb's *The Amazing Spider-Man 2*, praying that it could sustain a cinematic universe—or, in this case, a Spider-Verse—and that they could keep pace with their competitors.

"It was definitely intended to be bigger," Tolmach said about the scope of *The Amazing Spider-Man 2* and its task of rapidly establishing a much larger on-screen world for Garfield's hero.[3]

After surveying the casting news and contemplating the evolving shape of Webb's second Spider-Man movie, I wrote a column for CinemaBlend on January 29, 2013, titled "Marc Webb Isn't Making a Sequel, He's Mapping Out a Massive Spider-Man Universe." With Foxx's Electro tapped to be the main villain, it seemed evident that veteran character actors like Giamatti and Cooper, as well as rising stars DeHaan and Jones, weren't being brought on board for supporting roles in one film. Their appearances were meant to act as placeholders for larger story arcs that could be explored in subsequent sequels. You don't cast an actor of Cooper's caliber so that he can play a dying Norman Osborn in one scene. You convince Cooper to sign a contract to play the sinister Spider-Man villain in multiple movies, ensuring that Norman pulls the strings against Andrew Garfield's Peter Parker for years to come. And Webb had a wild plan for resurrecting Osborn in subsequent *Amazing Spider-Man* sequels.

There's a blink-and-you-missed-it moment in *The Amazing Spider-Man 2* where, following Norman's death, medical technicians strip the sheets off the bed where the corporate exec passed away. On the left-hand side of the bed, a horizontal green laser skims the mattress, first moving up to the headboard, then down toward the footboard. Norman definitely died. Webb swears that to be true. But the laser we spotted in that pivotal scene would have been explained if Webb had been able to continue because it was meant to suggest that Norman had his corpse decapitated and had his head cryogenically frozen in the Special Projects division of Oscorp.

Visual effects supervisor Jerome Chen confirms that his team built a head with Cooper's likeness so they could film a scene for the end credits of *The Amazing Spider-Man 2*, though it never got included. "We had a head, and we were showing it from behind, so you weren't sure who it was. It was suggested that it was [Norman's] head."[4]

Continuing on from my *The Amazing Spider-Man 2* prediction column in 2013, I wrote, "This is the kind of big-box, long-range thinking studios need to be doing with their franchise properties. No longer can (or should) a studio like Marvel or Sony be wondering how to best squeeze a trilogy out of a particular storyline. Screw that. Think bigger. *The Avengers* proved that you can, if you take the time to lay the foundation, cast properly, and spread your storyline out. I think that's what Webb is doing with this immediate sequel. I think he's being given the chance to plan for a few additional chapters. He's bringing in actors who can play important characters for multiple films, much like Samuel L. Jackson in the Nick Fury role or even someone as prominent as Robert Downey Jr. as Tony Stark. Lock the people up. Spread out how you use them over time."[5]

The afternoon that my speculative piece was published on Cinema-Blend, I received instant validation. Webb retweeted a link to my article, accompanied by a message for his social media followers that echoed my advice: "Think bigger." Webb made his intentions clear. He, Tolmach, and Arad would construct a larger on-screen universe that would expand on elements from the first *Amazing Spider-Man* while also planning ahead, placing a heavier emphasis on Oscorp, Norman Osborn's company and the place where Peter Parker's life changed forever. They would adapt the iconic "Death of Gwen Stacy" story from the comics, putting the gifted Garfield and Stone to great use for a tearjerker plotline. And they'd populate the movie with enough possible villains to one day stage a Sinister Six movie for Sony. The studio even staked its claim to November 11, 2016, as a possible release date for a Sinister Six spin-off film.[6]

"How cool is the idea that there are other villains out there? It portends all kinds of trouble for Spider Man down the road," Tolmach said, "[because] Oscorp is this sort of breeding ground for these creatures and these characters."[7]

First appearing in the 1964 comic *The Amazing Spider-Man Annual* number one, the Sinister Six is a high-powered gathering of the webhead's most infamous villains. Tentacled scientist Doctor Octopus assembled the original roster, which included Electro, Kraven the Hunter, Mysterio, Sandman, and the Vulture. It's a thrilling concept on paper, having multiple dangerous criminals joining forces to challenge Spider-Man over the course of one story. It's much harder to execute in live action, however—at least in any form that makes narrative sense.

Sony's ambitious plans for its burgeoning SpiderVerse of films wasn't stopping at a possible Sinister Six spin-off. By June 17, 2013—nearly one year before *The Amazing Spider-Man 2* opened in theaters—Sony had already announced release dates for *The Amazing Spider-Man 3* (June 10, 2016) and *The Amazing Spider-Man 4* (May 4, 2018). Leaking news to the trades showed confidence in Kurtzman and Orci's character development via the *Amazing Spider-Man 2* script. But it also placed enormous pressure on Webb's sequel, as the fates of Sony's future Spider-Man movies now rested directly on its metaphorical shoulders.

"Spider-Man is our most important, most successful, and most beloved franchise," said Jeff Blake, chairman of worldwide marketing and distribution for Sony Pictures at the time. "So we're thrilled that we are in a position to lock in these prime release dates over the next five years."[8]

Those sequels never happened. Sony's executives put their cart before the spider. Instead, by 2016, Sony had abandoned its *Amazing Spider-Man* series and negotiated a deal to send its new Spider-Man, played by Tom Holland, to Marvel Studios for the team-up film *Captain America: Civil War*. That film opened to raves on May 6, 2016. It's mind blowing how much can change in Hollywood over the course of two years.

The Thread Is Broken

What's frustrating about *The Amazing Spider-Man 2* is that the film manages to do almost as many things correctly as it does insufficiently, giving both supporters and detractors enough material to make a compelling case.

"I'm not sure I'll ever understand exactly what happened," Tolmach reflects. "I won't. That movie . . . I think there was a lot about it that was quite brilliant."[9]

Garfield similarly expresses dismay when remembering the pushback from audiences on *The Amazing Spider-Man 2* because he "genuinely loved" the Kurtzman and Orci screenplay but recognized that outside influencers tampered with it. "There was this thread running through it," he said. "I think what happened was, through the pre-production, production, and post-production, when you have something that works as a whole, and then you start removing portions of it—because there was even more of it than was in the final cut, and everything was related. Once you start removing things and saying, 'No, that doesn't work,' then the thread is broken, and it's hard to go with the flow of the story."[10]

Few people understand better what went wrong on *The Amazing Spider-Man 2* than the film's director, Marc Webb. And despite numerous attempts to get the filmmaker to open up on behalf of this book, his representatives politely but repeatedly declined, which is unfortunate because it's probable that Webb thinks his *Amazing Spider-Man* films were mistakes or failures that led to the dismantling of the Garfield series and Sony's need to appeal to Marvel for assistance. However, in a similar fashion to how Garfield received validation once he returned to Spider-Man for *No Way Home*, I believe Webb would hear affirmative messages from passionate Spidey fans who cherish his two films and prefer aspects of them to the other franchises in the series.

One fan-favorite element of *The Amazing Spider-Man 2* that worked extremely well was the Spider-Man suit upgrade conducted by Oscar-winning costume designer Deborah Lynn Scott. One of Scott's earliest gigs in the industry found her designing the puffy-vest look for an out-of-time Marty McFly (Michael J. Fox) in Robert Zemeckis's *Back to the Future*. In 1998, Scott collected her first and, to date, only Oscar for the exquisite designs she brought to James Cameron's Best Picture winner, *Titanic*.

The *Amazing Spider-Man 2* is Scott's only superhero property, and I can't see her topping the comic-accurate design she brought to Garfield's second suit. Garfield used words like "friendly" and "warmer" when describing the suit, adding that it's "closer to the Spider-Man we all know and love."[11] Webb's contribution was the larger design of the eyes on the *Amazing Spider-Man 2* mask.

"The eyes in this particular suit were a huge focus, and we really went back to the source material for that. The shape of them is very, very iconic," Scott said, pointing out that a slight change to an angle on the eyepieces can make Spider-Man look angry, mean, or sad, none of which were the desired effect.[12]

Scott also encountered production issues that Raimi's costume designer, James Acheson, encountered with regard to the coloring of the suit and the web patterns that cover three-quarters of the costume's surface area. Computer advancements did mean that Scott's team could use 3D models to perfect her designs, where Acheson and his team had to hand cut webbing to complete Tobey Maguire's costume.

From there, Chen and his visual effects wizards dipped into the sequel's increased production budget to improve on their VFX. Chen had more confidence in the procedures this time and was inspired to test more sophisticated visuals that they didn't have time to execute in the first *Amazing* movie. He praised the animators for the abundance of creativity they brought to Spider-Man's first scene in the film, a plummet from the sky that begins with a tight zoom on the hero's back before widening into a heart-thumping swing through Manhattan. Webb uses point-of-view shots to place the audience in Spider-Man's suit, while Hans Zimmer and the Magnificent Six's film score helps sell the pizzazz of the sequence.

"That second movie was the first time we approached the way we were simulating his costume over the body differently [with CGI] so that we could get that wind effect," said Chen. "Prior to that, the way it was constructed in the computer, there wasn't too much of a sensibility of the skin underneath. We faked the look of a cloth over the muscle, but we were just sculpting the suit to look like it, instead of having a simulation of cloth sliding over skin. As we got more sophisticated with our tools, and as the computing power became more powerful so that we could actually execute something like that, we started simulating his costume over an object underneath of it, and it looks much more convincing."[13]

Spider-Man's costume and his heroic gymnastics were expected carryovers from the previous Spider-Man movies. But the new villains introduced for *The Amazing Spider-Man 2* presented more significant challenges for the VFX artists. Electro's design was enormously complicated, requiring the creases of Foxx's actual face to appear underneath layers of scar tissue and energy. "We wanted the feeling that little lightning bolts were inside of his skin," Chen said. "They came up with a way of doing it. It was ridiculously elaborate, but it worked every time."

Chen also spent an inordinate amount of time traveling from the film's New York sets to Sony's Los Angeles offices to show Pascal tests of how the villain's lighting was going to look on-screen.

"Amy literally said the thing that you never want to hear, which is, 'I want to see lightning like it's never been done before,'" Chen said, totally unaware of the exact same orders his predecessor, John Dysktra, was given when working on Raimi's first Spider-Man.

The most time-consuming visual effects undertaking for Webb's *The Amazing Spider-Man 2*, though, was the re-creation of New York City's Times Square for an evening confrontation between Spider-Man and Electro. Chen admits that, in hindsight, he couldn't predict how difficult this entire sequence was going to be to pull off. Webb filmed only one physical scene in the actual Times Square location: the moment that Foxx's Electro stumbles into the tourist destination seeking more power. The rest of the confrontation was filmed on Chen's staged re-creation, which utilized six shipping containers lined with green-screen technology at Gold Coast Studios in Bethpage, Long Island.

To complete this sequence, a crew spent weeks taking pictures of every single Times Square storefront and cataloged all 211 digital billboards that threw light onto the real location so they could be mimicked on Webb's set. Chen estimates that the entire Times Square sequence, which lasts less than ten minutes on-screen, required a year of labor.

For all the hard work that went into *Amazing 2*'s visual effects, they're not what come to mind when listing the sequel's highlights. To me, they are eclipsed by Garfield and Stone, the magnetic pair who prevent the sequel from ever fully collapsing under the weight of its dense plotting. Their off-screen romantic relationship amplified the wattage on their already blistering on-screen chemistry, creating what I consider to be the most passionate pairing found in any of the Spider-Man franchises.

Because most audience members were emotionally invested in Garfield and Stone's Peter and Gwen, the gut-wrenching pain of Stacy's inevitable death landed like a roundhouse punch. Gwen Stacy's death in *The Amazing Spider-Man 2* is a brutally effective sequence and arguably the most devastating moment in Spider-Man's entire filmography. It was also the worst-kept secret in Hollywood during filming, no matter how badly Stone wanted the moment to shock audiences.

"I thought it would be like Bruce Willis in *The Sixth Sense*," she said. "And, obviously, it did not work out that way. There were photos online while we were shooting, and then in the trailers, she's literally falling. Everything is there except for [the death]."[14]

Comic fans likely drifted toward the edges of their seats the moment Harry Osborn (DeHaan) snatched Gwen off the ground at the end of the Electro fight at the Osborn power station and ascended into the skies on his glider. Any lingering hope they might have had that the movie would pull a punch and spare Peter's soul mate disappears, however, when Spidey and Stacy crash through the stained glass of the tower's ceiling and land on a narrow catwalk.

"You OK?" Peter asks, his voice filled with concern. Gwen is so rattled by fear that she barely responds, violently shaking her head no. Spider-Man and the Green Goblin's battle resumes in the cramped clock tower, and Gwen dangles by a thin strand of Peter's web until the gears of the clock turn—because Spider-Man's physically unable to stop time—and Stacy's lifeline severs.

The sequence that follows is masterfully edited by Pietro Scalia, slowing down to a crawl, then speeding up to demonstrate how quickly Gwen was falling to her death. Peter shoots one last web as he dives after Gwen, and Webb instructed his visual effects team to design the tips of the strand to look like fingers on a hand, desperately reaching out to catch Stacy. They do—but not in time. She's too close to the bottom of the clock tower. Her back bends, and her head smacks the floor, killing her instantly. The hands on the clock move to 1:21 a.m., a nod to the issue of *The Amazing Spider-Man* comic in which Peter's true love died.

Webb said Gwen's death "broke" him when he read it in the comics. "It stayed with me in a profound way. I was anxious and curious to explore it on the screen," he said.[15]

And he wanted this loss to hurt for audience members, many of whom probably refused to believe the franchise would kill off its extremely popular leading lady. "Emma is beloved, and that relationship is the heart of these movies. But that's also why we couldn't shy away from that. It has to have impact. It has to shock you. It has to be devastating. Anything else would be undermining the truth of it," Webb said.

Stone had been pushing for this Gwen story line since day one, admitting that her eventual death was "one of the reasons why I wanted to play the character." She jokes, after the fact, that the scene was "weirder to watch than to film" because on the day, all she had to do was lay still.

"I couldn't open my eyes to see Andrew," she said. "I could feel him, but to see his face, it's so heartbreaking."[16]

Chen added, "I remember when they were filming that scene, Andrew and Emma deliberately didn't see each other for a week. Andrew said, 'I don't want to see you! When we come into that scene, you have to pretend like you are dead to me.' It was very quiet. The sets were almost always very quiet. Marc likes to work very focused. So it was very quiet, a totally closed set. And I just remember Andrew coming in and just crying uncontrollably. It was just hours of that. That was gruelling, but powerful."[17]

Almost everything after the Gwen Stacy sequence in *The Amazing Spider-Man 2* diminishes the dramatic impact of her death in favor of clumsy world building in hopes of establishing the possibility of the Sinister Six. An imprisoned Harry meets with the mysterious Man in the Shadows, who informs him that Oscorp's Special Projects division is ready to move forward on villains inspired by an octopus, a vulture, and a rhino.

"We had to, storywise, bring in other characters to set them up and build a universe," Chen said. "And some of that may have clashed with the original storyline, which was trying to tell the story of Gwen. Trying to put the other characters in, I think, may have hurt it from a story point of view."

But Pascal and Tolmach remember *The Amazing Spider-Man 2* fondly, choosing to celebrate everything that worked instead of focusing on the components that didn't. "It was a really good family," Tolmach said. "We actually had a really good time making those movies. I have deep love for all those people." But he has come to realize that it's "hard to be the second Spider-Man franchise," and the desires of many ended up placing more responsibilities on the *Amazing Spider-Man 2* than one film could handle.[18]

If You Can't Beat 'Em . . .

The autopsy on *The Amazing Spider-Man 2* suggests too many causes of death to single out one as the reason for its struggles. Where Raimi's *Spider-Man 3* buckled under the weight of too many villains (including one the director had no interest in exploring), Webb's sequel struggled to juggle an obscene number of story lines it raised—some for this film and some for future films.

"One of the things we are probably guilty of in that movie is biting off more than we should have," said Tolmach. "We attempted to tell a ton of stories in a movie where any one of those stories would have been epic, and enough. And I do think there are places in the movie where we bit off more than we needed to."

That's not an exaggeration. *The Amazing Spider-Man 2* packs five pounds of story into a three-pound bag, rifling through the following: Electro's tragic origin story, the introduction of Harry Osborn, Peter and Gwen's high school graduation, the death (and cryogenic preservation) of Norman Osborn, Gwen applying to Oxford and potentially moving to London, the continued mystery surrounding Peter's parents and their connection to the Osborn family, Aunt May volunteering at a hospital, the sinister machinations of the evil scientists working in Oscorp's Special Projects division, Peter's promise to the deceased Captain Stacy to leave Gwen out of his crime-fighting adventures, our hero's inability to maintain that promise, Harry's rare blood disease (which he can cure only by obtaining a sample of Spider-Man's blood), Harry's transformation into the Green Goblin, and Gwen's devastating death at the hands of this new foe. Tolmach is correct when he says that any one of these plotlines would have been enough to carry the sequel. Taken all together, it's too much.

Then there were the factors going on both behind the scenes and in the entertainment industry as a whole that were out of Webb's control. Tolmach described 2013 as "a difficult time at the studio," likely referring to Sony Pictures CEO Michael Lynton's executive decision to shift the studio's focus from film production to "higher margin" television production. In an effort to increase Sony's profit margins, Lynton promised a "more onerous" process for getting films green-lit.[19] He claimed he'd start saying no to previously bankable movie stars asking for funding, and he'd keep directors on the financial hook when they soared past budget limits.

"Whereas I described the collective euphoria around the first Raimi movie, it didn't feel that way [for Webb's films]. Sony was having a difficult time, and the movie needed to be all things to all people in a certain way," said Tolmach. "It suddenly became encumbered, and that became the story."[20]

And finally, there was Marvel Studios, the 800-pound gorilla in the room against which Webb's *The Amazing Spider-Man* series and every other comic book property was going to be judged. MCU movies had become the gold standard for superhero storytelling by 2014. The studio was halfway through its Phase Two, having successfully delivered multiple movies for Iron Man, Thor, and Captain America, leading up to the critical and financial hit: 2012's *Marvel's The Avengers*. The Marvel Studios label grew so dependable that it guaranteed that C-level unknowns like the Guardians of the Galaxy could pack movie theaters, and Chris Pratt, best known as the chubby funny guy on the NBC sitcom *Parks & Recreation*, could reinvent himself as a comic book action star. Spider-Man fans undoubtedly looked at the uneven movies being produced around their favorite character and wondered why things couldn't be as good for the wall crawler.

"Marvel does this so brilliantly now, with the roadmap for where they're going," said Tolmach. "We were dancing a little bit. . . . Don't forget, you know, Marvel has all these characters. We had Spider-Man and the villains. It's not as easy to expand.

"[*The Amazing Spider-Man 2*] happened at a moment when I think fans were getting more, and expectations changed," Tolmach concluded. "And let's be honest, Marvel was crushing it out of the gate. And so the bar was raised, enormously."

Any imaginary obituary written for *The Amazing Spider-Man 2* would have to start by identifying the sequel as the film that ended Sony Pictures' solo Spidey universe, prompting the studio to break protocol and ask rival Marvel Studios for help. The creative team threw almost everything they could at this movie. Some of it stuck. Some of it didn't. So Pascal came to the painful conclusion that after five Spider-Man films, Sony had exhausted the majority of its options, and a drastic change was in order.

"There's only so many times that you can tell the story of, 'I really want everyone to love me, and if I tell them I'm Spider-Man, they'll love me . . . but I can't tell them!' We tried. We've told that story as many ways as I could figure out," Pascal said. "We needed to do something different. And we tried doing a lot of different things. . . . But the thing that we hadn't done was put him in the Marvel universe, and put him in a world where there are other superheroes."[21]

So the decision was made. Sony wasn't going to be able to beat Marvel, not with the assets they had at their disposal. Their best path forward, when it came to the creative and financial health of Spider-Man, was to join them.

CHAPTER NINE
SHAILENE WOODLEY'S MARY JANE WATSON

Considering Marc Webb's everything-but-the-kitchen-sink approach to *The Amazing Spider-Man 2*, it's hard to believe anything found its way to the cutting room floor, let alone the introduction of a seminal Spider-Man character played by an award-winning actress. But four scenes that were deleted from Webb's sequel have intrigued fans who speculate on the story lines that might have been explored if Shailene Woodley, star of the *Divergent* series and HBO's *Big Little Lies*, had been able to play Mary Jane Watson in *The Amazing Spider-Man 2* as planned.

Sony chose Woodley to be the first actress to play Mary Jane since Kirsten Dunst defined the character on-screen in Sam Raimi's trilogy. And Woodley was a red-hot Hollywood commodity at the time she was hired to join Webb's Spider-Man series. After establishing herself with recurring roles on the television series *The Secret Life of the American Teenager*, *The O.C.*, and *Crossing Jordan*, Woodley finally graduated to another tier with back-to-back critically acclaimed film performances in Alexander Payne's *The Descendants* (opposite an Oscar-nominated George Clooney) and the heartfelt coming-of-age romance *The Spectacular Now*. The latter likely convinced Sony brass that Woodley had the emotional chops to bond with Garfield and play Peter's famous love interest in Webb's film series.

Woodley also found herself near the top of the industry's casting wish lists when studios were looking for leads in larger franchises. Around the time she was shooting her Spider-Man scenes in New York City in 2013, Woodley also would have been prepping to film the first installment of *Divergent*, a three-film adaptation of Veronica Roth's best-selling science-fiction series. Sony seemed poised to lock Woodley into a crucial Spider-Man role right as the actress was preparing to take off as a box office commodity.

Her contributions to *The Amazing Spider-Man 2* would have been minimal—Woodley herself confirmed that Mary Jane was meant to appear in a total of only four scenes. But producers were eager to establish the character so that the actress could hit the ground running in the already announced *The Amazing Spider-Man 3*, but that sequel never happened. Woodley's performance as Webb's Mary Jane Watson got caught in the crosshairs of studio apprehension. Sony's leadership team seemed to be thinking one or two movies ahead instead of fully focusing on the story at hand. The confusion resulted in Woodley getting scrubbed from *The Amazing Spider-Man 2*, reserved for a sequel that never came to fruition.

"It didn't make sense," Woodley admitted when discussing her character almost showing up in an already busy *The Amazing Spider-Man 2*. "They [were] introducing so many new characters, it didn't make sense to introduce such a vital character to the comic books in a movie that had so much else going on."[1]

Everyone involved in the production swears the decision to cut Mary Jane Watson from the movie had nothing to do with either Woodley or her work.

"Shailene is a brilliant actress, and she did a great couple days of work," said Webb. "It was something we only discovered when we were shooting, and then in the edit room."[2]

"Shailene is an incredible talent. That's undeniable," added Garfield. "And the character not being in this movie had nothing to do with her, nothing to do with the scenes we shot, nothing to do with anything outside of, we realized there should only be one woman in Peter's life. And that woman is Gwen."[3]

Webb and his team committed to the Peter and Gwen relationship when they rebooted Sony's series with *The Amazing Spider-Man*. Gwen's tragic story helped the Webb films create narrative separation from the Raimi films, while the intense chemistry shared between Garfield and Stone remains the most memorable takeaway from that two-movie experiment. The spotlight for *The Amazing Spider-Man 2* always needed to be on Gwen, especially if her third-act demise was going to land the emotional punch the movie needed.

"It was very clear to us from the beginning that if Gwen was going to die, the entire movie was about her death," screenwriter Alex Kurtzman clarified. "It wasn't going to be a random turn-of-plot at the end. Everything needed to be leading up to that, and a reflection of this dilemma of being Spider-Man and the price tag, or the toll that it takes, on the people around you."[4]

There exists no evidence of sinister motivations for Woodley's removal from *The Amazing Spider-Man 2*, no grand conspiracy theories regarding studio manipulations, despite the rumors found in online chat forums. Mary Jane Watson is too important of a character in the Spider-Man mythology not to be included in the larger universe that Webb was designing. But trying to weave her into this already convoluted sequel probably would have diminished her impact and could have slighted a character who's crucial to Peter's development.

"There isn't some dark story here. We had gone one story too far," Tolmach concluded. "In a movie about the death of Gwen Stacy, our investment has to be in that love story. Not setting up another one."[5]

Three of Mary Jane's four scenes can be found online though only through candid photographs taken from moderate distances or grainy video with no accompanying audio or dialogue. Mary Jane would have been positioned as Peter Parker's new neighbor. "We had two or three scenes with me talking over the fence," Garfield recalled, "and there was one with us riding together on a motorcycle that we never got to shoot."[6]

In one confirmed sequence that Webb said was in the beginning of the film, Garfield would have encountered Woodley as she rode that motorbike down the alley that separated their homes in Queens. Decked out in jeans, leather boots, and a white helmet, Mary Jane appears to come across more like a tomboy than the superficial fashion model presented in her earliest Marvel Comics. This scene's unusual because Peter, in the sequence, has popped the hood on a car that's overheating, but there's no other moment in *The Amazing Spider-Man 2* where Peter owns or drives a car. The footage captured for this scene ends with a frustrated Peter reaching back into this broken-down automobile and taking out what looks like a book bag and some folders, suggesting that Mary Jane had offered to give him a ride someplace.

Emma Stone's Gwen Stacy also would have appeared in a long dialogue scene with Woodley's Mary Jane, this one taking place on the front porch of Peter's home. Footage exists of Stone arriving at the Parker house in a taxicab, walking up the steps, and knocking on the door labeled "36." (Part of this appears in the deleted scene "Is Peter Home?" on the *Amazing Spider-Man 2* Blu-ray.) No one answers the Parker's door, but Woodley's Mary Jane, sitting on her own front porch reading a book, saunters over to introduce herself. The conversation between Peter's current love and his future soul mate appears cordial, with Stone's Stacy laughing and smiling before the two shake hands. None of the footage available online includes the dialogue used in the scene. But as a melancholic observation, the purple outfit worn by Stacy in this eventually deleted scene is the same she wears throughout *The Amazing Spider-Man 2*'s final confrontation, including her tragic death, meaning that Mary Jane met Gwen moments before the latter left this world.

Woodley's third and final available scene shows Mary Jane working as a waitress in a New York City restaurant, and this one is remarkable because a blink-and-you-miss-it shot of Woodley's back remains in the final cut of

The Amazing Spider-Man 2. Mary Jane worked at the Cafe Select, which Webb includes in the film's closing moments right before the mechanized Rhino (Paul Giamatti) character marches into the frame. Woodley's sporting a blue denim shirt and a black and white striped apron. In the brief shot that remains in the film, you can spy Woodley on the right side of the frame as one car, which has been thrown through the air, smashes down on top of a parked vehicle. In extended footage that can be found online, Woodley's Mary Jane emerges from the eatery and investigates the chaos caused by the Rhino before Spider-Man swings onto the scene.

No matter how many different ways they looked at it, though, the team behind the sequel couldn't make Mary Jane fit into their narrative. "It was never something that worked particularly well in the script," Tolmach said. "And it became very clear that we were forcing it."[7]

When the decision to drop Woodley was made, *The Amazing Spider-Man 2* had ballooned into a 100-day production—excessive even by blockbuster schedule standards. It was essential that the unwieldy script started to shed stories. The buck stops with the director on any film set, and Webb does take full credit for making the creative decision to streamline the story by removing Mary Jane, spotlighting his movie's central romance.

"The relationship between [Peter and Gwen] is so sacred and so powerful, that it just didn't feel right," Webb said. "And it sucks because Shailene is such a fucking great actress, and so cool and magical. But it was just about having this obligation to this romance that I thought was sacred."[8]

Most fans view the omission with regret. Woodley, for her part, does not.

"It was not a bad thing," Woodley concluded. "It's always one of those things that people project on it, to be a really negative situation. But it really wasn't. I think it was a really smart decision on Sony's behalf"[9]—a decision that left both Woodley and Spider-Man fans with a tantalizing "what if" scenario that will forever remain unanswered.

Scrapped Sequels and Sinister Consequences

Woodley's truncated experience in the mechanisms of *The Amazing Spider-Man 2* illustrates a larger issue that has plagued virtually every major film studio in its attempts to construct superhero cinematic universes. Empowered by the end-credits scene included in Jon Favreau's 2008 origin story *Iron Man*, comic book movies too often dedicate valuable minutes in one film to teasing the next chapter in a series—whether that follow-up movie is guaranteed or not.

Studios like Sony, 20th Century Fox, and Warner Bros. haven't been as organized with their world building as Marvel, and so end-credit scenes shoehorned onto movies like *X-Men: Apocalypse* or 2017's *Justice League* led to dangling plot threads that never were explored because direct sequels failed to materialize.

Woodley's scenes were cut, but Webb's *The Amazing Spider-Man 2* still tacked on numerous teases to its third act in a gratuitous effort to world build, promising developments that were meant to be resolved in one of at least four announced Spider-Man movies. Only, much like Shailene, all four movies were canceled or indefinitely postponed in the wake of *Amazing 2*'s disappointing critical reception. We do know some details about the projects Sony planned. They included parts 3 and 4 in Sony's Garfield-led franchise. The studio also asked Alex Kurtzman and Bob Orci to sketch out their take on a Venom movie (which Kurtzman would have directed). Finally, Sony tapped Drew Goddard to shepherd a Sinister Six spin-off movie for the screen. The talented writer-director collaborated on the beloved TV shows *Buffy the Vampire Slayer*, *Angel*, *Alias*, and *Lost* in his earliest years, then broke out after helming the intelligent horror spoof *The Cabin in the Woods* for Lionsgate in 2011.

Of those abandoned projects, Goddard's *Sinister Six* sounded the most intriguing. He wanted his ensemble film to break the traditional rules of the comic book movie template, similar to the way he gleefully manipulated horror movie tropes in *Cabin*. Goddard wasn't overly concerned with the perceived obstacle of having too many villains in one movie. He cited classic films such as Robert Aldrich's *The Dirty Dozen* or Quentin Tarantino's *Reservoir Dogs* as proofs of concept because each character in those stories works as a protagonist. They just happen to be evil.

Garfield isn't sure how close Sony came to green-lighting Goddard's vision in the post-*Amazing* production cycle but remembers taking several meetings about the spin-off that got him excited about the possibilities. "We just got on like a house on fire. I loved his vision," Garfield said. "He's so unique and odd and off-kilter and unconventional in his creative choices."[10]

Sony never officially canceled Goddard's *Sinister Six*. Pascal even proclaimed interest in an all-villain Spider-Man spin-off movie as recently as 2018, though the inclusion of five classic antagonists in 2021's *Spider-Man: No Way Home* could have altered her intentions. Realistically, the Goddard script will remain in the limbo Sony created once it surveyed the landscape following *The Amazing Spider-Man 2* and realized it didn't make creative or financial sense to continue down this path. The project could surface again in the future, though chances are that it wouldn't look much like the movie Goddard envisioned in his imagination.

"This is the hard part of these movies. The 'We've got to do it again' conversations," Tolmach said. "And then it's the, 'What worked? What didn't work?' You do the whole post mortem."[11]

Editing out Shailene Woodley, unplugging *Amazing Spider-Man 3* and *4*, and shelving Drew Goddard's *Sinister Six* were the results of Sony realizing that the Spider-Man franchise desperately needed a change. The soft reboot of *The Amazing Spider-Man* felt too similar to Raimi's origin story, while the rapid franchise expansion performed in *The Amazing Spider-Man 2* underwhelmed audiences who preferred what was developing in the MCU around the same time. Financially, the Spider-Man films produced by Sony were leading to diminishing returns at the domestic box office, with *The Amazing Spider-Man 2* ($262 million) earning just over half of what Sam Raimi's 2002 *Spider-Man* ($407 million) earned in the United States.

Pascal, for her part, started to glance over at Marvel Studios, figuring a partnership with the comic book genre's top dog was the right way forward. But that decision closed the door on Garfield sooner than he likely anticipated. Garfield always believed he was borrowing the Spider-Man suit. Now he was being told to let another actor step into the costume.

Publicly, Garfield took the high road and found a silver lining every time journalists asked about his Spider-Man movies or the abrupt way his franchise ended. "There's not one part of me that regrets it at all. I feel so grateful for all the friendships and relationships I built, and the experience," he said. "I got to have that experience of being a part of that kind of behemoth kind of thing, and playing a character that has meant the world to me since I was three."[12]

The actor, in interviews, celebrated the fact that Spider-Man eventually got to appear in Marvel movies (something Garfield says he begged the studio to do the entire time he played the hero). He rightfully pointed out that contractually appearing in *The Amazing Spider-Man 3* for Sony would have prevented him from playing army medic Desmond Doss in Mel Gibson's war drama *Hacksaw Ridge*, a role that earned Garfield his first Academy Award nomination. He also likely would have missed out on the opportunity to collaborate on 2016's *Silence* with Martin Scorsese.

One time, however, Garfield let his emotional guard slip when discussing his time in the coveted suit for the two Webb films, and it provided an honest look at the genuine pain inflicted on the actor who started the assignment as a fan. In an interview conducted by fellow actor Amy Adams in 2016, Garfield confessed that Spider-Man wasn't just another job, that the role meant everything to him, but that the "machinery" of the studio system and the "corporate enterprise" that surrounds a superhero blockbuster disenfranchised him.

"There is something that happened with that experience for me, where story and character were actually not top of the priority list, ultimately, and I found that really, really tricky," Garfield said. "I signed up to serve the story. And to serve this incredible character that I'd been dressing as since I was three. And then it gets compromised. And it breaks my heart. I got heartbroken a little bit, to a certain degree."[13]

Garfield's contributions to Hollywood's on-screen interpretations of Spider-Man forever will be analyzed by journalists and fans, especially now that the conversation regarding his performance was reopened by 2021's *Spider-Man: No Way Home*. The discourse surrounding that movie moved the fan-approval needle deeper into Garfield's camp—thanks in part to his charismatic scene-stealing performance—and petitions immediately were generated online by supporters asking Sony to resurrect the idea of *The Amazing Spider-Man 3* with Andrew in the lead.

Writing for the *Washington Post* in 2022, pop culture columnist David Betancourt called for redemption for Garfield's Spider-Man reputation as he wrote, "Our Spidey senses failed us. Now we know we were wrong about Garfield. . . . [*No Way Home*] paved a path to Spider-Man redemption for Garfield that was more than just a quick cameo. But it wouldn't have worked if Garfield didn't still have a love and enthusiasm for Spider-Man that shined on screen whenever his mask was off—a love that never went away even when the character was taken from him."[14]

Garfield clearly made the most of the screen time he was given in Jon Watts's trilogy capper. And if that ends up being the actor's final swing in costume, supporters should be thrilled that, against all odds, he was gifted the opportunity to finish out his Spider-Man time on his own terms. Or, as Betancourt put it, "Garfield never needed our forgiveness for his performance, but we should hope that he can forgive us for overlooking it. In the end, his Spider-Man was nothing short of amazing."

CHAPTER TEN
LENDING SPIDER-MAN TO MARVEL

Tom Holland arrived at the Grosvenor House on the evening of March 24, 2013, ready to compete for an award. The five-star establishment located in London's upscale Mayfair neighborhood was playing host to the 18th annual Empire Awards. Holland, age seventeen, was nominated in the Best Male Newcomer category for his breakthrough role as Naomi Watts and Ewan McGregor's eldest son, Lucas, in J. A. Bayona's tsunami thriller *The Impossible*. Holland would take home the trophy that evening, but not before making the requisite pre-ceremony walk down the red carpet, fielding questions from an inquisitive press corps.

As his Empire Awards category implied, Holland was a newbie to the industry. London's theater crowd recognized him from a recent West End run in the musical *Billy Elliot*, but *The Impossible* marked Holland's feature film debut, so reporters who coaxed him to stop for a chat asked standard carpet fare, such as, "What types of roles would you like to play next?"

Holland played it safe when answering. "I mean, there are so many roles made every year, it's impossible to say exactly what you want to do," he deflected. "But, something that has a bit of action in it, or a bit of comedy. Maybe something that's less serious than *The Impossible*. Something a bit more jokey."[1]

If one didn't know any better, you could almost jump to the conclusion that Holland, on that March evening in 2013, somehow knew that he would be in consideration for the role of Spider-Man in a "jokey" MCU movie, one that would provide both a bit of action and a bit of comedy. The prescient nature of Holland's conversation only grew more intriguing when the reporter in question followed up by asking if there's a particular superhero the up-and-coming star could see himself playing.

"Oh yeah. Yeah, yeah, yeah," Holland belts out without missing a beat. "What kind of superhero would I want to play? Maybe Spider-Man in, like, 10 years time? Maybe. The reboot of the reboot, if they made one. I don't know. That'd be cool."

He wouldn't have to wait "10 years time." Two years after predicting this monumental career turn, all but willing it into existence, Holland found himself auditioning for Marvel and Sony, then filming his introductory scenes for Joe and Anthony Russo's *Captain America: Civil War* opposite Robert Downey Jr. and Marisa Tomei.

After several rounds of informal conversations and stop-and-start negotiations that spanned years, Marvel, Sony Pictures Entertainment, and the Walt Disney Company cleared a major logjam. Over an intimate meal with Amy Pascal, Marvel Studios President Kevin Feige finally convinced the studio executive to loosen her grip on Sony's most prized possession and relinquish creative control on Spider-Man. Pascal and Sony Pictures CEO Michael Lynton flew to Palm Beach, Florida, in early 2015 and sealed the deal over lunch with Marvel Entertainment CEO Ike Perlmutter. Spider-Man officially was on his way to the MCU, where so many believed he always belonged.

Feige couldn't wait to share this news with the brain trust behind the in-development sequel: *Captain America: Civil War*. From the moment negotiations between the studios turned serious, that 2016 film—which would kick off the MCU's Phase Three of films—was identified as the best possible story in which to introduce Marvel's take on Spider-Man. Christopher Markus and Stephen McFeely's *Civil War* screenplay would loosely pull inspiration from Mark Millar's comic book story line of the same name. A massive crossover event published in 2006, *Civil War* centered on a schism in the superhero community that began once the U.S. government passed the controversial Superhero Registration Act, which Tony Stark supported and Steve Rogers opposed. Spider-Man played a pivotal role in Millar's story line, serving as a vital negotiator caught in the middle of the warring factions. Working Spider-Man into the cinematic adaptation of *Civil War* would be poetic. It'd also be a crowning achievement for Marvel Studios and the MCU.

Clearing the studio hurdle meant that massive amounts of screenwriting and preproduction work needed to be revamped and reconfigured before shooting on *Civil War* concluded. But the moment Feige burst into a conference room at Marvel's headquarters and made eye contact with the Russos, Markus, and McFeely, words escaped him. The weight of the moment and the impact of crossing this imaginary finish line after years of running overwhelmed him. So Feige extended his arm, curled his fingers, and formed Spider-Man's signature web-shooting pose.

"We all lost it," Markus said, the joy still present in his voice years after the fact.[2]

To call the agreement "unprecedented" would be the understatement of the century.

"I've been in the business 30, almost 35 years, and I've never seen it," said Tom Rothman, the chairman and CEO of Sony Pictures Motion Picture Group. "I've seen studios co-finance movies before, but I've never seen studios share intellectual property before . . . so it's certainly unique. And because it's unique, it's inherently special."[3]

Pascal added, "Here's the thing that I want to emphasize, because I think this is really important, and I don't know if it will ever happen again in the history of the movie business. You had three studios that came together to have these movies get made. And no studio likes to share *anything* with anyone, let alone *three* studios."[4]

Sony Pictures Entertainment officially confirmed its deal to share Spider-Man with Marvel Studios on February 9, 2015.[5] Per the agreement, Feige and Pascal would oversee the collaboration, mapping out "a new creative direction for the web slinger." In the short term, Spider-Man would appear in *Captain America: Civil War*, then be the focal point of a solo picture that would be part of the MCU's connected story arc. Andrew Garfield would be replaced by an undetermined actor, chosen jointly by Sony and Marvel. Sony retained its ability to finance and distribute that Spider-Man film. But the deal allowed Feige unprecedented permission to bring Sony's most prized toy into his sandbox because he'd proven himself superior at building a superhero world.

Executives on all three sides justifiably called the deal a "win-win." Disney CEO Bob Iger praised Spider-Man as "one of Marvel's great characters, beloved around the world."[6] Feige celebrated Pascal's stewardship of the previous Spider-Man films and promised fans that Marvel's involvement in the development process would "deliver the creative continuity and authenticity that fans demand from the MCU."[7] Lynton talked about Sony's desire to collaborate with the industry's best and brightest creators to help grow their franchises, even if it meant reaching across the aisle to ask assistance from a competitor. Although the agreement required compromise—Sony showed corporate weakness by handing creative control to Marvel, while Disney loaned out one of its top employees (in Feige) for a fraction of the film's profits—this deal was the closest to a best-case scenario.

Sanford Panitch, president of Sony Pictures Motion Picture Group, summed it up nicely when he told the *Los Angeles Times*, "We're getting a superhero movie produced by the greatest superhero movie producer in the world."[8]

Industry analysts, however, were less understanding. Studio executives dream of establishing valuable IP that they can harvest, and few properties were more valuable than Spider-Man, who had earned Sony approximately $4 billion from five films over the course of fifteen years. Numbers like these prompted veteran Spider-Man producer Avi Arad to condemn the Sony–Marvel agreement as "the worst deal," laying the blame at Pascal and Lynton's feet. "They did it for money. Terrible," Arad said. "Like giving your kids away for adoption, just because you're not sure what to do with them."[9]

Sony tried for years to avoid this compromise. Marvel and Disney, through Feige, repeatedly inquired with their rival for almost a decade about bringing Spider-Man to the MCU, and Perlmutter frequently sent e-mails to Lynton, his old friend and former colleague, trying to convince Sony that it would be beneficial for both companies to somehow move Spider-Man into the MCU. Iger reportedly broached the topic with Sony's CEO Kaz Hirai during a 2014 summit for media moguls. And closer to ground level, Feige persistently pitched Pascal on the idea, making the best use of their long and productive history, which dated back to Feige's time as Avi Arad's assistant on Sam Raimi's first *Spider-Man*. The Hollywood legend states that Pascal's visceral reaction to Feige's initial suggestion of a Spider-Man partnership was to start crying and throw the sandwich she was eating at the Marvel boss's head. It was only when *The Amazing Spider-Man 2* struggled that the hypothetical "what-ifs" Feige loves so much turned into tangible negotiations.

It's worth remembering here that these negotiations between Sony and Marvel wouldn't have been necessary in 2015 if the former had accepted what now sounds like a ludicrous proposal from the cash-strapped comics company in 1998. Coming out of a debilitating bankruptcy, Marvel offered Sony the rights to every character in its arsenal, save for the Fantastic Four and the X-Men, which had been licensed to 20th Century Fox. The complete Marvel roster would have cost Sony $25 million—pocket change when you consider the revenues these characters eventually would generate. The studio's chief decision makers wrongly concluded that "nobody gives a shit about any of the other Marvel characters"[10] and purchased Spider-Man's rights for only $10 million. Seventeen years after that decision, Sony handed creative control back.

Feige wasn't mincing words when he elaborated on the impact of this deal. "So much of what we've done at Marvel Studios just started with very few people in a room going, 'Boy, it'd be really cool if we could do this.' Or, 'It'd be really cool if we could do that,'" he said. "This, by far, is the pinnacle of that.

"It's a testament to the character of Spider-Man that there's so much left to be done with him," Feige continued. "I think that's another thing that we wanted to prove. We really wanted to show people, 'You haven't seen what Spider-Man can be.' Because he was never created to be a hero by himself in a city. He was created to be an unbelievably different type of hero—younger, have other responsibilities—in contrast to the Iron Man and the Thor and the Captain Americas out there."[11]

It's unusual that Feige didn't have access to the enormously popular Spider-Man from the earliest days of the MCU. The executive couldn't have anticipated the contractual gymnastics that kept Spidey at Sony, preventing him from being part of the MCU's foundation. This makes it all the more impressive that Marvel Studios built its cinematic empire on the backs of lesser-known heroes like Ant-Man (Paul Rudd), Doctor Strange (Benedict Cumberbatch), and the Guardians of the Galaxy because any Marvel fan looking at the MCU from the outside had to recognize the Spider-Man–shaped hole.

Once, during an interview on the *Spider-Man: Far from Home* press junket, Feige let his guard down long enough to confess how much Spidey's absence in those early years irked him.

"Now Marvel has what DC has, what Harry Potter has, what Star Wars has, which is access to all of their characters," Feige said. "It's unusual for a company not to have access to all their characters. And the fact now that we have [them] back is pretty nice. It's pretty amazing."[12]

Sony, Marvel, and Disney ran their partnership through the public relations spin cycle, but everyone on the outside understood what was happening. Sony was admitting that after five feature films, they no longer could figure out how best to tell live-action Spider-Man stories in this shifting comic book movie landscape. Sony's road map through the two *The Amazing Spider-Man* films never solidified, and Marvel Studios demonstrated a proven knack for telling these types of stories better.

Pascal went so far as to call herself as "a Marvel groupie" when she met with a small circle of film journalists visiting the Atlanta, Georgia, set of Jon Watts's *Spider-Man: Homecoming*. The producer had evolved from competitor to cheerleader.

"They are meticulous, they are relentless. And one of the great things—I say this all the time—is [when] you're in a meeting with them, and they go, 'Okay, it's good—but how do we make it better?' I've never heard that before! . . . 'How do we go to the next place? How do we bless it?' That's their favorite word at Marvel. 'Are we *blessing* a scene?'"[13]

Pascal looks back on the 2015 deal and still describes it as "very tough to do" but also "very selfless" because by Hollywood's unwritten rule, three corporations are not supposed to come together and do what is right for a character. The agreement, more than anything, demonstrates the importance of Spider-Man and his movies to the film industry during this golden age of comic book adaptations.

"In the end," Pascal said, "I think we felt like we needed more characters, and we needed more challenges for Peter. Kevin [Feige] is a genius, and I wanted to work with him. And it just felt like we needed a different way to tell the story because I thought we were starting to repeat ourselves. You don't want to repeat yourself. And putting Peter in a world where there are other superheroes opened up a whole new world for us.[14]

"[We] realized that what was right for the character meant you might have to give up a little to get something better," Pascal said. "And I'm very proud of that."[15]

"I Didn't Carbon Date Him. He's on the Young Side"

Having shared the news that Spider-Man could appear in *Captain America: Civil War*, Feige had one mandate for screenwriters Christopher Markus and Stephen McFeely: make him a kid. Both Tobey Maguire and Andrew Garfield were in their mid-twenties when they stepped into the Peter Parker role. Then the Raimi and Webb franchises each shuffled Peter out of high school by their second installments, ignoring a decade of character development that's possible when you explore Parker's awkward teenage adolescence. Marvel Studios had no intention of doing that with its first official Spider-Man.

"That was always our goal when we started off with the idea of introducing Peter Parker to the MCU," said Tom Holland, the young British actor who eventually landed the life-changing part. "Obviously, in the MCU, you've got the billionaire, you've got the god, and you've got the soldier. And when I came in, it was now time to have the kid. Everyone goes to school, everyone does homework, everyone talks to their crush for the first time, and embarrasses themselves. And everyone wishes that they could be a superhero. So we really tapped into the idea of making him as relatable as possible. And I think it's been our secret weapon. Because people watch these films and look at Peter Parker, and can see themselves in him. Especially when he becomes Spider-Man."[16]

Like every hero in the MCU, Holland owes casting director Sarah Halley Finn for giving him his shot. Finn has been populating the Marvel universe with stars since 2008, when she convinced the up-an-coming studio to roll the dice on Hollywood bad boy and certifiable damaged goods Robert Downey Jr. to play Tony Stark. That inspired hire gave the MCU a charismatic but egotistical beating heart in the form of a billionaire playboy philanthropist who uses a homemade arc reactor to keep shrapnel away from his own vital organ in the center of his chest. Finn possesses an uncanny eye for pairing iconic talent with his or her signature role. Her casting coups include Chris Evans as the Star-Spangled Avenger, Captain America; Chris Hemsworth as the Mighty Thor; Scarlett Johansson as Black Widow; Chris Pratt as Star-Lord, the leader of the Guardians of the Galaxy; and the late Chadwick Boseman as Wakanda's King T'Challa, the Black Panther.

Holland was nineteen years old at the time of his audition and remains the youngest actor so far to ever don the Spider-Man suit on-screen. He reportedly endured six separate screen tests over the course of seven months before Finn finally told Joe and Anthony Russo, "This is the guy. You're going to love him."[17]

"That was intense, man," Holland recalled. "I was shooting other movies at the time, so I was lucky because I was preoccupied. I think if I wasn't working, I would've imploded just waiting to hear [about] this movie."[18]

Holland recruited acting friends Joel Kinnaman and Jon Bernthal to help him record audition reels for Marvel. One of his very first official script reads had nothing to do with Spider-Man and instead was an intense scene between Miles Teller and J. K. Simmons—J. Jonah Jameson himself—from Damien Chazelle's 2014 movie *Whiplash*. Eventually, Holland read scenes involving dialogue for the wall crawler, but even then, the true nature of the project for which he auditioned remained a mystery.

"My agents at one point were like, 'We don't know who you're auditioning for.' I was like, 'But my lines are for Spider-Man—so who else could I possibly be auditioning for?' They were like, 'We don't know.'"[19]

The Russo brothers trusted Finn implicitly, having collaborated with her on *Captain America: The Winter Soldier*. In addition, they were blown away by Holland's charisma, physicality, and range in these auditions. Pascal cherished the fact that Holland had been a dancer, even once playing the lead role in the West End production of the musical *Billy Elliot*.

"He understood what it meant to tell a story physically, [which] was wonderful for us," Amy Pascal said.

"His dance background imbues [the character] with a sense of wonder and enthusiasm," Downey added.[20]

The Russos brought their recommendation to Feige, who carried it up the ladder to his new partners at Sony. But the Sony Pictures Entertainment executives hesitated and were unwilling to commit to Holland on the spot. Anthony Russo believes it was because Sony had never actually allowed a teenager to be cast as Peter Parker. Joe Russo speculated that giving in to Marvel's casting suggestion meant Spider-Man no longer truly was theirs, and that reality was jarring. No matter the cause for the cold feet, they ended up being short lived. Both Sony and Marvel overcame most of their jitters the moment they watched Holland screen-test opposite his eventual MCU mentor, Downey.

Heading into filming on *Captain America: Civil War*, Downey had become the big, beaming planet around which the rest of the MCU rotated. So it was a significant deal that he'd agreed to read opposite six potential Spider-Man candidates on the *Civil War* set in Atlanta, of which Holland was one. Downey admitted to *GQ* magazine in 2021 that he understood the weight that came with finding the next Spider-Man. "That character is the gold standard in the MCU. Iron Man? Whatever. When I became Iron Man, few had even heard of the character, ergo less pressure," Downey said. "But Spider-Man? Everyone knows Spider-Man."[21]

The scene given to the six candidates to learn ended up being Peter Parker's very first moment in the MCU, a conversation with Tony Stark that occurs when Peter comes home to his unassuming Queens apartment and finds the genius eating walnut date loaf with Aunt May. Holland's agent ordered him not to improvise in the scene, warning that Marvel preferred actors who memorized the lines as written.

"And then, on the first take, Downey just changed the scene completely," Holland said.[22]

Downey was testing the kid. He'd already read with a few other candidates that day but wanted to gauge Holland's composure and his ability to keep material fresh and interesting in the moment. Prior to their read, Downey reportedly pulled Holland aside and passed along some sage advice, saying, "I've been through this before and it is incredibly stressful. Enjoy the process and let your body take over." Holland says he still applies that logic of letting his physicality overcome his mental state on film sets to this day.

"I think that's the piece of advice that got me the Spider-Man job ultimately," Holland said.[23]

Not right away, however. Following the May 30, 2015, reading with Downey on the *Civil War* set, Pascal and Feige narrowed their pool down to Holland and *The Golden Compass* costar Charlie Rowe, who, ironically, played the younger version of Andrew Garfield's character, Tommy, in Mark Romanek's 2010 drama *Never Let Me Go*. Sources confirm that Holland ultimately earned the role because he aced the last challenge: a physical fight sequence opposite Evans as Captain America. But Holland found out he got the part the same way most of us heard about it: on the internet.

As he remembers, he'd just returned from playing golf with his father when he checked Instagram and saw that Marvel had posted a cartoon image of Spider-Man. A message accompanied the photo, telling fans to go to Marvel's official site to find out who had been cast as the new web slinger. Holland immediately assumed he didn't get the role, mainly because no one from Marvel or Sony had called him.

"I was like, 'I'll just go and check,'" he said. "I got my computer, and my dog was sitting next to me. I type in 'Marvel.' I've still got the article saved on my computer. It said, 'We would like to introduce our new Spider-Man, Tom Holland.' I broke my computer, because I flipped it up in the air.

"The craziest thing is, I found out online, the same way everyone else did," Holland continued, the disbelief still coating every word. "No one had texted me prior to me finding out. Of all the people that I know that could have texted me, I found out first. It was so bizarre how it happened."[24]

Tom Holland: A Spider-Man and a Beekeeper

While Pascal and Feige waffled back and forth about who was going to play Spider-Man in *Captain America: Civil War*, the Russo brothers, Christopher Markus, and Stephen McFeely were wrestling with *how* they'd introduce the pivotal character into what had become a fairly complex screenplay. The team sequestered themselves in a conference room for weeks, hammering out the movie's multiple story lines and trying to make every plotline gel.

"That movie had a number of moving pieces," Markus remembers.[25]

That's an understatement. In addition to serving as a traditional Captain America sequel, *Civil War* had to establish the Sokovia Accords—restrictive legislation put in place following a public battle that resulted in several innocent bystanders getting injured. The law stripped away the Avengers' rights to operate as a private team and placed them under the jurisdiction of a United Nations panel. As the story played out, *Civil War* also drove a wedge between Steve Rogers (Evans) and fellow Avenger Tony Stark (Downey), found motivation for a manipulative new villain named Baron Helmut Zemo (Daniel Bruhl), and showcased the Wakandan ruler Black Panther (Boseman, also making his MCU debut), who had a vendetta against Cap's best friend: Bucky Barnes (Sebastian Stan).

Very little was guaranteed to the creative team as they schemed out *Captain America: Civil War*. "There was one point where it didn't look like we were going to get *Robert*," Markus said, referring to the report that the penny-pinching Perlmutter ordered the screenwriters to remove Iron Man from the script so that he wouldn't have to pay the actor's escalating rate. "So there were a few chess pieces that we were moving around going, 'Well, maybe we could do this?'"

As these balls floated in the air, Marvel and Sony's ongoing negotiations over the terms of the Spider-Man settlement began cutting into the Russo's prep time, and the delays began to drive the siblings insane. The brothers dedicated precious time to developing their interpretation of Spider-Man and cementing him into their *Civil War* story. Failure to secure Spider-Man's rights would have sent the Russos back to the drawing board on *Captain America: Civil War*, a terrifying scenario that would likely have prevented them from hitting Marvel's announced release date.

Specifically, the brothers singled out a sequence that they loved so much that they would have been devastated by having to cut it. Having just lost track of the Winter Soldier (Stan) in Berlin, Natasha Romanoff (Scarlett Johansson) and Tony Stark lament the fact that their pro-registration half of the Avengers is severely understaffed. Tony suggests that he might know a guy. Black Widow asks where this person is, and the film's next scene smash cuts to a title card reading "Queens."

The Russos could almost forecast the reaction of the opening-night crowd. Every Marvel fan sitting in the audience would squeal, knowing that Queens was home to Peter Parker. When it looked like Sony might refuse to share its toys, Markus and McFeely briefly floated the idea that Tony Stark's "guy" could be Black Panther since Boseman's casting was confirmed and Marvel

Studios planned to use *Civil War* as the movie that sets up the solo *Black Panther* feature. But that didn't make sense storywise. The audience would have met Boseman's T'Challa in the first act of the film. Also, as Markus astutely points out, it wouldn't have been nearly as much of a "holy shit!" moment as introducing Spider-Man into the MCU at that time. The smash-cut scene works only if *Civil War* could use Spidey.

"During the time that it takes you to convince the powers that be to make the jump and let you do that, you've engrained the character so deeply into the story at that point that you'd have to destroy the story to take him out," Joe Russo said. "So, by the time we found out that he'd be in the movie, it wasn't so much elation than, 'Thank God! We don't have to blow the whole movie up.'"[26]

If the *Civil War* team's first creative mandate was "keep Peter young," then its second order of business would have been "skip the origin story." By this point, audiences had seen it on screen twice before, and the last thing anyone needed to sit through was Uncle Ben's death a third time. Instead, Markus and McFeely treated that now infamous bedroom scene in May Parker's apartment, where the veteran Avenger recruits the kid to the team, as the table setter for this fresh interpretation of Spider-Man.

"That scene in the bedroom in *Civil War* really is the heart of what we wanted to launch. When he says, 'Somebody's gotta look out for the little guy,'" Feige said. "Basically, while all of these Avengers are flying around, dealing with very big things, who's here taking care of the little guy? And that's what Peter's always been about."[27]

It's in this scene, though, that Marvel implements some of its most interesting (and some would argue controversial) changes with regard to the Peter Parker introduced into the MCU. Not only did *Civil War* choose not to show Uncle Ben getting shot and killed by a thief Peter let's slip past him, but the movie avoids mentioning Ben altogether. The bedroom scene contains what Markus describes as "a nice, fumbly rephrasing" of the classic "With great power" mantra. "But you don't get that. You don't get those words, and you don't get any kind of explanation," Markus continues. "He's talking about something that's a lot like Uncle Ben's death. I could not even tell you whether, in MCU canon, that has happened. We never talked about it."[28]

It's surprising that the screenwriters dissecting the introduction of a pivotal Marvel character into the MCU never discussed the specifics of his very familiar origin story, especially given how neurotic and detail oriented Marvel fans are about these films. But when I asked Holland point-blank at the *Spider-Man: Homecoming* press junket if his version of Peter Parker was responsible for his Uncle Ben's death, Holland replied, "I don't know." And he meant it.

Feige backs his leading man and the *Civil War* team, saying Marvel fans are savvy enough to fill in those story gaps. "That was a very purposeful decision we made to not retread that ground," he said. "There are little things that are said here and there that people can read into. What the specific facts are in the past, we haven't revealed yet."[29]

One other crucial component of Spider-Man's origin that the *Civil War* team didn't discuss? The radioactive spider bite that gives Peter his extraordinary powers.

"I mean, God knows there would have to be something not unlike that, probably," Markus said. "But no, I wouldn't say . . . I mean, I think he was bitten by a radioactive spider on a field trip. We never talked about *that* either, but I think that's what happened."[30]

The spider bite didn't concern *Spider-Man: Homecoming* director Jon Watts either as he assembled Marvel's first solo Spidey movie in the MCU. While he says he has "a couple sort of vague ideas" about how the bite happened for his Peter Parker, he thought of it only in terms of ways he'd need it to hold his story logic together. "It was just so nice to skip past it and just deal more with the repercussions," Watts said, "and just explore it from the perspective of someone else finding out about it, and having a lot of questions."[31]

It's remarkable how different the creative choices could be now that Spider-Man was being introduced into a universe already populated by superheroes. There was no need for screenwriters to overly explain a kid with the proportionate speed, strength, and agility of a spider when the MCU audience was privy to sorcerers, aliens, and Asgardian gods. It's the presence of the existing heroes that actually gave Holland's Spider-Man his most significant change over Maguire and Garfield because his Peter Parker ends up having Tony Stark as a mentor.

Markus and McFeely loved the dynamic between Peter and Tony as characters on the page. They're both genius-level intellects, though one's a tech entrepreneur and the other dumpster dives for used computer equipment. Stark's a billionaire inventor, and Parker occupies a tiny bedroom where he manufactures homemade webbing with tensile strength that's off the charts.

But there is a crucial interplay to that bedroom scene that isn't written, merely understood. The circumstances of the conversation required Holland, a teenage actor who was brand new to the giant Marvel franchise, to trade lines and verbally spar with Downey, a megawatt Hollywood star who already was the heart of the franchise. "And the worry as a filmmaker at that point is 'Jesus, Robert's going to eat this scene!'" Markus said. "Are we making a mistake, taking the person the scene exists to establish, and we're putting Robert in there, who could crush him? But it worked perfectly for the dynamic between those characters."[32]

Downey says he spotted these formidable dramatic qualities in Holland back during their audition scene in Atlanta. He wasn't just helping Marvel and Sony find the next actor to step into a suit that two men already have worn. He was identifying the one person strong enough to carry the mantle of Spider-Man, a daunting responsibility not everyone has the power to meet. And he compliments Holland sincerely when he refers to him as "a beekeeper" type of actor.

"Me, Tom, the Marvel guys, we're beekeepers. It's not sexy. It's hot under those damn suits. You can't see us. We're sweating to make the sweet, sweet syrupy nectar to be consumed for our leaders," Downey said.[33]

The Tony Stark mentorship became a point of contention for Spider-Man purists who didn't fully embrace the MCU interpretation of the character. As the relationship expanded through *Spider-Man: Homecoming* and the back-to-back chaos of *Avengers: Infinity War* and *Avengers: Endgame*, Holland's Spidey detractors dismissed him as "Iron Boy Jr." They were annoyed by Peter's reliance on Stark tech for his suits and gadgets, including the Iron Spider suit he received in *Infinity War*. It's valid criticism given that teenage Spider-Man in the comics struggles to keep up with his well-funded counterparts and charmingly sews his battle-tattered costume late at night in his Queens bedroom (a fact that's finally captured in the closing moments of 2021's *Spider-Man: No Way Home*). But Marvel wanted to zig in all of the places that the previous Spider-Man franchises had zagged. And so, giving a wet-behind-the-ears teenage superhero his own mentor felt both different from the previous incarnations and authentic to Holland's take.

Especially because Holland himself had a superhero role model he claims to have looked up to his entire life: Tobey Maguire's Spider-Man.

"The thing I had to remind myself of most, before I took on this character, was [that] Tobey Maguire's Spider-Man had such a huge impact on me as a kid. He was my role model growing up. He was my favorite character," Holland said. "So I had to keep reminding myself that I was going to have that same impact on kids, and a generation. So I really wanted to do them proud, and to be a solid role model for them."[34]

CHAPTER ELEVEN
"A FILM BY PETER PARKER"

om Holland couldn't have received a stronger vote of confidence than the one he got from Stan Lee following his casting. Asked what he thought of the choice of Holland for the role, the Marvel icon proclaimed, "Tom is just the way I had pictured Spider-Man being when I created Spider-Man."[1]

Holland usually deflected compliments of that nature. Instead, when asked questions about his approach to the character, Sony's next Spider-Man paid homage to the men who swung before him. During a break from filming on the *Spider-Man: Homecoming* set, Holland told a small group of reporters, "It's difficult not to take influence from Tobey and Andrew because they both had such great versions of the character. I think from Tobey, I'm taking his sort of less cool side of things, whereas Andrew was very cool and very contained. But then with Andrew, I thought his Spider-Man was fantastic. I thought that when he was in that suit, he really came to life. So there are two things I am taking from both people."[2]

Nineteen-year-old Holland likely would have melted into a puddle if someone had told him on the *Homecoming* set that day he'd share the screen with both Maguire and Garfield in a Spider-Man movie that reached theaters six years after he was hired for the gig. That's one of the many reasons why *Spider-Man: No Way Home* feels like a love-letter fever dream, an impossible construction of cinematic fan fiction that shouldn't exist yet somehow does.

Excitement over Holland's hire and Marvel's increased influence didn't stop with Stan Lee. Months before filming on *Spider-Man: Homecoming* began, MTV caught up with *Spider-Man* icon Sam Raimi to ask what he thought of the direction of the MCU Spider-Man. "I'm really glad that Marvel's taking it to high school. I think that's going to be refreshing, and just like my favorite of the Spider-Man comic books," the director said.[3]

As Raimi reflected on aspects of the character he, too, would have liked to explore deeper when he was the steward of the series, the director admitted, "I'd like to go into his high school life, and his relationship with Gwen Stacy. I love Flash Thompson. The difficulty of going through high school is so unique to a superhero. It's unique, and that's what Spider-Man is all about. That they are going to explore that head on is very exciting."

So when the screenwriting team of Jonathan Goldstein and John Francis Daley accepted an offer to pitch Sony and Marvel Studios on their unique approach to Spider-Man, the duo referenced a filmmaker who had absolutely no connection to superheroes but was synonymous with teenage angst: John Hughes.

From 1984 to 1988, the Michigan-bred filmmaker helped amplify the voices of an entire generation of high school students by putting their stories on-screen in the comedic staples *Sixteen Candles*, *Weird Science*, *Ferris Bueller's Day Off*, *Pretty in Pink*, and *The Breakfast Club*. Goldstein and Daley came from a similar comedic background, having penned two *Horrible Bosses* movies, *Cloudy with a Chance of Meatballs 2*, and a sequel to Hughes's *Vacation*, starring Ed Helms and Christina Applegate. But they understood mainly that the teenage relatability found in the Hughes filmography paired perfectly with an MCU movie based on that universe's youngest hero—going so far as to write a Ferris Bueller–inspired sprint through multiple backyards into *Homecoming*. You even see Hughes's 1986 crowd-pleaser on a television set in front of which Spider-Man runs.

Never mind the fact that *Ferris Bueller's Day Off* opened in theaters ten years before Holland was born or the fact that Hughes's influential filmography was relatively new to the *Homecoming* cast, which is why Holland ordered pizzas one afternoon and invited the entire cast to his rental home in Atlanta for a one-day Hughes Film Festival that included *Breakfast Club*, *Bueller*, and *Pretty in Pink*.

Reflecting on the attributes that got them the *Spider-Man: Homecoming* gig, John Francis Daley said, "We did want to put an emphasis on the realism of it, bridging the gap between this larger-than-life superhero and the audience. To make him this vulnerable kid who is really sweet, and has trouble talking to girls, and is smart, and has a very, very small group of friends. Namely, the one. Having been on *Freaks and Geeks*, and knowing that they were wanting this John Hughes type of experience, it was easy to tap into, for sure."[4]

It's impressive that Goldstein and Daley's *Spider-Man: Homecoming* proposal connected with Marvel's executives because the duo whipped up their presentation over the course of one weekend. Their manager received a call late one Thursday night from Marvel asking for a meeting. But they were told it would take place four days later, on Monday. This meant they had Friday through Sunday to map out an entirely new Spider-Man movie that adhered to the tenets of the character but still differentiated itself from previous on-screen iterations.

"It was the most rigorous writing we've ever done," Daley said. They hunkered down in Daley's living room, bouncing ideas off the wall from morning to night. They knew the comics and Peter's origin story. They also knew they didn't want to rehash it since that field had been plowed so many times already. Instead of lifting ideas from preexisting Spider-Man or super-hero movies, they examined the teen comedies of their youth and pulled what worked from those beloved films.

Daley said, "We thought in those few days, 'What are the staples of that genre, and how do we incorporate them into this?' My wife was milling around sometimes, and would say, 'Oh, you should have a party scene, obviously.' And we went, 'Of course, of course.'"

Writing for a teenage Spider-Man in 2016 also meant incorporating updated contemporary facets of Peter Parker's everyday life, using things that wouldn't have been available to Tobey Maguire's nerdy version, like You-Tube. "One of the first things we came up with in our pitch was that idea of him YouTubing himself, basically creating a Spider-Man YouTube channel, because that felt like what a kid would do," Goldstein said. "He would go out and set up a camera and show himself doing cool stuff, and then get followers. Because that's how you feel validated as a teen."

While the studios sought scribes to shape Spider-Man's debut MCU solo adventure, Amy Pascal zeroed in on indie filmmaker Jon Watts as her top choice to helm *Homecoming*. After cutting his teeth on Fatboy Slim and Death Cab for Cutie music videos, Watts started turning heads in 2015 with the lower-budget indie drama *Cop Car*. The small-scale story centered around two young boys who hijack an abandoned police vehicle to take it on a joy ride, not realizing that the car belongs to a corrupt sheriff (Kevin Bacon) trying to cover up some heinous deeds. Pascal, in particular, appreciated how Watts overcame a limited budget on *Cop Car* to tell a compelling story through his balance of action and character development. She also praised his work with the two kids as his leads. "The performances that he got from those little boys, I thought, was really something. Plus, he scared you. He made you feel hopeful. And he surprised you," Pascal said. "He did things with, like, $8,000 that people can't do with eighty."[5]

Watts also connected deeply with the developing Spider-Man movie's John Hughes inspirations and contributed valuable insights into the makeup of the diverse community that he felt needed to surround this version of Peter Parker.

"Our director came in and said, 'I want the world to look like high school. I don't want it to look like a Hollywood high school movie. Because, we've all seen those. I want it to look like what a high school would look like today. With a lot of nerdy kids, because it's a school for smart kids,'" Pascal claimed. "He wanted it to reflect the world that we live in. . . . He brought a whole other modern sensibility to it that I think is really fresh."

Part of that preproduction development included sending Holland to a science-focused school in the Bronx borough of New York, where for three days, the actor hid behind a fake name, refined his American accent, and learned how best to blend in with kids that age. "Some of the teachers didn't even know. It was a science school, and I am in no way a science student," Holland said. "Some of the teachers would call me up in front of the class and try to get me to do science equations and stuff. It was so embarrassing!"[6]

That anonymity even extended to the students, many of whom didn't recognize Holland from either his earlier films or his Marvel debut in *Captain America: Civil War*. "I actually have videos on my phone of me interviewing people, and asking them what they thought of the new Spider-Man in *Civil War*. They were like, 'Oh he's great. I love him.' And then some people were like, 'Nah, I don't love him. He's not great.' And I was standing right in front of them!" Holland remembered with an enormous laugh.

With Watts on board, Holland in training, and a script in development, it was time for Marvel to officially put its creative stamp on a Sony-produced Spider-Man motion picture.

Spider-Man: Homecoming

If Marvel's prime directive on *Captain America: Civil War* was "make Spider-Man a kid," then the marching orders for *Spider-Man: Homecoming* appears to have been "do things we have never seen in a Spider-Man movie."

"We had this sort of M.O always to just, if we can . . . let's take Spider-Man out of his comfort zone and put him on the Washington Monument, or put him in the suburbs," Watts said. "We've never seen that before. That's the point of making a movie like this, to show people things they've never seen before."[7]

This mind-set impacted everything from the supporting characters surrounding Peter Parker at his high school to the sequences on which *Homecoming* would linger as it fleshed out this interpretation of the Marvel hero. Watts faced some of the same obstacles Marc Webb encountered as he tried to swim upstream against the current established by the seminal Sam Raimi trilogy. How do you make something fresh but also familiar that's not a carbon copy of any Spidey movie that's come before you? This time, however, the existence of those previous movies also gave Watts the opportunity to drill deeper into moments in Peter's on-screen lore that fascinated him as a storyteller and explore important moments that he felt were shortchanged in earlier films.

"Like in the other movies," Watts said, "[there would be] a quick 'learning your skills' montage, and then it's onto the next thing. Whenever I would see that, I would be like, 'No! Do more of that. I want to see more of the 'learning of the skills.' That's the best part."[8] Daley and Goldstein confirmed that they sketched out several more scenes of Peter mastering the art of swinging and overcoming his fear of heights. "All of the things that aren't built into getting bit by a spider," Goldstein said.[9]

Watts also studied the physical movements of Maguire and Garfield in their Spider-Man suits but not so he could mimic them for his movie. He instead instructed Holland to go in the opposite direction during his preparation—for a deliberate reason.

"I definitely used them as a reference, but with the idea that this Spider-Man isn't that good yet," he said. "You see these awesome key-frame poses getting hit in the other movies. My direction to Tom and the stunt team [was] that he's not there yet. This is a movie about Peter Parker on his way to becoming that, but he's not even close to that yet."[10]

Holland, meanwhile, pushed hard to build flaws into this overzealous but inexperienced Peter Parker. "The opening act to the movie, you see Peter really trying to discover who he is and what he can do, which is something I feel like we haven't really explored massively in the previous movies, seeing Peter make mistakes and try to rectify them, and learn exactly what he can do," Holland said. "That was something I was very passionate about, and I know Jon was as well—and from the first draft that was always in the script."[11]

And when it came down to the hero's physicality and stunt work in the stunt pieces, be it the Washington Monument or the Staten Island Ferry, the team once again factored Peter's youth and naïveté into their choreography. "We tried to . . . add a lot more things like him being unsure about being up really high, and a couple of wobbles when he lands, and having his arms sort of flail around to keep that feeling of gravity and weight," Watts said. "The whole movie is about growing up and learning and coming of age, and I wanted to apply that to the physicality and the action, as well."[12]

This "be original" mantra also helped dictate which villains Spider-Man would face off against on-screen in *Homecoming* and its sequel: *Spider-Man: Far from Home*. Pascal wasn't afraid to admit that Sony had recycled its story lines and characters one too many times on the Webb movies. "At least for now, I don't know how many more times we can do the Green Goblin," the producer admitted on the set of *Homecoming*, giving one obvious example. "I've certainly tried to do it fifty [times]."[13]

Taking Norman or Harry Osborn off the table for the time being made it easier for Goldstein and Daley to suggest the Vulture (Michael Keaton) as the film's primary antagonist, with the added bonus of plucking numerous side characters from Spidey's colorful rogues' gallery. Goldstein and Daley's *Homecoming* script weaves the Tinkerer (Michael Chernus); the Shocker (Logan Marshall-Green, then Bokeem Woodbine); Mac Gargan, aka the Scorpion (Michael Mando); and Aaron the "Prowler" Davis (Donald Glover) into supporting parts, effectively populating Spider-Man's corner of the MCU with potential future threats.

"It always comes from, 'What does the movie we're currently making need?' It needed these characters that are selling these illegally retrofitted alien tech weapons under a bridge in a van," Feige said. "So we need somebody that they may be selling it to, and somebody that will come back later in the story, and that's the Donald Glover character. 'Oh, what if he is Aaron Davis? Then we can also mention the crawlers.' So it always is, 'We're going to have a character in this scene. We're going to have a character that needs to carry a particular element of the story that we're making. And when you have so many characters to pull from, you may as well use one of the characters in the comics."[14]

Giving a rare peek behind the curtain of his planning process, Feige references a seemingly insignificant moment from a Captain America movie. Because his mind is always thinking ahead to the next few Marvel projects, be they movies or television shows, Feige made an instant mental connection to the Spider-Man movie he was mapping out in his imagination.

"I remember leaning over to people when we were screening *Civil War*. When Crossbones' gauntlets are pounding Cap, and Cap rips one off and throws it aside, I'd lean over and go, 'The Shocker's going to get that!'"

The European-set *Spider-Man: Far from Home* then continued this trend, structuring its plot around a vintage Spider-Man antagonist we'd never seen on-screen. For *Far from Home*, it was the fishbowl-headed master of illusion, Mysterio (Jake Gyllenhaal), who fooled S.H.I.E.L.D. specialists Nick Fury (Samuel L. Jackson) and Maria Hill (Cobie Smulders) by conjuring Elementals that resembled second-rate Spidey villains Molten Man, Sandman, and Hydro-Man. These antagonists wouldn't be engaging enough to carry a sequel on their own but ended up being entertaining components of a larger villain's story.

During an interview with Feige on the 2019 *Far from Home* press tour, though, I asked him if iconic Spider-Man villains Doctor Octopus and the Green Goblin were unavailable to Watts and his team because Raimi's movies used them before and to such terrific effect. His answer was very telling given the events of the multiverse-busting *Spider-Man: No Way Home*.

"Not necessarily," Feige said. "It just depends on, 'Is it the right story? Is that the right time? Is there a right angle to do it again in a way that feels fresh, and doesn't feel like, here it is again!' Because Spidey, as you know better than anyone, has a great roster of villains. And Mysterio and Vulture being two of the best that hadn't been brought to the screen before. But I think it all depends on what the story is. It all depends on what the angle is."[15]

Feige likely knew at the time what he wanted to have happen in *Spider-Man: No Way Home*—maybe not the complete details but definitely the blueprint sketch of Peter having his secret identity revealed, then turning to Doctor Strange (Benedict Cumberbatch) to reverse the damage, tearing open a multiversal rift that allowed series veterans Otto Octavius (Alfred Molina), Norman Osborn (Willem Dafoe), the Lizard (Rhys Ifans), Electro (Jamie Foxx), Sandman (Thomas Hayden Church), and the two previous Spider-Men (Tobey Maguire and Andrew Garfield) to swing into Holland's world. That's the angle to which Feige was referring back in 2019 and to which he delivered in 2021.

None of this happens if Sony doesn't relent in 2015 and allow Marvel to drop Spider-Man into an already established MCU. Goldstein and Daley rarely skip an opportunity in *Homecoming* to remind audiences that this Spidey—unlike Maguire's or Garfield's—exists in a world that is influenced on a daily basis by the presence of Marvel's heaviest hitters. The very first thing we see when *Spider-Man: Homecoming* begins is a child's cartoon drawing of the Avengers, held by Adrian Toomes, Keaton's criminal character. "Things are never going to be the same now," Toomes growls, and while he's referring to the arrival of alien threats and superpowered saviors, the comment also applies to the future of Spider-Man movies. Once you've paired him with Earth's Mightiest Heroes on-screen, there's no going back to the way things used to be.

The Marvel associations hardly stop there. Toomes's villainous motivations also are tied to Marvel's top team. When the opportunistic, blue-collar salvage expert attempts to cash in on Manhattan's wide-scale cleanup efforts following *The Avengers'* Battle of New York, Toomes gets undercut by the Stark-funded Department of Damage Control, helping establish a serious grudge. Once the movie catches up with Peter (Holland), he's being escorted to Germany by Tony Stark's manservant, Happy Hogan (Jon Favreau), so he can join Team Iron Man in the conflict with Captain America (Chris Evans). While at school, Peter's classmates make jokes about dating Black Widow (Scarlett Johansson), they study the Sokovia Accords from *Civil War* in history class, and they're forced to watch fitness videos starring Steve Rogers while in gym class. Even when Spider-Man confronts street-level crooks who are using alien technology to rob ATMs, the criminals wear store-bought Thor, Iron Man, and Hulk masks.

According to Watts, the full weight of his movie's MCU connections finally landed with him the day he filmed a *Spider-Man: Homecoming* scene that shows up late in the story. The Vulture has been vanquished by our friendly, neighborhood, teenage superhero. Happy picks Peter up at school and drives him to the renovated Avengers compound in upstate New York for an impromptu meeting. There, Tony finally offers the fifteen-year-old the one thing he's been chasing for the entire movie: the chance to graduate to the big leagues and fight as an official member of the superhero team.

"That big moment in the movie was always there," Watts said. "That was really fun to shoot. And just such a nice moment to see this kid, with this really goofy t-shirt on, smiling and staring out at Avengers compound with that big 'A' behind him. It feels like, 'Wow, Spider-Man is really in the Marvel universe!'"[16]

Spider-Man: Homecoming answers the question, "What would a Spider-Man movie set entirely in the Marvel Cinematic Universe look like?" And the majority of film critics reacted positively, describing the film as "fizzy and funny,"[17] "an utter gas,"[18] and "the best Spider-Man movie of the bunch."[19] But not every audience member embraced Feige and Pascal's shared vision. Doing something different and giving fans something they have never seen before also means that your Spider-Man movie won't look like the previous ones they might have loved. Change is hard, and some resisted. The loudest complaints aimed at Holland's interpretation came from fans who didn't appreciate an on-screen Spidey whose primary motivations were driven by existing Marvel characters. They rejected the amplified presence that Tony Stark has in MCU Peter Parker's life, captured, essentially, by the multi-million-dollar "Stark" suit tricked out with 576 different web shooter combinations, enhanced reconnaissance tools, its own JARVIS-style artificial intelligence, and, of course, an Instant Kill mode. Giving Peter access to Stark tech might make sense in the context of a Marvel Studios movie that establishes tech-savvy Tony as the web slinger's "father figure." But it also drastically changes Peter's characteristic struggles as a broke teenage superhero in the Marvel Comics. That science whiz invented his own spider-shaped tracking devices, often dealt with empty web cartridges in the middle of battle, and endured late-night sewing sessions to repair the damage done to his one and only homemade costume. By the end of *Spider-Man: No Way Home*, MCU Spidey had worn eight costumes, four of them created for him by Iron Man, S.H.I.E.L.D., or Doctor Octopus and his nanotechnology. But it was the final minute of *No Way Home*, which featured Peter swinging through a snowy New York City in a comic-accurate costume he sewed himself in a dingy apartment, that corrected these thematic mistakes with one majestic conclusion.

Spider-Man purists bothered by Stark's function in *Captain America: Civil War* and *Homecoming* gripe that Tony essentially occupies the influential Uncle Ben role from the comics, even delivering the movie's equivalent of a "With great power" life lesson when he tells Peter, "If you're nothing without this suit, then you shouldn't have it."

The way Daley explains it, though, the writing team was intrigued by Tony Stark as an estranged father figure for Peter, primarily because he's not an ideal father figure in any sense of the term. "He'll give you all the fun toys, but he isn't going to show you how to use them," Daley said. "We always likened the suit that Tony gives him to a Ferrari that's a stick shift, and he doesn't even know how to drive. Wielding that power, I think, gave him this false sense of confidence that I think most kids would get if they had these newfound powers and this suit. And so we really just wanted to explore the idea of him putting too much value on the suit and who Spider-Man is, and not enough value on who Peter Parker is."[20]

The Ben-to-Tony comparison could have been sidestepped if either *Homecoming* or *Far from Home* explained in greater detail what happened to Ben before Peter met Tony in *Captain America: Civil War*. But Feige, cagey as usual, said they made "a very, very purposeful decision . . . not retread that ground."[21]

"We did talk about there being a scene where [May] references him directly," Daley remembered. "It was when [Peter] was getting ready for homecoming and the wardrobe she was giving Peter was all Uncle Ben's clothes. It was a nice moment, but we also knew that it veered away from his arc. If you're going to talk about someone's death, you don't want it to be a throwaway."[22]

Then there are those who dismissed Jon Watts's *Spider-Man: Homecoming* as a blatant cash grab, one that had no chance of being as good as Sam Raimi's original trilogy of films. Or perhaps that was only *Spider-Man* star Kirsten

Dunst, who told *Marie Claire* magazine in 2017, "We made the best ones, so who cares? I'm like, 'You make it all you want.' They're just milking that cow for money. It's so obvious."[23]

Such criticism overlooks the note-perfect sequences in *Spider-Man: Homecoming* that breathe life into fan-favorite moments from Spider-Man's legacy because the film re-creates some of the hero's most memorable comic book panels with impressive detail. The most notable, arguably, is the nod *Homecoming* makes to The Amazing Spider-Man #33, titled "The Final Chapter," which Feige wanted to see done properly in a movie. After Peter confronts Toomes in a warehouse, the villain distracts our hero long enough to get his mechanical wings in the air, then uses the device to collapse a chunk of the concrete structure down onto Spider-Man's shoulders. Pinned and helpless, Peter must summon all of his strength to lift the overwhelming weight of the rubble, just as the character did in that iconic comic issue in order to obtain a serum that would cure his ailing Aunt May.

"I will say, here's a little bit of trivia, what we had originally intended when he was stuck under the rubble and trying to get himself out," said Daley, "the thing that gets him out, originally, is not telling himself 'You're Spider-Man,' but 'You're Peter Parker,' and putting value on himself. We thought that was really interesting."[24]

"That's one of the best Spider-Man moments of all time," Watts added. "And I think it's a lot of really big Spider-Man fans' favorite moments, too. So to be able to put that in the film was an honor."[25]

Such an honor, in fact, that Holland cherishes a memory he has of visiting the Queens, New York–based Silver Age Comics during shooting on *Homecoming* and asking the shop's owner, Gus Poulakas, what his favorite Spider-Man moment was. Poulakas singled out "The Final Chapter" and the unforgettable Steve Ditko art showing Spider-Man overcoming exhaustion to lift an unbearable weight. Poulakas had no clue it was going to appear in the movie. So Watts reached into his pocket, took out his cell phone, and showed Poulakas photos of how his interpretation of the sequence would look on-screen. The lifelong comic book collector lost his mind.

The other fan-friendly homage Feige worked into *Spider-Man: Home-coming* isn't as old as The Amazing Spider-Man #33, which Marvel Comics published in 1965. But similarly, it was a Spider-Man plot twist we'd never seen on-screen before and one that Marvel's president had been lobbying to include for years. It's the final shot in the film, where Peter removes his mask without knowing that his Aunt May (Marisa Tomei) is standing in his bedroom doorway. Just like that, Spider-Man's secret identity has been blown.

"J. Michael Straczynski did an issue when he was doing his run of Spidey many years ago where [May] discovered the secret. I think it was in the laundry, or something, and they had a sit-down scene," Feige said. "Probably going back to [Raimi's] *Spider-Man 2*, I would carry that issue around and go, 'We should do this some day!' It was great luck that it hadn't been done yet. So that was always part of the plan. And very much like our instinct to say, 'Let's have Tony Stark say "I am Iron Man" at the end. Well, what does that mean for the next movie? I don't know! But it will force us to do something unique!' We did not want to do the secret identity thing at that point in the MCU. And now, same thing. The dynamic now is forced to be something fresh and something unique going forward."[26]

Again, we wonder how much Feige already had dreamed up about Spidey's future MCU plot twists when mapping out *Spider-Man: Homecoming* in 2016 because the fragile nature of Peter Parker's secret identity—and the way that it gets revealed—creates a ripple effect that flows through his entire *Home* saga. By the end of *Spider-Man: Far from Home*, Michelle (Zendaya) has deduced that Peter is Spider-Man, joining Ned (Jacob Batalon), May, and Happy in the hero's close-knit circle of trust. Then the staggering *Far from*

Home cliffhanger of Mysterio's public reveal acts as the catalyst for Peter and Doctor Strange (Benedict Cumberbatch) to open up the multiverse as well as a slew of fascinating story-line potentials in 2021's *Spider-Man: No Way Home*. These big-swing plot turns can be traced back to May seeing Peter without his mask as *Homecoming* ends, setting up years of storytelling for Holland's version of the hero.

"Going forward [from *Far from Home*], it'll be fun to see Spidey back in his element, out of the shadow of Tony, out of the shadow of the other Avengers as his own man now, his own hero," said Feige. "And now facing his own challenges that aren't coming from Avengers fighting, like *Civil War*, or aliens coming, like *Infinity War* and *Endgame*."[27]

Placing Spider-Man in the MCU during *Civil War* did allow Joe and Anthony Russo to heavily showcase him alongside the Avengers and take the character to places he truly has never gone before in back-to-back Avengers features. It also created a headache for Watts he couldn't have anticipated when he signed on to the series.

Spider-Man: Far from Home

Sam Raimi and Marc Webb encountered their own unique challenges when attempting sequels to their initial Spider-Man movies. But they were nothing like the obstacles intimidating Watts as he prepared to make his second Spidey feature, 2019's globe-trotting *Spider-Man: Far from Home*. Because of where this movie fell in the overarching story line of Marvel's entire Infinity Saga—which pit the MCU's heroes against Thanos the Mad Titan (Josh Brolin)—*Far from Home* wasn't just a sequel to *Homecoming*. It also needed to work as the first Marvel movie released into theaters after *Avengers: Endgame*, a monumental game changer of a blockbuster that stuck the landing on ten years of storytelling and temporarily held the title of the highest-grossing movie of all time (until James Cameron's *Avatar* conducted a 2021 rerelease in China and earned just enough to reclaim that distinction).

No pressure whatsoever, following up that juggernaut.

It's charmingly naive that Watts went out of his way to showcase an inexperienced Spider-Man in *Homecoming* because by the time he got his "toy" back from the Russo Brothers, Peter had experienced a lifetime's worth of thrills. Tobey Maguire's most significant set piece occurred on a moving train. Andrew Garfield fought "a Russian guy in a rhinoceros machine," as he explained in *Spider-Man: No Way Home*. But Holland's Peter Parker traveled to space with Iron Man, Doctor Strange, and the Guardians of the Galaxy to fight Thanos on the ravaged planet of Titan. He rode on the back of Valkyrie's flying horse while carrying the Infinity Gauntlet. He watched his billionaire, genius mentor—Tony Stark—die. Watts needed *Spider-Man: Far from Home* to absorb and process all of that while also sending Peter on a European jaunt where he'd match wits with Mysterio: the master of illusion.

Bringing the focus back to Peter meant Chris McKenna and Erik Sommers's *Far from Home* script could burrow into character development for which *Infinity War* and *Endgame* had no time. Having survived the Blip, the five-year period in the MCU when half the world's population was snapped out of existence by Thanos, Parker enters this sequel with an uncharacteristically selfish and laissez-faire attitude, wanting nothing more than to enjoy a carefree summer vacation with his classmates. His Aunt May seems okay with her nephew's secret identity and even pushes him to take his Spidey suit on his trip with him in case trouble surfaces. Peter, however, has other plans. In addition to rest and relaxation, he hopes to get closer to Zendaya's quirky Michelle and see if there's chemistry between them.

Nick Fury (Samuel L. Jackson) interferes because MCU Spider-Man takes advantage of his adjacency to the on-screen Marvel roster every chance he gets. The S.H.I.E.L.D. director recruits Parker into action after ecological creatures dubbed Elementals begin attacking random locations in Mexico, Italy, and the Czech Republic. Over the course of the movie, Peter ventures to Berlin in his alternate Stealth suit, gets sent to a Netherlands jail cell, confronts Mysterio at London's famous Tower Bridge, and earns the nickname "Night Monkey" thanks to best friend Ned's quick thinking.

Don't expect any deeper meaning behind that nickname by the way. "It was just like, 'What is the dumbest thing we could think of?'" Watts said with a laugh. "He's dressed in black, and he's swinging around like a monkey swinging on vines. So that's what Ned would think of."[28]

Some might dismiss *Spider-Man: Far from Home* as a frivolous Spidey solo adventure, an international lark that doesn't advance the character much beyond where we meet him in the film's opening. Looking back on it, though, *Far from Home* begins constructing the unexpected bridge between Holland's MCU franchise and the preexisting Maguire and Garfield Spider-Man movies, proving it possible to dip back into those stories without drastically rocking the boat. During its end-credits scene, *Far from Home* introduced J. Jonah Jameson into the Marvel Studios mix. But in a clever move that now reads as foreshadowing, Watts recruited Raimi's original Jameson, J. K. Simmons, to once again play the part. The conversations regarding Jameson evolved organically. Watts knew that Peter's secret identity was going to be revealed by the end of the film and that the media would somehow be involved. The team knew the *Daily Bugle* always had been the main media outlet in Spider-Man's world, but it would have to be updated to make sense in a contemporary time.

J. Jonah Jameson, however, would not be updated. "There was never any discussion about it being someone else," Watts said. "It's got to be J. K. Simmons." The biggest uncertainty was whether the Oscar-winning character actor would agree to revive one of his signature parts. It took very little convincing. Once he agreed, the challenge was keeping his return a secret so that the surprise could have maximum effect once the movie screened for fans.

"We shot [his scene] in a conference room at Marvel with a green-screen set up," Watts explained. "It was funny, because it was the exact same set up as we shot the kids' news from the beginning! It was just him and a desk and a green screen. He just launched into it, and it was amazing. I asked him, 'Is this weird?' And he said, 'It's a little weird.' But he just stepped right back into the role, and I had goosebumps."[29]

There's also a now important conversation in *Far from Home* that references the multiverse, establishing the possibility of its existence so that Watts could continue expanding on it in *No Way Home*. When Peter Parker officially meets Jake Gyllenhaal's Quentin Beck in Italy, the villain claims to be from an alternate Earth—Earth 833 to be exact. It's a lie. Beck's a con artist, pulling the wool over Peter's eyes. But the "Nick Fury" in that scene also happens to be the Skrull leader, Talos, which Watts believes lends credence to Beck's fib.

"The fact that Nick Fury, who's actually Talos, completely believes this story about a multiverse makes me wonder," Watts said, proving that even in 2019, the director was contemplating the credibility of the multiverse in the MCU.

So *Far from Home* does its fair share of projecting forward. It also, however, dwells heavily on one lingering element of Peter's past: the long shadow Tony Stark cast over Parker's day-to-day existence. Even in death, Tony lives in Peter's head, impacting his decisions and operating as a measuring stick against which Spidey forever will compare himself.

"I thought it was a nice comparison to what happened at the end of *Iron Man*," Watts said about his main character's identity reveal. "Because for so much of *Far from Home*, we're having the world ask Peter, you know, 'Are you going to be the next Iron Man? Are you going to step up and be the next Iron Man?' And he makes his decision not to be the next Iron Man, but to be the first Spider-Man.

"And it's Peter Parker, and nothing ever goes according to plan," Watts continued. "So we thought as soon as he was starting to have things figured out, we would pull the ultimate reversal on him. Which is, Tony chose to reveal himself to the world. And now this time it's Mysterio. And it just made sense in this movie that's all about lies and deception that Peter's greatest secret would get revealed."[30]

The impact of *Far from Home*'s final scene should reverberate through Sony and Marvel's shared Spider-Man franchise for years. The identity reveal fueled the plot twists that drove 2021's *Spider-Man: No Way Home*, which picked up its story right where *Far from Home* left off. The consequences of the reveal prompted Peter Parker to ask Doctor Strange to cast a memory-wipe spell on the entire planet, which goes wrong, and opens up the multiverse. The *Far from Home* finale also linked the MCU to Sony's Spider-Verse in the end-credits scenes of both *No Way Home* and the Sony sequel, *Venom: Let There Be Carnage*, when Eddie Brock pitstopped in the MCU and left a half-dollar-sized drop of alien symbiote behind, which means there's very little doubt that the complete ramifications of that scene have run their course in Parker's on-screen life.

CHAPTER TWELVE
SPIDER-MAN, THE AVENGER

The first time that audiences laid their eyes on Tobey Maguire's Peter Parker, he's shown chasing after a school bus. Sam Raimi even framed Parker in the vehicle's rearview mirror, visualizing the sad truth that Peter exists outside of the student body. His classmates literally have left him behind. Mary Jane Watson (Kirsten Dunst), out of pity, has to order the smirking bus driver to slow down and let Peter on. Naturally, nobody wants to sit with the sweaty boy as he searches for a seat. And as Peter makes eye contact with the redheaded girl of his dreams, mustering the courage to attempt a smile, a bully sticks out his foot and trips him, sending Parker's clunky eyeglasses flying. During these first steps of his cinematic history, Peter's as far removed as possible from the high-flying, wisecracking superhero he's destined to become.

Flash-forward to the moment we first see Tom Holland's Peter Parker in Joe and Anthony Russo's *Avengers: Infinity War*, and the stark difference (no pun intended) could give you whiplash. Once again, a school bus is involved. Beyond that, nothing about Holland's Parker reminds you of Maguire. To begin with, Peter's already on the bus—a small detail that's still worth noting simply for the social acceptance that it implies. After his spider sense alerts him to danger, the hairs on his arm standing straight up, Peter looks out his window but doesn't spy a grimy Queens neighborhood. He sees a gigantic circular spaceship that's bearing down on Manhattan. Peter taps his best friend—something Maguire's outcast teenager would have cherished—and tells him to create a diversion. Once Peter's classmates have turned to stare at the alien craft, our hero slaps on his web shooters, exits the moving vehicle, pulls his mask over his face, and swings off to battle space invaders alongside Iron Man (Robert Downey Jr.), Bruce Banner (Mark Ruffalo), and Doctor Strange (Benedict Cumberbatch) as an honorary member of the Avengers.

Two school bus sequences, separated by sixteen years, but they illustrate exactly how far our wall crawler progressed in a relatively short amount of time. The conversation continued in 2021's *Spider-Man: No Way Home* once the three on-screen Spider-Men were able to share scenes for the first time. When comparing the scale of the villains they've faced over the years, Holland's Peter impresses the other two by stating he has fought an alien in space. Later, in an attempt to coordinate their attacks and establish teamwork, Holland brags ever so slightly that his Spider-Man learned how to fight alongside other heroes because he was a member of the Avengers. It's played for a laugh because Maguire and Garfield's Peters have no clue what the Avengers are. "Is that a band? Are you in a band?" Garfield asks excitedly.

It wasn't just the Spider-Man character who had evolved in that sixteen-year span. The comic–book movie genre, as a whole, had matured. By 2018, Hollywood's superhero revolution led to theater screens occupied by Lego movies dedicated to Batman and his Gotham cohorts, Oscar-nominated neo-westerns with Hugh Jackman's Wolverine in the lead, and an R-rated franchise centered around the foulmouthed mercenary Deadpool. Genre popularity is cyclical—and usually at the mercy of the audience's tastes. But comic book movie success has lasted decades and inspired rapid maturation from screenwriters, VFX artists, producers, and directors.

Still, there's no possible way that Kevin Feige, working for Avi Arad on the set of Raimi's 2002 *Spider-Man*, could have predicted a cinematic reality where Marvel's friendly neighborhood Spider-Man would cling to the side of a spacecraft piloted by Black Order member Ebony Maw as Iron Man unlocks compartment 17A at the Avengers compound, rocketing an Iron Spider suit into the Earth's stratosphere. "I should have stayed on the bus,"

Peter laments as a panel door closes, locking him on the spaceship, except by this point, both physically and metaphorically, Peter is so far beyond "the bus" that there is no going back.

The Death of Spider-Man

The unwritten promise Marvel and Sony made to show Spider-Man fans things they'd never seen before in a Spidey film was amplified once Christopher Markus and Stephen McFeely wrote the web slinger into the Avengers films and the studios fully embraced Peter Parker's role inside the vast and growing MCU.

There's comic book precedent to Spider-Man appearing alongside the Avengers, dating as far back as 1966's *The Amazing Spider-Man* annual #3, titled ". . . To Become an Avenger." After interviewing Daredevil about Spider-Man's character traits and getting the blind superhero's seal of approval, the Avengers offer Spidey the rare opportunity to be tested for membership on their team. Unlike Tom Holland's version of the wall crawler, however, the 1966 hero as written by Stan Lee sports a serious chip on his shoulder and bristles at the notion he'd have to prove himself worthy to other crime fighters. The lone-wolf superhero has a confident arrogance that comes with youth, so he enters the meeting in a defensive mood and ends up physically lashing out at Marvel's top team, damaging his chances of ever fitting in.

Spider-Man's outcast status with the Avengers lasted only so long. The hero fought alongside these colleagues many times over the years and even went on to hold numerous leadership positions on different iterations of the team, including the New Avengers and the Uncanny Avengers. In those earliest interactions with Earth's Mightiest Heroes, however, lie traits in Peter Parker that are vital to his makeup but detrimental to his odds when in the heat of battle: he's impetuous and can be overly proud. Because the teenaged

Peter gets picked on and bullied by his classmates, he's often quick to lash out at the Human Torch, Captain America, Wolverine, or any hero offering him assistance.

"He didn't trust them," Markus points out about these classic comic confrontations. "Because as much of a good boy as he is, he's also an outlaw, in his own way. That's what I love about him, is that he has invented this on his own. The other characters were either developed by the Russians, or H.Y.D.R.A., or the U.S. Army, or Tony [Stark] had a vast company to do it. Peter Parker is a kid who came up with this in his bedroom as a way to deal with a problem. And he's never sure it was a *good* idea. So he's not going to sign on immediately for stuff, because he's not all that confident it's a good thing."[1]

When given their own opportunity to write Spider-Man into an onscreen adventure opposite the MCU's Avengers, Markus and McFeely scaled back on this inherent distrust and instead embraced the unfiltered adolescent excitement they predicted Peter would have when interacting with his idols. "Like, 'Yeah, I know I'm about to have to fight Captain America. But gee, look! It's *Captain America!*' You don't get to play that note too often, and you can't play it more than once," Markus said.

That's an astute observation. The initial deal reached between Sony, Marvel, and Disney was finite. It allowed Spider-Man to appear in *Captain America: Civil War*, two MCU Avengers films, and two solo Spidey features that Feige would help develop. It gave the creative team permission to attempt a few important events that hadn't happened in a Spider-Man story before. But they had only one real shot to get these aspects right because once the deal expired, there was a very real chance Feige and his team wouldn't get the opportunity to try this all over again. And so, as part of his MCU tenure, Peter Parker rattles off a bevy of on-screen "firsts," cementing Holland's place in the wall crawler's history. MCU Spidey ventures into outer space for the very first time on-screen. He wears a mechanized Spider-Man suit (the Iron Spider) made of Stark nanotech. He playfully introduces himself to fellow New York City protector Doctor Strange, then gets "knighted" by Tony and inducted onto the varsity team. ("Kid? You're an Avenger now.") He fights Thanos the Mad Titan (Josh Brolin) alongside Star Lord (Chris Pratt), Nebula (Karen Gillan), Drax (Dave Bautista), and the Guardians of the Galaxy.

And he dies.

Death and loss are integral parts to Spider-Man's story. Gwen Stacy. Norman Osborn. Captain George Stacy. Peter's own parents, Richard and Mary Parker. Uncle Ben. Never before, though, had fans witnessed Peter's death on-screen in a Spider-Man movie. And it hurt, even more than many Marvel fans could have predicted.

"He had the most painful death in *Infinity War*, where it really broke people's hearts to see him pleading with Tony and not wanting to go. And then fading out," Markus said. "I think that was the one when people watching that movie went, 'Oh, they're really doing this. And they're doing it in an on-screen way where the emotions are going to have to be real, and we're going to have to feel them.'"

Peter wasn't the only hero on the chopping block. In the closing minutes of *Avengers: Infinity War*, Thanos successfully decreased the galaxy's population by half, completing his genocidal mission of bringing balance to all of existence. The ramifications of the Snap spread far and wide, claiming Scarlet Witch (Elizabeth Olsen), Sam Wilson (Anthony Mackie), Nick Fury (Samuel L. Jackson), Peter's best friends Ned (Jacob Batalon) and Michelle (Zendaya), and half the roster of existing MCU superheroes.

Yet every eradication in *Infinity War* was driven by story and emphasized through character. Bucky Barnes is the first person to dust following Thanos's snap, and his death is viewed from the perspective of Captain America, his closest ally. When Black Panther dusts, the warrior is holding the hand of

Okoye, whose chief responsibility as a member of the Dora Milaje is protecting her Wakandan king. The shock of failure registered on her face was being felt by every audience member watching the movie for the first time. "To see those characters react in those situations is very powerful and resonant," Anthony Russo said.[2]

Peter's final moments in *Infinity War*, therefore, are spent in the arms of his MCU mentor. Tony Stark ushered Peter Parker into this universe. He'd have to stand there and watch his protégé fade out. It was intentional that Spidey's dusting appeared to take longer than the other MCU heroes, if only by a few seconds. It wasn't just to torture Stark, though that was a powerful side effect. Per codirector Joe Russo, Peter's intense desire to survive, coupled with his incredible spider strength, postponed the inevitable long enough for the teenager to say "I'm sorry" to Tony. Then he collapsed into dust.

This devastating loss underlines Tony's journey from *Infinity War* to *Endgame*, the specter of Peter's death eating away at the egotistical billionaire who naively believed he could solve any problem. The second thing Tony says to Steve Rogers (Chris Evans) on returning to Earth in *Endgame* is, "I lost the kid." In time, though, the same guilt that clouds Tony's vision ultimately ends up being the motivator Stark needs to decipher time travel, giving the Avengers the advantage they needed to defeat Thanos.

Going into *Avengers: Endgame* as an audience member, Jon Watts knew most of the screenplay's important story beats. Feige had to fill him in given the fact that the director was heavily plotting *Spider-Man: Far from Home*, the movie tasked with picking up the MCU baton post-*Endgame* and running with it.

"Remember when Bart Simpson goes to the MAD magazine headquarters on *The Simpsons* in New York? Do you remember that one? And he looks in the door, and it's exactly what you'd expect? That's sometimes what it feels like working at Marvel," Watts said. "You're walking through the hallways, and you'll peek around the corner into a conference room, and there are all these tantalizing hints of what could come. And then someone slowly pushes the door closed."[3]

That's how Watts believes the Russos managed to include one scene in *Avengers: Endgame* he wasn't aware of, and it doubled down on the narrative importance of Tony and Peter's relationship.

"I didn't realize that the very last thing that Tony was going to look at before he decided to crack the time travel problem [in *Endgame*] was that photo of him and Peter," Watts said. The scene takes place in the Stark kitchen, late at night. Tony's finishing up cleaning the dishes, and he gets distracted by framed photographs on a nearby shelf. "It's behind a picture of his dad, and you think he's looking at the picture of his dad, and then he reaches behind that and takes out the picture of him and Peter with the Stark scholarship certificate. He's holding it upside down. That really hit me. So I had one genuine surprise during *Endgame*. I got a little choked up."

Out of all of the things the Avengers lost between *Infinity War* and *Endgame*, it's "the kid" that wakes Tony up. It's Peter who drives him, inspires him to finish the mission, and helps bring everyone back from the dead. Markus and McFeely devised a powerful and symmetrical through line, having Peter motivate Tony when it was Tony who motivated Peter all through *Spider-Man: Homecoming*. Even Tony and Peter's sweetest moment in *Avengers: Endgame*, the reunion hug they share on the battlefield in the midst of so much chaos, is a callback nod to the non-hug Stark delivers in the backseat of his car during *Spider-Man: Homecoming*.

And that moment originally wasn't supposed to be in Watts's movie. Downey Jr. improvised the line, "That's not a hug, I'm just grabbing the door for you," on his first day of *Homecoming* shooting.

"A lot of that sequence, the stuff we started with, is all of Peter's cellphone footage of him secretly filming," Watts remembers. "It wasn't a traditional shoot in any sense. Basically, I gave the camera over to Tom. We had these mini high-def cameras that were mimicking the phone footage. And I just closed the door of the car—we were on a green-screen stage—and just let them go. So I was like, 'This is pretty easy! Just hand the camera over!'"

Spider-Man's future in the grand scheme of the MCU remains uncertain. The agreement Sony and Disney extended to keep Feige on through *Spider-Man: No Way Home* included one additional Spider-Man appearance in a to-be-determined MCU crossover film. Feige and Pascal also revealed preparations for a fourth Tom Holland–led Spider-Man movie in the wake of *No Way Home*, though details were being kept under wraps. Nothing's stopping the studios from returning to the negotiating tables at any point in the future to continue the partnership. Or new leadership at either studio could step in, evaluate the deal, and deem it imbalanced or unfair, severing the historic ties and sending Spider-Man back to Sony for use in its Sony Pictures Universe of Marvel Characters (SPUMC). Groundwork has been laid for just such a transition, with Eddie Brock (Tom Hardy) showing he could move back and forth between the worlds in the mysterious mid-credit scenes for *Venom: Let There Be Carnage* as well as *Spider-Man: No Way Home*.

Whatever happens moving forward, though, it will never erase the fact that for a few years, Feige and Pascal pulled off what seemed to be impossible. They let Peter Parker share the screen with his Marvel Comics counterparts, as he had done in the pages of the comic books for decades. They incorporated him into the epic *Avengers: Endgame*, still one of the most financially successful movies in Hollywood history. And they shattered the cinematic universe blueprint with *No Way Home*, devising a first-of-its-kind multiverse adventure that dissolved long-standing boundaries between live-action Spider-Man franchises, making the Raimi and Webb films canon.

CHAPTER THIRTEEN
A LEAP OF FAITH

Long before Sony Pictures, Marvel Studios, and Walt Disney Studios agreed to share Spider-Man in 2015, the companies spent years trading ideas that could have set up a mutually beneficial creative collaboration. And these on-again, off-again conversations weren't limited to live-action projects.

Talks between the studios regarding a potential animated Spider-Man feature-length comedy made significant progress in late 2014, landing on the desks of studio heads Kaz Hirai (Sony) and Bob Iger (Disney) for consideration. Longtime Spider-Man conservator Avi Arad, who had developed popular animated Marvel stories for Spidey and the X-Men, referred to this as "a Eureka moment"[1] in the expansion of Sony's Spider-Man. This feature tentatively would have been produced by Marvel, with Sony retaining marketing and distribution responsibilities as well as creative control of the story and script. This picture also would have coexisted alongside Sony's ongoing efforts to lend a live-action Spider-Man to Marvel for inclusion in its MCU movies.

Arad urged Sony to use Spider-Man as a means of revitalizing Sony Pictures Animation (SPA), which had slipped into a creative rut and was losing its top talent to the competition. Returning the Spider-Man character to his animated roots made sense. Despite the fact that Sony just spent several years and millions of dollars helping Sam Raimi and Marc Webb figure out how to bring a live-action Spidey to life, the Marvel superhero's agility and physicality were first perfected on comic book pages and in animated television programs. The absence of physical limitations in animation meant that designers could accomplish awe-inspiring Spider-Man sequences that stuntmen, actors, and visual effects artists would struggle to achieve no matter how sophisticated VFX technology had gotten year over year.

Amy Pascal agreed with Arad that a proper Spider-Man project had the power to rejuvenate Sony's animation division, which was letting sequels for existing franchises like *The Smurfs* and *Hotel Transylvania* drive its production slate. So she and Sony Pictures Chief Executive Michael Lynton spent the bulk of 2014 recruiting a creative brain trust at SPA that would replicate the creative environment that animators were finding at Pixar Animation Studios, the gold standard in computer-animated features. Pascal and Lynton's wish list included Brad Bird (*The Iron Giant* and *The Incredibles*), Will Gluck (*Easy A* and *Friends with Benefits*), and SPA veterans Phil Lord and Chris Miller, the duo behind the studio's 2009 hit *Cloudy with a Chance of Meatballs*.

"Those guys are superheroes," Sony Pictures Motion Picture Group Chairman and CEO Tom Rothman said about Lord and Miller. "They are mega-talents."[2]

Yet, when Sony offered Lord and Miller the keys to the car and a blank slate on which they could create an original Spider-Man movie, the duo almost decided against it—with valid reason.

"I was initially skeptical about doing a Spider-Man movie because it is such a saturated character in the culture, and in film," Miller said.[3]

Few would argue that point. The hero was well represented in the movies, books, comics, video games, and television shows that occupied our pop-culture landscape at the time. Spidey was such a sought-after character that even visionary theater director Julie Taymor (*The Lion King* and *Salome*) tried to mount a glitzy Broadway musical based on his adventures. *Spider-Man: Turn Off the Dark* (2010) boasted a songbook with music and lyrics by famed U2 front man Bono and guitarist The Edge but ended up being a disaster-plagued failure—a creative misfire that was savaged by theater critics and cost its investors millions of dollars. The Broadway flop indirectly supported

Miller's concerns that he and his creative partner might not find a suitably fresh Spider-Man story to tell.

That's saying something because prior to tackling their Spider-Man story, Lord and Miller built their reputation by reinventing offbeat properties that, on paper, looked like they shouldn't work until the twosome figured out how to make them sparkle. The pair earned a Golden Globe nomination in 2010 for their adaption of Judi and Ron Barrett's children's novel *Cloudy with a Chance of Meatballs*. From there, Lord and Miller reconfigured the campy television drama *21 Jump Street* into a raunchy buddy-cop vehicle for odd couple Channing Tatum and Jonah Hill. That 2012 movie generated enough box office revenue and positive audience feedback to spawn a sequel. Producers and studio executives around Hollywood were starting to take notice of the way that Lord and Miller embraced seemingly ridiculous concepts and figured out how best to present them to mainstream audiences, finding the right balance of nostalgia and contemporary humor. Still, those wins didn't prepare audiences (or the industry) for the movie magic this duo would weave with a simple toy from our childhoods: the Lego brick.

Lord and Miller's 2014 computer-animated adventure *The Lego Movie* plunged audiences into a shape-shifting world of Master Builders and minifigures, where an optimistic worker bee named Emmet Brickowski (voiced by a jubilant Chris Pratt) teamed up with the action-savvy Wyldstyle (Elizabeth Banks) and Batman (Will Arnett)—yes, Batman—to stop the sinister Lord Business (Will Ferrell) from conquering the world. The imaginative film earned raves as well as $468 million in worldwide ticket sales. Salon.com's Andrew O'Hehir summarized the critical consensus on *The Lego Movie* when he called it "surprisingly enjoyable and satisfyingly dense family entertainment that pays tribute to the spirit of free play and individuality."[4] After all, Legos are the types of toys that thrive in the hands of creative people, designers who refuse to follow the step-by-step instructions provided in the kits to instead build whatever inspires them. That perfectly describes how Lord and Miller make movies. They rarely adhere to Hollywood's rules, instead taking all the ingredients at their disposal and whipping them into something authentic, original, and crowd pleasing.

They brought those sensibilities to Spider-Man. Instead of viewing the character's market saturation as a roadblock, Lord and Miller embraced the reality that Spider-Man is extremely well known and made his inherent cultural omnipresence part of their narration. They rooted their story in a world where Spider-Man already was an established superhero, then manifested drama for their main character by having the shadow of Peter Parker—and the weight that comes with being Spider-Man—hang over almost every decision made on-screen. These steps put the duo on the right path toward crafting a Spider-Man film that would be demonstratively different from the six on-screen, feature-length stories that had come before it.

Success wasn't guaranteed. It just required a leap of faith.

"It Always Fits . . . Eventually"

Tom Rothman announced plans for Sony's animated feature *Spider-Man: Into the Spider-Verse* in 2015. It marked another groundbreaking achievement for Spider-Man as a character, as no other comic book hero, past or present, could claim to have both a live-action and an animated feature film backed by a major studio heading to movie theaters around the same time.

"Now, it seems like a no-brainer," Rothman said. "But I'm proud of Sony for having greenlit that film, because it was very risky to take our most prized asset—our number one piece of intellectual property—and animate it and do a kind of thing that had never been done before. I think that was very brave of Sony. It was doable because of the level of belief that we have in [Phil Lord and Chris Miller], and how talented they are. But even still, that was a brave greenlight. And boy, we've been richly rewarded."[5]

Pascal and Arad joined Lord and Miller as producers on the film. The team hired Rodney Rothman, Peter Ramsey, and Bob Persichetti to codirect *Spider-Man: Into the Spider-Verse*, working off an original script by Rothman and Lord. Every Spider-Man project mounted in the wake of Raimi's debut did as much as possible to offer fans a fresh experience, and *Into the Spider-Verse* was no exception. Instead of Peter Parker, the main story in *Into the Spider-Verse* focused on Miles Morales (voiced by Shameik Moore), a biracial Brooklyn teenager first introduced by acclaimed Marvel comic book writer Brian Michael Bendis and artist Sara Pichelli in 2011.

Morales's origin is tied to Parker, as the boy is bitten by an enhanced spider that happens to be carrying a unique formula synthesized from Parker's blood. But the two have foundational differences that contribute to the type of hero each one becomes.

"Miles has his family. His mother and father, he's being raised by them actively. He also has good friends and his little circle," said Bendis, who served as a creative consultant on *Into the Spider-Verse*. "Peter was an orphan with a very old aunt. Peter was a very depressed young man and [was] being treated very badly by everyone around him. That's just the environment they are growing up in. It's enormously different, so they react to it differently."[6]

Not having to rehash the traditional story of Peter, Uncle Ben, and Aunt May, *Into the Spider-Verse* instead spun a vibrant story around Miles's unique living situation. Morales isn't an academic genius like Parker. The artistic teen can't emotionally connect with his police officer father (Brian Tyree Henry) and prefers to hang with his rule-bending Uncle Aaron (Mahershala Ali) instead of bonding with his boring boarding school classmates.

It was Lord's idea to focus *Spider-Man: Into the Spider-Verse* on Morales, mainly because he echoed his partner's concerns about saturation and figured a Miles movie would allow them to "get everything that's cool about Spider-Man" but also to "do something that was distinct from all of the other portrayals of the character."[7] It also furthered the duo's core belief that we all have the potential to be Spider-Man because Spider-Man, under that costume, is more like us than any other hero.

"He wears a mask that covers his entire face. So anybody can imagine themselves being behind that mask," Miller said. "And that was really important, thematically, for the movie that we made. But I think it's also why, when you go into the Mexican neighborhoods here in L.A., they're selling Spider-Man masks everywhere. Because everyone can put that thing on, and they can be the hero. They look at the character in the comic books, and it could be them."

Unlike the Raimi and Webb films, though, *Into the Spider-Verse* faced the challenge of having its hero stand apart from a live-action Spider-Man that Tom Holland was playing at the exact same time. Because of that, the *Into the Spider-Verse* team kept Spider-Man's legacy, both past and present, in its periphery as they worked. As codirector Rodney Rothman explained, "You don't look right at it. You don't overstudy any of the versions, or all of the minutia. You learn a bunch of it and then you kind of put it slightly to the side and start to tell your version of his story."[8]

Spider-Man: Into the Spider-Verse tackles the issue of character familiarity in its opening frames. In an inspired stroke of storytelling, *Into the Spider-Verse* opens with an acknowledgment that the world doesn't actually *need* another introduction to Spider-Man. "Alright, let's do this one last time," a graciously impatient Chris Pine voices before the movie regurgitates the main plot points of the familiar Spidey mythology. An animated montage showcases Peter's Uncle Ben, pokes fun at Tobey Maguire's embarrassing dance scenes from Raimi's *Spider-Man 3*, and re-creates a handful of heroic moments culled from *Spider-Man 2*, a feature that Lord and Miller say taught them important lessons about the character.

"The Raimi films, especially the second one, do such a good job of reminding you that you're in a story about a teenage kid and his friends and family, and you never really forget it," Lord said "That movie abuses Peter Parker pretty brutally. For an hour, he just gets his butt kicked in every possible direction. And so we spent a lot of time thinking about why that was so successful, even though our movie is quite different. And even though our movie starts by saying it's not going to be anything like those movies, it is, at its heart, still trying to get you to fall for a kid who's not having his best day."

Some elements you simply can't escape when telling a Spider-Man story. The hero has to be a relatable kid. The lesson of responsibility should be learned, usually due to a life-altering loss. But good storytellers will evolve these ideas and push the familiar into unfamiliar territories, which explains why, when *Into the Spider-Verse* arrives at its second-act plot turn, Miles is joined on-screen by a plethora of spider-men and spider-women from parallel dimensions, all looking for a way home.

Embracing the mantra "Anyone can wear the mask," Persichetti, Ramsey, and Rothman felt free to bring beloved but unexpected comic characters such as Spider-Ham (John Mulaney), Spider-Gwen (Hailee Steinfeld), and Spider-Man Noir (Nicolas Cage) to life in a logical story. This choice instantly distanced *Into the Spider-Verse* from any of its predecessors, at least until Jon Watts did a live-action take on the multiverse in 2021's *Spider-Man: No Way Home*.

Populating *Spider-Man: Into the Spider-Verse* with multiple spider heroes also meant, though, that the creatives doubled down on a challenge that plagued every Spider-Man movie to date: who's the best person to cast in the pivotal heroic role? As Lord and Miller argued over the voice cast for the multiverse of characters, they wanted to make sure the "team" they assembled felt distinctly different from each other both visually and vocally. As part of the casting process, Lord and Miller sat in a room with their three codirectors and tossed out coveted celebrity names to see what would stick.

"When the name Nicholas Cage came up [for Spider-Man Noir], everybody just stopped for a second and went, 'Well yeah, of course.' And that was the case for everybody, really," Miller said.

Into the Spider-Verse is a Miles Morales story, but it also needed a Peter Parker. Once again, in an effort to steer clear of all the Spider-Man movies that preceded it, Lord pitched another offbeat idea. He suggested that audiences meet a seasoned, almost burned-out, adult Peter Parker, who has to reluctantly step into a mentor's role—creating a version of the character that had never been done on-screen before. Lord also wrote his version of the character, Peter B. Parker from an alternate universe, with his close friend and *New Girl* costar, Jake Johnson, in mind.

"The thing about Jake is that he just seems like he's seen it all before, and he's kind of floating above it a little bit," Lord explained. "He just seems like a regular guy. We keep coming back to this theme, which is, [Spider-Man's] not an incredibly high-status character. He's a low-status character from Queens. So he feels right when he's being played by someone who doesn't pump themselves up."

Strangely enough, Johnson has no deep connection to the Spider-Man mythology whatsoever. He claims to have never even seen any of the previous live-action Spider-Man movies that came before his film and has no real passion for superhero storytelling.

"I'm not kidding. If it wasn't Spider-Man—if it was an indie movie called *Older Mentor, Younger Mentee*—that [still] would have been one of the best scripts I had [read]," Johnson said. "So the fact that it was Spider Man and connected to that world is cool. But what really pulls me into Peter B. Parker is the story of somebody who used to have something great, and it has faded. And maybe it's still in them. But really, maybe it's also time to pass it on."[9]

Lord even pulled off some casting trickery to ensure that Johnson secured the role. While in London, hammering out the screenplay, the producer phoned Johnson and asked him to record a few pages of Peter B. Parker dialogue, which Lord then included as part of the test animation reels that were being sent to Sony. Lord believed that once the studio heads back in Los Angeles heard Johnson's charming line deliveries, they'd love the choice as much as Lord and Miller did. They also wanted to avoid a potential casting snafu where executives reached for the stars, literally, because they didn't understand the project.

"If we'd gone through a more deliberate process," Lord said, "I was afraid that people would start getting greedy and want [Peter B. Parker] to be played by Tom Cruise. I was like, 'I don't think that's the idea.'"[10]

Cruise, ironically, *was* written into the *Spider-Man: Into the Spider-Verse* script during an early development stage because Lord and Rothman peppered their screenplay with endless homages to Spider-Man's legacy. As the movie starts, the Marvel logo fades away, and a title card announces that *Into the Spider-Verse* is "Approved by the Comics Code Authority." Older fans will recognize the stamp from the covers of early Marvel comics, referencing an organization that loosely governed the comics industry and kept harmful or offensive subject matter out of the story lines. Additionally, when Miles wakes up in the movie and encounters his unusual spider powers for the first time, his exaggerated reactions mirror the exact origin-story moments found in original Spider-Man comics.

In what would have been the most meta joke of the entire production, though, Lord constructed a sequence that referenced both Cruise and director James Cameron's brushes with the Spider-Man franchises. Cameron notoriously tried to mount a Spider-Man adaptation for Carolco in the 1990s, while Cruise was B-movie director Joe Zito's choice to play Peter Parker in his Cannon-backed feature from the mid-1980s. Lord crafted a scene where Miles, in an effort to learn how to be the next Spider-Man, studies commentary tracks on the DVDs of Spider-Man movies that were produced in his world. One of those movies would have starred Cruise as Peter, working for director James Cameron.

"Miles watched the commentary of the movie to learn clues about how to be a better Spider-Man," Miller said.

"It didn't make the cut," Lord said, "but it was a lot of fun. I think, actually, the commentary was supposed to be Tom Cruise and Jim Cameron."

"We were really ambitious," Miller said. "We were just like, 'Sure, why not?'"

"It's easy when you're writing a screenplay," Lord added, "I think mostly they were saying really boring commentary stuff. Like, 'Man, it was cold that day.' And Miles was frustrated that he couldn't learn more."

Whenever possible, *Spider-Man: Into the Spider-Verse* considered big risks like this in an effort to remain different. Those gambles led to huge rewards. Critics praised the film, and critical organizations showered *Spider-Verse* with trophies. Tom Holland threw his support behind the feature when he labeled *Spider-Verse* "one of the coolest films [he has] ever seen."[11] And on the morning of January 22, 2019, *Spider-Man: Into the Spider-Verse* received its highest acknowledgment to date: an Oscar nomination in the Best Animated Feature category.

And the Oscar Goes To . . .

Spider-Man: Into the Spider-Verse producers Phil Lord and Chris Miller had zero expectations that their animated adventure comedy would appeal to Academy voters. "Spider-Man's not the thing where you think, 'Oh, that's Oscar bait,'" Lord joked. Additionally, codirector Rodney Rothman had no real expectation that an animated Spider-Man movie would carry them to the Academy Awards. However, from the moment the trio emerged from the SPA editing bays, they started to suspect that they might have created something remarkable.

For starters, positive awards buzz began swirling around *Into the Spider-Verse* before audiences had the chance to screen it. The creative team actually received its first award for *Into the Spider-Verse* before they finished working on it. The New York Film Critics Circle named *Spider-Man: Into the Spider-Verse* the Best Animated Feature of 2018, but Rothman recalls getting the winning e-mail while they were still in the mixing stage, with ten days of work still left to complete.

From the moment the movie reached theaters, the team rode what Rothman described as "a Spider-Man-sized wave" of accolades generated by the fandom's love and enthusiasm for Spider-Man, Peter Parker, Miles Morales, Aunt May, Mary Jane Watson, Spider-Gwen, Spider-Ham, and all things tied to the wall crawler.

"It was a routine experience for us to go to a press junket or an interview and the journalist interviewing us had a Spider-Man tattoo that they got when they were 17 or 18 that they would show us," Rothman remembered. "That was normal during that period. By the time we made it to the Oscars, it had been going on for months. And that was obviously a really memorable, special time.

"Really, that whole period was special," he continued. "Not just because of winning awards, but also viscerally feeling connected to millions of people. People were finally seeing the movie and responding to it, and emotionally connecting to it. So many people were feeling these connections to this thing we'd worked so hard on. . . . You realize that you have been working on something that millions of people are interested in and excited about. But you're just representing something. You're there to represent something. You're just kind of carrying the [Spider-Man] flame for a moment."[12]

The *Spider-Man: Into the Spider-Verse* crew carried that flame all the way to the Academy Awards ceremony on February 24, 2019. Their movie competed in the Best Animated Feature category against Pixar's *Incredibles 2*, Wes Anderson's *Isle of Dogs*, the Japanese feature *Mirai*, and Disney's sequel *Wreck-It Ralph 2: Ralph Breaks the Internet*. Rothman admits that in the minutes before their category was announced, he started to believe a little bit of his movie's own press.

"I don't know if anyone else that worked on the movie will say this, but I will say that at that point, we'd had people shouting to us that we were going to win for weeks and weeks beforehand. So there was an element of, you know, at that point, my hopes were kind of up," he said. "But there also was a sense of, 'Oh well of course this probably isn't going to happen.' There was that kind of Charlie Brown sense of just, 'Well, everyone's been saying this might happen. So probably it won't.'"

Except it did. Oscar copresenters Michelle Yeoh and Pharrell Williams came onstage that evening to announce the nominees for Best Animated Feature. All Miller remembers is that he and Lord were holding hands "as though we were on a first date or something." Williams opened the envelope, but he and Yeoh read the winner aloud together. Spider-Man won an Academy Award.

"I mostly blacked out," Lord admits. "I remember when they called the name, and just that feeling of, 'Yep, here we go! Get ready to be embarrassed in front of the world!'"

The Dolby Theatre stage quickly filled with the power brokers and creatives behind *Into the Spider-Verse*'s success. Amy Pascal stood off to one side, hugging Jake Johnson. Shameik Moore embraced Peter Ramsey as the codirector held his Oscar statue. And perfectly positioned in the center of Lord and Miller as they gave their speeches was Avi Arad, sporting a black suit, a black shirt buttoned up to the collar, and a black stocking cap that had an animated Spider-Man emblem on the front.

Miller was hardly surprised. "I don't think I've ever seen Avi not wearing at least one piece of clothing that has a character that's part of his world."

"If you've been to Avi's house," Lord added, "you know that the whole house is merch. Not just from all the movies he's produced. He also used to make toys for a living. So it's got all the toys that he used to make. So it's not surprising that he would be wearing licensed material at one of the most important moments of his career."

A winner's time on the Oscars stage is short because the house band stands ready to play you off the moment your speech goes long. Team Spider-Verse was prepared. Estimating that they each would get eight seconds to speak, they rehearsed who would say what and in what order they would go should the win happen. Their acceptance speech reiterated the film's central message of inclusion, which was integral to Morales's interpretation of the Spider-Man lore.

Miller stated, "There's 800 filmmakers who pushed boundaries and took risks to make people feel powerful and seen."

Lord then added, "So when we hear that somebody's kid was watching the movie and turned to them and said, 'He looks like me,' or, 'They speak Spanish like us,' we feel like we already won."

Even with the preplanning, Bob Persichetti's comments were cut off by the music. It stings because Persichetti's planned lines were a touching tribute to Steve Ditko and Stan Lee, who'd passed away on November 12, 2018—a few months prior to this ceremony.

Time will tell if the 91st Academy Awards serve as a watershed moment for comic book movies, a turning point where the industry begins to treat the genre with more respect. Prior to this year, superhero movies such as Tim Burton's *Batman* or Richard Donner's *Superman* settled for nominations and wins in below-the-line categories such as Visual Effects, Set Design, or Art Direction. Heath Ledger's posthumous Oscar win in 2009 for playing the

Joker was the exception that proved the rule. But the 2019 nominations suggested a palpable shift. Alongside *Spider-Man: Into the Spider-Verse*'s win in the prestigious Animated Feature category, Marvel secured its first Best Picture nomination for Ryan Coogler's *Black Panther*. Then 2021's *Spider-Man: No Way Home* generated serious Oscar buzz in the weeks following its release.

Lord and Miller refuse to take credit for the increase in Academy attention for comic book movies. But they agree that it was long past time for Academy members to honor the artistry in superhero movies as opposed to banishing them to also-ran categories.

"Why should they be treated any differently than a Western? I believe *Unforgiven* is a Western that won a bunch of Oscars," Lord said. "Why is it any different than a crime picture? *Traffic* won some Oscars. These genres maybe started out as B-pictures. When a great one happens, I'm not sure why it's any different than anything else."

No matter the impact *Spider-Man: Into the Spider-Verse*'s Oscar win has on the industry at large, nothing will diminish the remarkable weight it lent to the character's cultural influence. Socially awkward Peter Parker, who never felt like he fit in, ends up being celebrated at Hollywood's most prestigious event. The Marvel superhero garnered industry prestige, and Sony green-lit two more animated adventures—*Spider-Man: Across the Spider-Verse*, and *Beyond the Spider-Verse*—as a result. People still hate spiders. Stan Lee's boss was correct in that assessment. But the Academy of Motion Picture Arts and Sciences had embraced Spider-Man, and a trail had now been blazed for subsequent superhero features to follow.

CHAPTER FOURTEEN
SONY'S SPIDER-VERSE

When Sony Pictures Entertainment struck its initial deal to share Spider-Man with Marvel Studios in 2015, webhead snagged the bulk of the industry headlines—and rightfully so. The coveted character had earned Sony billions of dollars in revenue and was expected to provide a sizable bump in interest for the already dominant MCU. "I never thought we'd be able to make a Spider-Man movie set in our universe, and here we are," Kevin Feige told the *Los Angeles Times*. "It truly was a dream-come-true scenario."[1]

But while pundits focused their analysis on the impact made by one character swinging from Sony to the MCU, Sony Pictures Motion Picture Group Chairman Tom Rothman and President Sanford Panitch shifted their focus to the more than 900 Marvel characters with direct ties to Spider-Man whose licensing rights remained under Sony's umbrella.

"We don't really think of our 900 characters as the Spidey-Verse," Panitch told the trade site Variety in May of 2021. "We have a Marvel universe."[2]

And they were ready to do something historic with it. The studio might not have been successful in constructing a cinematic universe using Marc Webb's two-film *The Amazing Spider-Man* series. But the lucrative concept of a shared on-screen world still appealed to the executives, and loaning Spider-Man to Marvel didn't halt Sony's forward progress on a universe of Spidey adjacent characters who could hold down their own films and eventually intersect.

You can pinpoint the exact moment when the fuller potential of this on-screen world shifted into focus for the general public. During the end credits of Andy Serkis's 2021 sequel *Venom: Let There Be Carnage*, audiences caught up with Eddie Brock (Tom Hardy), the disgraced journalist turned reluctant antihero, as he lay on a bed in a dingy motel room, staring at the ceiling. On the television set, a soap opera couple appeared to be dealing with a shocking pregnancy reveal, standard fare for a daytime drama. Brock was only half paying attention to the dialogue, but Venom—the chatty alien symbiote who lives inside Eddie like a parasite—adores the program and provided a running commentary. Because of some devious betrayals that were happening on the soap, Eddie and Venom started their own conversation about secrets and the damage they can cause to friendships when they are kept.

"We all have a past, Eddie," Venom warns, prompting his human host to probe a little further. Venom cautions that if he dared to expose Eddie to all of the information that the symbiotes have absorbed over "80 billion light years of hive knowledge across universes," it would fry the poor man's brain. As a compromise, Venom agrees to provide Eddie with a small taste of things the symbiotes have experienced. Before he is able to, however, another outside force interferes. The hotel room shakes, floods with a blinding light, and physically transforms before our very eyes.

Both Eddie and Venom are confused by what's happening, proving this is not Venom's handiwork. The nighttime sky spotted outside the window becomes day. The motel room morphs into what looks like a beachside vacation cabana. And in the background, the soap opera disappears from the television set, replaced by footage of *Daily Bugle* publisher J. Jonah Jameson (J. K. Simmons). The newsman rants about a "shocking revelation" regarding Spider-Man, and we realize we are watching the *Spider-Man: Far from Home* end-credits sequence, only from a different perspective. As Jameson continues to rail against "the Spider Menace," we see Tom Holland on the television screen, unmasked but wearing his newly crafted red and black Spider-Man costume. Venom leans close to the screen, murmurs, "That . . . guy," and licks the screen.

Somehow, Venom and Eddie Brock landed in the MCU courtesy of this game-changing mid-credits sequence. And a tantalizing scenario teased by Marvel Studios President Kevin Feige suddenly had become a reality. When Sony Pictures Entertainment and Marvel agreed in September 2019 to extend their partnership for at least one more film, Feige coyly described Spider-Man as "the only hero with the superpower to cross cinematic universes." He went on to say that because Sony was hard at work on an individual Spidey universe of films, starting with two *Venom* films and expanding to include Jared Leto's *Morbius* and a Kraven the Hunter movie, fans should remain on the lookout because they "never know what surprises the future might hold."[3]

Tom Hardy's Venom teleporting into the same universe as Tom Holland's Spider-Man qualifies as one of those surprises. The trip ended up being temporary. By the end of the *Spider-Man: No Way Home* credits, a drunk Eddie and his symbiote partner beamed back to the universe from whence they'd come—but not before leaving a small piece of the symbiote behind, no doubt to cause extreme headaches for Holland's costumed hero in a future MCU movie.

Sony had, in fact, been brainstorming this crossover for years. The studio made it clear that it was constructing what they referred to as the SPUMC so that the web slinger could join it when the time was right.

"Those movies will all take place in the world that we are now creating for Peter Parker," said Amy Pascal when discussing Sony's in-development slate while Marvel worked on *Spider-Man: Homecoming*. "They'll be adjuncts to it. There may be different locations. But it will all still be in the same world, and they will be connected to each other."[4]

Still, there's an ironic component—one that can't be overlooked—that it's Venom, a character whose inclusion in *Spider-Man 3* helped bring about the end of the Sam Raimi run of web slinger movies, who jump-started Sony's universe and made such a monumental crossover possible.

We Are Venom

Sony's roster of Spider-Man characters includes a fascinating mix of recognizable heroes and villains (Doctor Octopus, the Green Goblin, Black Cat, and Mysterio), long-standing comic book supporting characters (Betty Brant, Flash Thompson, Liz Allen, and Gwen Stacy), and obscure names that promise the possibility of alternate live-action origin stories on the big screen (the Scarlet Spider and Spider-Man 2099). The available stable also features heroic teams and criminal gangs like the Enforcers, the Spider-Man Revenge Squad (also described as the Legion of Losers), and the Wild Pack—a band of mercenaries led by the mysterious Silver Sable. Strangely, two characters remain nonexclusive to Sony and came with specific stipulations as to how they can be shared between the studios: Wilson Fisk, the Kingpin of Crime (who has been played on-screen by *Full Metal Jacket*'s Vincent D'Onofrio since 2015), and Jessica Drew, aka Spider-Woman.

Over the years, projects meant to either launch or expand this Spider-Man universe were announced to the Hollywood trades with interesting directors attached. One of Panitch's goals for these stand-alone stories has been to embrace and explore diversity both in front of and behind the camera when bringing these unique heroes, villains, and antiheroes to multiplexes.

"What's exciting about the comic book characters that we have—which are part of Sony's Marvel universe, and includes animation too—is that the characters are incredibly complex," Panitch said. "They're not two-dimensional. They have back stories. They have challenges. They're morally conflicted. They make for great characters. That's what we're trying to do with our projects—to make the best characters. Whether they be antiheroes, or heroes."[5]

Specifically, Sony seemed eager to bring more female Marvel characters to life on-screen. That push led to a series of exciting hires, including *Booksmart* director Olivia Wilde having her name attached to a female-centric Marvel film (rumored to potentially be Spider-Woman), S. J. Clarkson (*Jessica Jones* and *The Defenders*) being hired to develop a feature film about the clairvoyant character Madame Web (with *50 Shades of Gray* star Dakota Johnson in the lead role), and a proposed but ultimately shelved production titled *Silver & Black*, which would have been a team-up vehicle for Spider-Man characters Silver Sable and Black Cat, directed by Gina Prince-Bythewood (*Love & Basketball* and *The Old Guard*).

Sometimes these potential projects originated from so far out of left field that you knew they had next to no chance of getting a green light. For example, *Do the Right Thing* director Spike Lee reportedly circled a film about a little-known costumed vigilante named Nightwatch. The Oscar winner eventually denied his involvement in 2018, placing the project back on the development shelf. Other times, the characters being discussed by Sony made sense because they possessed deep backstories and provided a roster of engaging supporting players who were capable of sustaining a feature film or spin-off television series. This is where we'll likely see the characters of Cindy Moon/Silk and Spider-Gwen in years to come.

The abundance of announced projects illustrated Sony's eagerness to test-drive Marvel characters who potentially could lure audiences into a Spider-Man film universe that, for the time being, didn't include Spidey. As was the case with Raimi's third and final Spider-Man movie, it was the popularity of Toy Biz's Venom line that drove some of the behind-the-scenes decisions once the studio got serious about its live-action features. By Avi Arad's estimates, the toy company's Venom sales were neck and neck with those for Spider-Man in 2016. The statistics proved to Arad what he'd always told people: kids love Venom and think he's cool.

"We had Jon Favreau come to the set when we were working on *Spider-Man 3*. His son Max was a little boy at the time," Arad remembers. "[The child] couldn't care less about Spider-Man. He just said, 'Where is Venom?'"[6]

The concept of a Venom movie drifted in and out of development hell for decades, with Gary Ross (*Seabiscuit* and *The Hunger Games*), Roberto Orci (*The Amazing Spider-Man 2*), and *Deadpool* scribes Paul Wernick and Rhett Reese all taking a stab at cracking the formula for a stand-alone story. New Line Cinema gets credit for mounting the first serious attempt in 1997 when it toyed with adapting David S. Goyer's Venom screenplay into a vehicle for *Rocky IV* and *The Punisher* star Dolph Lundgren. Decades later, several ideas from the Goyer script found their way into Serkis's *Venom: Let There Be Carnage*, which was written by Kelly Marcel from a story conceived by Tom Hardy. Goyer's Venom origin story, for example, opens with a young Cletus Kasady creating chaos in St. Estes Psychiatric Hospital. It develops the maniacal symbiote Carnage as the movie's chief antagonist, showcases She-Venom when the symbiote takes over an integral female character, and even has an action-heavy set piece where Kasady survives state-mandated execution, giving birth to his villainous alter ego. (Goyer employed the electric chair for his sequence, while *Venom: Let There Be Carnage* hooked Woody Harrelson up to a lethal injection machine.)

In one of the screenplay's most ambitious flourishes, Goyer detours his story to Venom's home planet of Klyntar, spinning an origin tangent that has the alien symbiote (dubbed the Other) arriving on our planet via a transport pod before bonding with Brock, a down-on-his-luck failure. *Venom* producers Arad and Matt Tolmach say they experimented with a similar sequence during preproduction on their 2018 film, but the idea was scrapped so that an astronaut named John Jameson could bring the symbiote to Earth. Comic readers, naturally, recognize this character as the son of *Daily Bugle* publisher J. Jonah Jameson. In the comics, John transforms into a wolf-like humanoid creature dubbed Man-Wolf, though there's no indication the SPUMC will explore that character in the future.

The most interesting facet of Goyer's Venom script has to be the absence of Spider-Man, unusual given how crucial Peter Parker is supposed to be in the character's formation. Raimi remained relatively faithful to Venom's comic book origin story when he tackled the villain in *Spider-Man 3*, showing a dejected symbiote bonding with a suicidal Eddie Brock (Topher Grace) over their shared hatred of our friendly neighborhood web slinger. By leaving Spidey out of his screenplay, Goyer foreshadowed one of the largest creative obstacles current filmmakers faced once Sony hired them to work on the symbiote franchise: create a universe of Spider-Man movies, but do it without using Spider-Man.

Venom director Ruben Fleischer (*Zombieland* and *Uncharted*) referred to the absence of Spidey as a challenge when he signed on to helm the feature but claimed that the creative detours the team took in crafting their story helped their film stand apart from its comic book peers. While accurate, *Venom* also arrived during a time when the pop-culture landscape was getting more adventurous with comic projects that didn't lean heavily on the participation of a traditional hero. Joaquin Phoenix, for example, earned an Academy Award for playing the Clown Prince of Crime in a Batman-free *Joker* movie for Warner Bros. And for five seasons, Fox's television program *Gotham* generated suitable ratings by showcasing Riddler, Penguin, Catwoman, and the denizens of the title city's criminal underworld, introducing the Caped Crusader only in the closing scenes of the series finale.

This small sampling proved that classic villains could carry their own story lines as long as their projects received proper attention and care. That's why *Venom* co-screenwriter Jeff Pinkner accepted the contractual Spider-Man handcuff as "heartbreaking" but quickly added that "once we accepted that as a truth, we just set about trying to remain honest and true and authentic to the spirit and the nature of the relationship of those characters, and to what we found appealing about Venom in the first place."[7]

One way *Venom* did that was to pull inspiration from multiple comic story lines that separated Eddie Brock from Peter Parker. Pinkner and Scott Rosenberg's script dutifully mapped out an open-world narrative set in San Francisco, the location of David Michelinie and Mark Bagley's popular 1993 Venom comic book run *Lethal Protector*. They wove in just enough small-scale Spider-Man components throughout the feature (John Jameson and *The Daily Bugle*) to keep the film tangentially connected to the wall crawler's world. And they collaborated with Hardy to hone in on a comedic tone for the Eddie–Venom relationship that critics and fans didn't anticipate from a Venom feature.

"Here is a film that answers the question, 'What if the lead actor thought he was in a goofy comedy, and everyone else thought they were in a dour thriller?'" Josh Spiegel wrote in *The Hollywood Reporter*'s review of *Venom*.[8]

Arad and Tolmach say they pushed for humor in the very first planning meetings for *Venom*, but Fleischer credits Hardy with much of the decision to embrace broader physical comedy and prop-driven slapstick. "He was fully on board with exploring the more comedic aspects of Eddie," the director said. "Tom led us in that direction very early on with his interpretation of Eddie as [having a] more funny reaction to the experience of being taken over by an alien. There's the more horror version that you could play, that we've seen in [David] Cronenberg films and *An American Werewolf in London*. But for us, like *American Werewolf in London*, there's a lot of humor to be drawn from it, as well.

"And so his reactions to things happening," Fleischer continued, "like when he's beating guys up with these tendrils that he's not even in control of, and he's apologizing to them. 'I'm so sorry about your friends!' And then he throws him through a table. There's inherent comedy to that version of it. Part of it was in the script, and part of it was Tom's own genius."[9]

One specific scene in the first *Venom* movie deftly captures the tone Hardy sought for this burgeoning franchise. At the same time, the scene probably felt clumsy and awkward to any fans who bought a ticket to *Venom* hoping for an R-rated, blood-soaked iteration of the alien symbiote on-screen. While confronting his love interest Anne (Michelle Williams) in a swanky bistro, Eddie is forced to feed the perpetually starving alien symbiote that has over-taken him. So he climbs into a lobster tank and starts feasting on the crusta-ceans, shells and all.

"That was something that we hadn't planned. We went to rehearse the scene at the set, and the production designer had planned for a giant lobster tank in the middle of the restaurant," Fleischer remembers. "And Tom goes, 'Well, I must get in that giant lobster tank. There's going to be a giant lobster tank. Of course I'm going to go in it!' For me, that's a really fun moment in the movie that's really unexpected. That was all just Tom leading us in that direction, which ended up being such a great instinct."

Equally unexpected was *Venom*'s spectacular box office performance. Despite near-unanimous negative critical response, *Venom* opened on Octo-ber 5, 2018, to an impressive $80.2 million in the United States and went on to post a massive $856 million in global ticket sales during its complete run, a fact of which Hardy remains particularly proud. "It didn't carry any water with the critics. They literally panned us," the actor said. "But the audiences turned out in droves, which was so lovely about it. It was like watching an underdog be lifted up and be presented, enjoyed, and relished for what it was, and what it is. And certainly for the joy we have in playing within the sand-box, and enjoying the work that we do with Venom. That was a tremendous sense of spirit."[10]

Venom's financial success also was considered an enormous vote of con-fidence from the audience regarding the film's tone, humor, and exagger-ated visual style. Hardy and replacement director Andy Serkis took that momentum directly into the sequel, doubling down on the looney facets from *Venom* and amplifying them for *Let There Be Carnage*. Improved visual effects let Hardy expand on his one-man Three Stooges routine with the symbiote that lives inside of him. Costar Woody Harrelson was encouraged to amplify his silliest instincts to play the love-struck serial killer Cletus Kasady. And screenwriter Kelly Marcel could race past the symbiote's origin story, which bogged down the first movie, and spend more screen time coloring in Eddie and Venom's dysfunctional relationship.

Marcel said, "You can see from *Venom* that Tom was never going to play Eddie as the archetypal hero, which he kind of is in the comics. He definitely wanted to make the choice to be real. How would you feel if an alien suddenly appeared in your life, and decided to take over your body? You would be fucking terrified, and very panicked. And Eddie, he's quite a selfish character as well. So this is a real pain in the ass, to have this thing living with you. And so we just really wanted to play with that version of it [in *Let There Be Carnage*]."[11]

Reflecting on his own relationship to Eddie Brock and the Venom symbiote that overtakes him, Hardy commented during a press day for the first movie that he considered Eddie to be "a professional coward," so it made complete sense that an alien parasite could easily slide in and take full advantage of him.

"There's a part of [Eddie] which galvanizes as a strong crusader for morality, fighting for the underdog, and speaking up for those who are unheard. But it's a deeply self-centered narcissism that also surrounds him, because he does it to the detriment of the people he loves and cares about," Hardy said. "And then Venom turns up, and it's an audacity for this thing to turn up and live inside him. That conflicts Eddie. He then has to negotiate the terms of somebody else's ethical framework, which is from another planet. This forces his feet to the fire, to actually understand his own idiosyncrasies and flaws."[12]

This approach to the Venom character changes the audience's opinion of the symbiote. In the comics as well as in Raimi's *Spider-Man 3*, the alien invader was a manipulative creature, something terrifying that needed to be rejected by well-intentioned hosts. By the end of *Venom: Let There Be Carnage*, Brock views the symbiote as a power that can be used to clean up the streets and protect the innocent.

Should Sony continue to establish Eddie Brock as this universe's centerpiece, *Venom* could end up being the studio's equivalent of *Iron Man* in the MCU—the debut film in an organically cultivated cinematic universe that sets the larger tone for the Spider-Man films that will follow for years. Serkis's *Venom: Let There Be Carnage* certainly amplified the slapstick physical comedy and the sweetly symbiotic relationship hinted at in the first movie. Daniel Espinosa's *Morbius* and J. C. Chandor's *Kraven the Hunter* can expand on this intentionally campy landscape when they introduce biochemist Michael Morbius (Jared Leto) and Russian tracker Sergei Kravinoff (Aaron Taylor Johnson), keeping an overarching vibe for Sony's Spider-Man films. Or those movies can drastically shift gears, keep the audience guessing, and contribute to a feeling of uncertainty regarding what this universe is and where it has the potential to go.

"What Will Be Best for the Fans?"

At the very least, *Venom* and its sequel, *Venom: Let There Be Carnage*, laid a foundation for an unprecedented on-screen universe that should gradually make room for more characters from Sony's vast roster. The fact that Sony initially did this without having access to its crown jewel, Spider-Man, makes the achievement all the more impressive. But now the game-changing sequence on everyone's mind as 2021 draws to a close is Venom's arrival in the same universe as Tom Holland's Spider-Man and the remnant of the alien symbiote that was left behind in a bar when Eddie Brock "beamed" back to his traditional world.

These events could lead to a hasty meet-up movie pitting Venom against Spider-Man. If Sony and Marvel choose an alternate path, the abandoned symbiote left on the bar by Brock could bind with a new host, creating an MCU Venom who exists separately from Tom Hardy. Over in the SPUMC, Serkis or some other filmmaker might continue to explore interesting sidebars in the VenomVerse, leaving Holland's Spidey free to embark on a new trilogy within the MCU. There also were persistent rumors in the weeks following the release of *Spider-Man: No Way Home* that Andrew Garfield could resume his position in the SPUMC and be the Spider-Man that faces Hardy's Venom for the first time. All of these options appeared to be in play in the wake of *No Way Home*. The financial performances of *No Way Home* and *Let There Be Carnage* ensure sequels to both features. Now Sony has given itself options.

It's not essential for Venom and Spider-Man to rush into a shared feature, even knowing what happens in the final scene in *Venom: Let There Be Carnage*, mainly because the sequel did more than enough world building to sustain more stories centered around the symbiotes that don't require the friendly neighborhood web slinger. Ravencroft Institute for the Criminally Insane, a facility we first saw in Marc Webb's *The Amazing Spider-Man 2*, played a significant role in *Let There Be Carnage*, housing Cletus's love interest, Shriek (Naomie Harris), and an assortment of hardened criminals that could populate this world. In fact, Serkis referred to the prison that's featured in his sequel as Ravencroft West, confirming that there's also a Ravencroft East that's likely situated in upstate New York, as is the case in the Marvel Comics. Marcel went on to add, "As you probably know from the comics, Ravencroft holds all kinds of interesting characters. And we do have a character in Ravencroft called Siegfried, played by this incredible artist called Scroobius Pip, who was actually in *Taboo* with Tom as well. If you look him up, he's very well known in his own right. And he's someone we'd love to work with again, so who knows?"[13]

Another tease written into the end of *Venom: Let There Be Carnage* involved Stephen Graham's police detective: Patrick Mulligan. Comic readers know that this officer eventually transforms into the antihero Toxin, a creature spawned from the symbiote that was controlling Cletus Kasady. Although it's unclear how Mulligan gets infected with the symbiote, the detective's blue eyes betray a transformation, leaving Serkis (or a replacement filmmaker) another non-Spidey plot thread he or she could pick up and explore in a sequel while Spider-Man sits on the shelf.

The partnership between Marvel and Sony will continue to evolve following the massive success of *Spider-Man: No Way Home*. It's interesting to learn that *No Way Home* screenwriters Erik Sommers and Chris McKenna "definitely discussed" including Venom as an antagonist in the final battle of that 2021 sequel. "The idea is that the symbiote has knowledge of other universes. Buried in his brain is some knowledge of that connection [to Spider-Man]," McKenna said when opening up about their thought process.[14] In the end, the screenwriters opted to use Eddie Brock in an end-credits scene that Jon Watts directed. But even without showcasing Venom opposite the multiversal villains, Sony already found itself in a much stronger storytelling position at the conclusion of *No Way Home* than it was when *The Amazing Spider-Man 2* struggled to entertain global audiences. Allowing Marvel Studios to help get Spider-Man on the right track freed up Sony to shift its focus to the Spider-Man–adjacent characters and start developing a stable world where Spider-Man eventually could fit. In fact, those bridges might already exist.

Eagle-eyed fans spotted a mural drawing of Spider-Man on an alley wall behind Dr. Michael Morbius (Jared Leto) in the trailer for 2022's *Morbius*. Some fans went one step further and speculated that the mural has the word "Murderer" scrawled over the Spider-Man sketch because Sony plans to use

Andrew Garfield in that universe, and the label ties into the actor's *No Way Home* speech to Tom Holland, when he stopped pulling his punches after the death of Gwen Stacy (Emma Stone). Strangely, the mural scene didn't make it into the final cut of *Morbius*, and Espinosa claimed in interviews following the film's release that it was never his decision to include that shot in the trailer. Then there is the appearance of Michael Keaton in Sony's *Morbius*, suggesting that Adrian Toomes, the villain he portrayed in *Spider-Man: Homecoming*, also crossed the imaginary line that separates the universes. He meets with Leto's Michael Morbius in the movie's closing moments and suggests a team-up between the duo. So many roads are now open for Sony.

Panitch explained Sony's intentions as it figures out how to carry all of these plot threads forward by saying, "You have this overarching idea of, 'What will be best for the fans?' And that, ultimately, is the unique thing about comic books or comic book movies. It's this relentless desire to make sure that the core fans feel satisfied."[15]

It's possible the mid-credits scenes in both *Venom: Let There Be Carnage* and *Spider-Man: No Way Home* that temporarily moved Eddie Brock to the MCU and back officially kicked open the door to Spidey's triumphant return to the SPUMC. But if that crossover doesn't happen overnight and Holland gets to embark on a "College Trilogy" of MCU films, then Sony now finds itself in an enviable position of not needing such a headline-grabbing team-up film—not immediately anyway.

Panitch sounded extremely confident about Sony's future when speaking with *Variety* in 2021. The Sony executive knew exactly what waited for fans on the distant landscape of Spider-Man movies, including an announced Kraven the Hunter feature with Aaron Taylor Johnson (*Kick-Ass* and *Avengers: Age of Ultron*) dated for January 13, 2023, and two more Untitled Marvel/Sony projects that were scheduled to arrive in June and October of that year.

So he tried to present patience and confidence for a curious crowd of comic book readers.

Panitch said, "The great thing is we have this very excellent relationship with Kevin. There's an incredible sandbox there to play with. We want those MCU movies to be absolutely huge, because that's great for us and our Marvel characters, and I think that's the same thing on their side. . . . There's lots of opportunities, I think, that are going to happen.

"There actually is a plan," Panitch concluded.[16] And fans will hear all about it whenever Sony and Marvel determine that they are ready to share.

CHAPTER FIFTEEN

AN ABRUPT BREAKUP, A DRUNKEN SAVE

ony and Marvel's 2021 multiverse movie *Spider-Man: No Way Home* is nothing short of a Hollywood miracle. The culmination of two decades of Spider-Man storytelling, *No Way Home* merges three once-disconnected franchises into an interlocked universe of Spider-Man heroes, villains, and supporting characters. It visualizes the fullest potential of the shared-universe concept, cooking up a credible story involving spells and portals that allowed preexisting Spider-Men Tobey Maguire and Andrew Garfield to step into Tom Holland's MCU and help him correct some egregious mistakes. *No Way Home* also gave those two series stars closure following the abrupt endings of their respective franchises and rewarded fans with a team-up that never seemed possible due to the amount of red tape studio executives would need to sever to permit creatives to dream this up and pull it off. As the character has done so many times before, Spider-Man rewrote traditional Hollywood rules of storytelling and broke new ground regarding the possible connections between franchise reboots and their predecessors.

Also in true Spider-Man fashion, it almost didn't happen.

Fans probably don't realize how close the unprecedented *Spider-Man: No Way Home* came to dissolving on the production table during the pivotal planning stages for the third Sony–Marvel Spider-Man collaboration. At a time when the studios should have been raising toasts to the critical and financial success of Jon Watts's *Spider-Man: Far from Home*, top executives found themselves at odds about how to move the franchise forward. The reasons for the division, predictably, boiled down to money. Disney bosses felt their studio deserved a larger share of the first-run profits from the Sony Spider-Man movies they were helping to create. In their minds, contributions from the Marvel Studios team are what helped Sony reach previously unattainable heights. It would be hard to argue against the influence that Marvel President Kevin Feige and his crew had on Sony's two Tom Holland–led Spider-Man movies, particularly given how much Sony struggled with Garfield's *Amazing Spider-Man* series. The monetary value of that guidance and feedback, however, suddenly was up for debate.

In August 2019, the details of a Disney–Sony "divorce" over Spider-Man started to go public. Unhappy with the existing agreement, Disney reportedly sought a fifty-fifty split of all first-run profits on Spider-Man as well as merchandising revenues. This would have been a massive increase from the Sony-friendly 5 percent the studio was paying Disney on *Spider-Man: Homecoming* and *Spider-Man: Far from Home*. Assuming it had enough leverage to squeeze Sony, the Mouse House played hardball by removing its most valuable chip—Feige's guiding hand—from the equation. If Sony didn't yield, Feige no longer would serve as a producer on the Spider-Man franchise and would instead turn his attention to the numerous film and television projects in development at Marvel Studios.

To the shock of several industry analysts and Spider-Man fans around the globe, Sony didn't blink. They called Disney's bluff, thanked them for their contributions to *Homecoming* and *Far from Home*, and expressed confidence in their own ability to chart Spider-Man's course moving forward.

"Spider-Man was fine before the event movies, did better with the event movies, and now that we have our own universe, he will play off the other characters as well," Sony Pictures Chairman and CEO Tony Vinciquerra said during *Variety*'s Entertainment and Technology summit on September 5, 2019.[1] He was referring to the *Venom* films produced by Sony, as well as the announced features planned for supporting Spider-Man characters Morbius (Jared Leto), Kraven the Hunter (Aaron Taylor Johnson), Spider-Woman, and more. "I think we're pretty capable of doing what we have to do here."

Not only did Sony defy Disney's push for increased profit sharing, but publicly they laid the blame for the split at the feet of Marvel—and specifically Feige—in the most diplomatic way possible. In a statement released once the separation was announced, Sony pointed to mischaracterizations in reporting regarding the extent of Feige's role in plotting out *Homecoming* and *Far from Home*. The studio went so far as to suggest that the wunderkind producer and on-screen world plotter simply didn't have enough room on his overloaded plate to focus on non-Disney features.

"We hope this might change in the future," the statement read, "but understand that the many new responsibilities that Disney has given [Feige]—including all their newly added Marvel properties—do not allow time for him to work on IP they do not own. Kevin is terrific and we are grateful for his help and guidance and appreciate the path he has helped put us on, which we will continue."[2]

The benefit of hindsight makes the separation seem less hostile. We know the conflict gets resolved. And Sony Pictures Motion Picture Group CEO and Chairman Tom Rothman downplayed the severity of the potential split when he clarified in 2021, "All that really was, the honest truth about it, was that negotiations shouldn't be public until they're final. It was just a point in time. And that happens on every negotiation. . . . It was greatly, greatly exaggerated. And I always felt it would resolve. I'm equally happy and glad that it did resolve, and hopeful and optimistic that things will continue going forward."[3]

But it's worth documenting the real-time details of the messy breakup because it's one of the rare examples of a rival studio barking back at the perceived Hollywood "Big Dog" that is Disney. Plus, the backlash leveled at Sony from the Spider-Man fandom was both immediate and intense. Frustrated patrons rightfully pointed out that Sony admitted failure on the *Amazing Spider-Man* franchise front just four years earlier, prompting the studio to swallow its pride and allow Marvel to help show them the way. They doubted Sony's ability to do better with the character than Feige and Marvel, citing the $1.13 billion in ticket sales for *Spider-Man: Far from Home*. And very few approved of the idea to remove Spider-Man from the MCU—where he had participated in two Avengers team-up movies—and plug him into the still-developing SPUMC. Twitter users, as a joke, shared the *Avengers: Infinity War* scene of Holland's Peter Parker clutching Robert Downey Jr.'s Tony Stark as he faded to dust, pleading, "I don't want to go. Sir, please. Please, I don't want to go."

Some did use social media to chastise Disney—a company that already owned the lucrative Marvel, Lucasfilm, and Pixar brands—for demanding more money out of Sony and placing Spider-Man's MCU future at risk. Industry analysts, meanwhile, used this unexpected disruption as an invitation to dissect Disney's monolithic presence on the entertainment landscape, paying close attention to then-CEO Bob Iger's strategic maneuvers. Disney earned its powerhouse reputation through acquisition and internal growth but did find itself facing new pressures created by upstart content producers like Netflix and Amazon staking larger claims of the landscape. One drastic way Disney decided to remain competitive in 2017 was to purchase a direct competitor in 20th Century Fox.

"But Sony wasn't having that," business entertainment reporter Steven Zeitchik wrote in the *Washington Post* in 2019. "And thus Disney faced a quandary: Should it let Feige keep guiding the movies despite unfavorable financial terms? Should it keep its subject close, not allowing a studio in a far corner of its empire to go off and do what it would with an important property?"[4]

Caught in the crosshairs of this public divorce was Holland, the first Spider-Man actor who was permitted to interact with his Marvel superhero colleagues on-screen but who also was an employee of Sony Pictures Entertainment and therefore beholden to its executive decisions. "It was almost like, two parents are getting divorced. And then the little kid was like, 'Mom and dad, please don't do this. I don't want to have to do this without you guys,'" Holland said. "And then they were like, 'Oh, we should listen to him. Because he's so cute!' And then they fell in love again."[5]

From the moment Sony announced its split from Marvel and Disney, fans groused and analysts spilled ink over what would be next for the three studios. Vinciquerra wasn't wrong when he said Sony was prepared to move forward independently. The studio spent years constructing its universe of live-action Marvel movies, with plans in place for it to gradually expand. Spider-Man eventually would have returned to Sony and shifted into this world of stories. This contractual squabble merely sped up the process.

But behind the scenes, the top executives at Sony, Disney, and Marvel continued to discuss solutions and make progress to the point where the parties finally succeeded in reaching an agreement that allowed Holland to hop on his social media account for a very special—and character-appropriate—celebration. The running joke in the MCU Spider-Man movies is that Peter, who is much younger than his Avengers counterparts, references "old" movies to explain plans he concocts to defeat an opponent. He brings up "that really old movie," *The Empire Strikes Back*, when fighting Giant-Man in *Captain America: Civil War*. Tested by Tony (Robert Downey Jr.) in *Avengers: Infinity War* to come up with a plan to rescue Doctor Strange (Benedict Cumberbatch) from the clutches of Thanos's henchman, Ebony Maw, Peter brings up a scene from James Cameron's *Aliens*. Referencing classic movies to make a point is Peter's thing, so it felt right that Holland himself did it to share Sony and Disney's news.

On September 27, 2019, a scant thirty-nine days after Sony severed ties with Disney, Tom Holland posted to his Instagram one the most memorable scenes from Martin Scorsese's 2013 stockbroker comedy *The Wolf of Wall Street*. In it, Leonardo DiCaprio's hedonistic Jordan Belfort stands before his loyal Stratton Oakmont employees, prepared to temporarily depart the company before the FBI closes in on him. But Belfort is far too egotistical to step away from the corporation he built, so he whispers "I'm not leaving" into the microphone before working up a full and defiant lather: "I'm not leaving!"

It's a funny meme, but it also communicated Holland's message loud and clear. His Peter Parker was staying in the MCU.

"I Think This Is Bob Iger. But I'm Drunk"

Feige credited the change of heart to a commitment to story, confident that the financials would work themselves out. "Luckily, Tom Rothman and Bob Iger and Alan Horn and Alan Bergman and Tom Holland himself all realized, 'Wouldn't it just be more fun if we just kept doing it? Let's not get business or politics in the way,'" Feige said. "Because the deal always started with Amy Pascal and I, having nothing to do with numbers or contracts or politics. It had to do with story, and a love of Spider-Man and Peter Parker and the Marvel universe."[6]

That sounds very kumbaya, and Feige slings hope and optimism for the power and joy of Marvel Studios storytelling with the best of them. But Rothman echoed that mission statement when he said, "I think all parties would tell you that it's been very much for the greater good. It's been for the good of the fans. It's been for the good of the movies. And it's been for the greater good of the companies. So I'm pretty sanguine about the future. You never know, but the likelihood is that the companies will find a way to continue, because it's been as mutually satisfying as it has been."[7]

As for Iger, he joined the bandwagon of positivity during a guest spot on *Jimmy Kimmel Live*, downplaying the business side of the decision in favor of the boost the extension would give to fans. "You know what happens? Sometimes companies when they are negotiating, or people when they're negotiating with one another, they kind of forget that there are other folks out there who actually matter, and that was the case here," Iger said. "There's a whole Parker family out there."[8]

And at the head of that family is Holland, who admits he cried when he told Iger how much his tenure as Spider-Man meant to him and why the hero deserved to stay in the MCU.

But that might be because he was drunk.

"Because I was really upset that I wasn't going to be in the MCU anymore," Holland defended with a laugh.[9]

A few days before this fateful conversation, Holland stood on stage alongside Chris Pratt and Julia Louis-Dreyfus promoting Pixar's animated film *Onward* at the Disney fan exposition D23, in Anaheim, California. By this point, news of the Disney–Sony breakup had gone public, so an emotional Holland ended the D23 panel by thanking the fans, followed by a delivery of Downey Jr.'s signature *Endgame* line: "I love you 3,000."

Backstage, the reality of his expulsion started sinking in as Holland watched his Marvel costars laughing, sharing stories, and posing for group pictures. The other MCU cast mates weren't purposely excluding Holland, but he did feel uncertain about whether he was even permitted to appear in pictures with these people anymore or whether he was in violation of a contractual agreement. Seeking some closure of his own, Holland asked for Iger's e-mail. "I just wanted to say, 'Thank you, this has been an amazing five years of my life. Thank you for changing my life in the best way, and I hope that we can work together in the future,'" Holland said.[10]

To Holland's surprise, Iger responded rather quickly, asking if Holland would be free for a phone call in the near future. The actor said yes, then started to wait—and wait. Days passed with no communication from either Disney or Iger—until the Holland family decides to spend a night playing pub trivia in their local town. As luck would have it, that's when Iger decided to ring.

"I'm three pints in," Holland remembers. "[I] haven't eaten much. And I get a phone call from an unknown number. And I have a feeling. I'm like, 'I think this is Bob Iger. But I'm drunk.'"[11]

He answered the call anyway at his father's urging. And as he planned, Holland thanked Iger for the opportunity Disney gave him to play Spider-Man in the MCU. "We spoke about my passion for the character. I think I spoke about the importance of Spider-Man in the MCU, and what I can offer, and what I can bring to the table," Holland said. "I think that really resonated with him. And he really heard how much I love this character and how much I believe in him. I think, through that conversation, he then opened up a bigger conversation between himself and Tom Rothman and Tony Vinciquerra. And they were able to make a deal."[12]

Holland, to this day, humbly downplays any part he played in the renegotiations that kept Spider-Man in the MCU. "You know, lots of people think that I was on the phone, orchestrating these business meetings," he said, implying that this isn't quite the case. But if Holland didn't take his unprovoked steps to patch up this division, *Spider-Man: No Way Home* would not have happened, at least not in the form that it currently exists. According to Holland, Sony went so far as to formulate a plan during the brief period where the studio had Spider-Man back, just in case the MCU really was off the table. Director Jon Watts pitched his star on a Kraven the Hunter–focused story for their third Spider-Man collaboration during this cycle before the idea of the multiverse materialized, though *No Way Home* co-screenwriter

Chris McKenna jokingly states, "I feel like there's always a Kraven the Hunter pitch. [laughs] Even on movies that aren't Marvel movies, we're like, 'What if Kraven the Hunter showed up?'"[13]

Holland was contractually obligated to participate in that third Spider-Man movie no matter how the negotiations between Disney and Sony played out. But he made it clear on which side of the equation he wanted his Spider-Man to fall. Maybe he didn't orchestrate the actual conversations between Iger, Rothman, Feige, and Vinciquerra, but he definitely sold all parties on the need to maintain the status quo, and it worked out—for one more movie, at the very least, and more than likely beyond.

Iger certainly acknowledges Holland's part in sealing the deal. He sent a Christmas Day tweet in 2021 as *Spider-Man: No Way Home* crushed box office records and simply said, "Hey @TomHolland1996 . . . I'm glad we had that discussion about Spider-Man and congratulations on the success of @SpiderMan No Way Home! Merry Christmas, too!"[14]

The same day that *Spider-Man: No Way Home* opened in U.S. theaters, Kevin Feige confirmed to the *New York Times* that Sony and Disney were "actively beginning to develop"[15] the plot of Holland's fourth Spider-Man movie, getting ahead of any unfounded speculation that a messy and protracted divorce might once again be in the cards.

Pascal echoed her support for the partnership, seemingly giving Holland's Spider-Man hope for the future when she said, "I love working with Kevin. We have a great partnership, along with Tom Rothman, who runs Sony and has been instrumental, a great leader with great ideas. I hope it lasts forever."[16]

CHAPTER SIXTEEN
NO WAY HOME AND SPIDER-MAN'S HOLLYWOOD FUTURE

Two days before Sony released *Spider-Man: No Way Home* to a global audience, Sony Pictures Motion Picture Group CEO and Chairperson Tom Rothman sat in his Los Angeles office, surveyed the theatrical landscape, and projected a sense of cautious optimism.

"We're trying to do something that's literally never been done," he said with a palpable mix of excitement and uncertainty.[1] You might think Rothman's trepidation silly, given the Spider-Man sequel's record-breaking financial success, but *No Way Home* was anything but a slam dunk for exhibitors in December 2021. Surges in COVID cases at that time threatened to impact audience turnout, with the rapidly spreading omicron variant creating the second-largest spike in U.S. infections since the coronavirus pandemic began. Restaurants, bars, and entertainment venues in major metropolitan centers faced debilitating closures following outbreaks among their already depleted staff. Hospitals, meanwhile, packed their emergency rooms to near capacity as a fatigued medical community labored to keep up with the health care demand. Rothman was right to be prudent on the eve of the release of an extremely important feature film for Sony. There was always a chance that audiences would choose to stay home.

"If we can get people to the movie theaters in the face of a two-year pandemic," he reflected, "then Spider-Man will absolutely have proven to be the greatest superhero of them all."

Rothman's statement echoed the thesis of this book. Two decades after his feature-film debut, Spider-Man had established himself as a proverbial blue-chip stock on the Hollywood exchange, an industry leader and a dependable commodity in a genre that had been floating all boats. But now, during an extended period of uncertainty for studios and theater chains alike, the franchise was being asked to defy expectations and do what no other film had managed since the beginning of the pandemic: bring global audiences back to the multiplex. As I've proven, success in the face of overwhelming odds defines Spider-Man. No matter the obstacles, this hero finds a way to prevail. So maybe we should have anticipated the outcome because Rothman laid down a gauntlet and Spider-Man picked it up, fulfilling the executive's prophecy beyond a shadow of a doubt.

Sony opened *Spider-Man: No Way Home* in the United Kingdom on December 15, 2021, followed by a U.S. bow two days later. The movie was a box office juggernaut immediately out of the gate, shattering records on virtually every day of its release. By the end of its opening weekend, *No Way Home* had posted $260 million in domestic ticket sales, the second-highest domestic weekend in history (behind only the $357 million earned by *Avengers: Endgame* in 2019). Globally, *No Way Home* surpassed $600 million in that opening frame, making it the third-largest worldwide debut ever. On December 23, seven days after its release, *No Way Home* crossed the $813 million mark worldwide, making it the highest-grossing movie of 2021. And finally, following a dominant Christmas weekend performance marked by sold-out showings around the globe, *No Way Home* hit the $1 billion mark worldwide.

It took only twelve days.

Veteran box office analyst Paul Dergarabedian tried to put the movie's achievements into perspective when he wrote, "What this represents is quite mind-boggling. These numbers would be very impressive in the pre-pandemic era, but for *Spider-Man: No Way Home* to sprint to a billion dollars in this marketplace is really hard to wrap your mind around. The monumental achievement of *No Way Home* hitting this number cannot be overstated for this industry right now."[2]

The third film in Sony and Marvel's Spider-Man *Home* trilogy accomplished this by connecting the character's present to his dissociated past, tapping into the full resources of the MCU to make such a franchise-bridging story possible.

"'Surreal' is the word I keep coming back to," director Jon Watts said of the premise he helped conceive.[3] *No Way Home* opened the door to the multiverse, a complicated concept suggesting that alternate universes coexist in the MCU but have the possibility to intersect, usually with devastating consequences. Andrew Garfield, returning to the role that was ripped away from him in 2015, called Amy Pascal and Kevin Feige's pitch for *No Way Home* "immediately undeniable."[4]

"It sounded incredibly fun, incredibly spiritual—trippy and thematically interesting," Garfield added. "On a base level, as a Spider-Man fan, just the idea of seeing three Spider-Men in the same frame was enough."

Peter One, Peter Two, Peter Three

Spider-Man: No Way Home deals with the aftermath of Mysterio (Jake Gyllenhaal) revealing Peter Parker's (Tom Holland) secret identity in the closing minutes of *Spider-Man: Far from Home*. That was always the launch point, though nobody associated with the sequel knew the full extent of the consequences that news would have on Peter and his inner circle. "Sitting in a room, in this case it was a conference room at Marvel Studios, with the team is always my favorite part of the process. Where anything is possible," Feige said. "We knew coming out of *Far from Home* that we didn't want to shy away from the fact that his identity is now revealed. It's out there. And that was certainly always the starting point."[5]

The obstacles created by *No Way Home* allowed Marvel Studios to expand on unexpected corners of its already large universe. When co-screenwriters Erik Sommers and Chris McKenna first tackled the sequel's outline, they wrote what they described as the "kitchen sink" version of a multiverse story, where every major legacy character from a previous Spider-Man movie was on the table. They didn't concern themselves with actor availability or contract status. They just tried to include everyone they deemed important—to the detriment of the overall story.

"We went down different roads with different characters that just didn't fit," said McKenna.

"The first draft, we bit off more than we could chew," Sommers added.[6]

They were also plotting out a story line that was supposed to follow the events of Sam Raimi's *Doctor Strange in the Multiverse of Madness*, until COVID-related production delays forced Marvel Studios to shift that sequel to a 2022 release date. This shift affected mostly Benedict Cumberbatch's Doctor Strange, who originally was meant to have intimate knowledge of the dangers of multiversal shenanigans due to his sequel's adventures and instead had to be rewritten as a curious but cautious helping hand for Peter Parker.

As McKenna and Sommers whittled down their bulky cast list, they locked in on exciting new characters that both made sense to *No Way Home* and fleshed out the MCU. J. K. Simmons continued to beef up his reimagined J. Jonah Jameson, keeping public heat on Holland's Parker. For one scintillating scene, fan-favorite Netflix actor Charlie Cox returned to the role of attorney Matt Murdock, who masquerades as Daredevil, to clear Peter of any legal issues tied to Mysterio's death. He's expected to play a larger role in MCU feature films and Disney+ television series moving forward.

"We had so much fun working with Charlie. It's really interesting doing a scene between two superheroes that has no real superhero stuff in it. Apart from the bit when he catches the brick," Holland recalled.[7]

When a litany of colleges start to reject Ned (Jacob Batalon) and Michelle (Zendaya) because of their close associations with Spider-Man, however, Parker heads to 177A Bleecker Street to pay Doctor Strange a visit and pitch an abnormal request: Can the sorcerer cast a spell that will make the world forget Mysterio's devastating revelation? Can Strange put things back the way they were when only a few close confidants knew Peter's secret identity?

The arrogant Sorcerer Supreme accepts the challenge, but this is Peter Parker we're talking about. Nothing ever goes according to plan for our hard-luck hero. Because Peter interferes during the casting of the spell, Strange's effort doesn't make people forget Spider-Man. Instead, it brings every character from any universe that *knows* Peter's identity into the MCU.

That intriguing premise created the type of crossover bucket-list ensemble that's usually reserved for internet fan-fiction sessions. Spider-Man and Strange temporarily permeated the barrier between the MCU and the multiverse, allowing villains and heroes from preexisting Spider-Man franchises to appear and share the screen with Holland, Cumberbatch, Batalon, and Zendaya. This included Willem Dafoe's Green Goblin, Alfred Molina's Doctor Octopus, and Thomas Haden Church's Sandman from the three Sam Raimi *Spider-Man* movies. It included Rhys Ifans's Lizard and Jamie Foxx's Electro from the two Marc Webb *Amazing Spider-Man* films. And in an unprecedented move that generated waves of goodwill in the fanbase—and no doubt powered repeat business that bolstered *Spider-Man: No Way Home*'s box office totals—the sequel returned original stars Tobey Maguire and Andrew Garfield to their signature roles, allowing each actor to finally participate in a full-fledged Marvel Studios movie and achieve forms of closure after their respective franchises ended so abruptly.

Given the restrictions that hamper a standard Hollywood production, *Spider-Man: No Way Home* shouldn't exist. Securing the talent necessary for such a collaboration and contractually securing their participation should produce an Olympic-level amount of legal negotiations, studio compromise, and paperwork—even for a company like Marvel Studios, which blazed similar trails for *Avengers: Infinity War* and its sequel *Avengers: Endgame*. *No Way Home* screenwriters Chris McKenna and Erik Sommers reportedly constructed the sequel's narrative without ever knowing with 100 percent certainty that Maguire and Garfield could participate because beyond the crossed "t" and dotted "i" on a legal document, there were emotional hurdles the previous Peter Parkers needed to consider.

Pascal and Feige first reached out to Maguire, who was intrigued by the love and celebration for the preexisting franchises that he heard in the *No Way Home* team's intentions. "I wanted to join that," he said. "I'm a big fan of Tom and those movies. And [of] Andrew. So it was definitely intriguing, But yes, I was also going, 'Well, what are we going to do?'"[8]

Maguire admits he had personal issues he wanted to resolve by returning to the role of Peter Parker for the first time since 2009. They likely paled in comparison to Garfield's, who was being asked by Pascal to return to a cherished role to which he'd committed his heart and soul completely, only to watch it collapse beneath a heap of creative decisions that were out of his control. But Garfield took the high road, identifying *No Way Home* as a coveted opportunity to answer lingering questions that remained for his Peter. He expressed gratitude for the invitation he never thought he'd receive. And he confessed that once Maguire signed on, it really left him with very few options.

"I was just waiting to see if Tobey was going to do it. And if Tobey was going to do it, I was like, 'Well, I have no choice,'" Garfield said with a laugh. "I follow Tobey to the ends of the Earth. I'm a lemming for Tobey."[9]

No Way Home literally and figuratively is a movie about receiving second chances. Peter appeals to Strange because he wants Ned and Michelle to get the second opportunity he believes they deserve to get into their dream college: MIT. Once the preexisting villains arrive in Holland's MCU, our hero embarks on a fool's errand to "cure" them all, believing it will give them a chance to return to their home universes unscathed. And the movie's climactic battle takes place on the Statue of Liberty, which Holland's Peter acknowledges as a symbol for second chances sought by immigrants arriving in America.

But beneath the surface of the plot, *No Way Home* gave Maguire and Garfield, the cornerstones of the Spider-Man film franchise, a second chance to bring texture, nuance, mature reflection, and unbridled comic book passion to a shared character who clearly means a lot to them. Garfield appeared to relish the two weeks he spent filming on the set—whether he was cracking Maguire's back as they prepared for battle or sweeping away cobwebs on the ceiling for Ned's Lola (Mary Rivera). If Maguire assumed the elder statesman's role, then an effervescent Garfield plugged into a happy-to-be-here vibe that counterbalanced the movie's inherent severity.

"We talked a lot about mentorship," Garfield said about the preparation shared by the three actors. "We talked a lot about brotherhood and about what it is to be the older brother, younger brother, and the middle brother."[10]

Additionally, *No Way Home* gave the MCU's interpretation of Peter Parker a second chance to implement the classic, character-shaping line, "With great power comes great responsibility." Marisa Tomei's Aunt May speaks the mantra in Watts's third movie, but the line returns later in the film so that all three Peters can better comprehend their cosmic connections and the valuable life experiences that will always bind them together as Spider-Men.

No Way Home's most memorable moments involve character-driven callbacks to the painful and inspirational moments in Garfield and Maguire's franchises. When Holland and Garfield pepper Maguire with questions about the organic webs that shoot directly out of his wrists, he recalls a time when the webbing stopped working for him (in Sam Raimi's *Spider-Man 2*), blaming it on an existential crisis. During a pivotal point in the third-act battle, as the Spider-Men are figuring out how to work together, Holland brags that he has experience working with a team because he was on the Avengers. Naturally, Tobey and Andrew have no clue what that means.

Some of the fan-favorite beats are quieter but no less effective. A healed Otto Octavius (Molina) reunites with his one-time science protégé, Peter Parker (Maguire), in the film's final act and appears shocked at how the boy he once knew has grown. "How are you?" Octavius asks the hero with warmth and genuine curiosity. "Trying to do better," Maguire's Peter replies, a tender nod to their classic *Spider-Man 2* interactions. After Electro (Jamie Foxx) is subdued by the trio, he confesses to Garfield's Spider-Man that he wrongfully assumed the hero was Black. "There's gotta be a Black Spider-Man out there somewhere," Foxx laments, and Garfield nods as the audience awaits a live-action Miles Morales.

It's Garfield, however, who takes his progression the farthest in one of *No Way Home*'s most cathartic sequences. An explosion created by the Green Goblin (Dafoe) in the final confrontation knocks Zendaya's M.J. from the scaffolding surrounding the Statue of Liberty. Holland dives to catch her, but he's intercepted by the Goblin on his glider. Without hesitating, Garfield dives after the falling Michelle, snags her in midair, and webs a post so they're able to safely land on the ground. "Are you OK?" he asks her, almost fearing the answer. But once she nods her head, Garfield allows a powerful combination of relief and pain to overwhelm him. His facial reaction conveys a hard truth—saving M.J. isn't going to bring his Gwen (Emma Stone) back, but it might provide the closure that will allow his healing to begin.

"My Spider-Man got to save his younger brother's romantic relationship, potentially. And to heal the most traumatic moment of his own life through doing it for his younger brother," Garfield said of that moment. "There's something cosmically beautiful about that."[11]

No Way Home deeply connected with audience members, as proven by the film's box office success and the 98 percent Fresh audience score on the aggregate review site Rotten Tomatoes. Words can't properly convey the emotional satisfaction that fans no doubt felt seeing the three live-action Spider-Men swinging simultaneously, producing cures for their antagonists in a science lab, dutifully re-creating the "Spider-Man Pointing" meme, or trading stories about the weirdest villains they've ever fought. Their chemistry was wonderful. Their admiration for each other was undeniable.

"It wasn't like they were just asking us to come and say hi, and then leave again. They actually [wanted to] have our presence be in service to Tom's journey and, and where he is as Peter Parker," Garfield explained. "I love the destiny feeling of the multiverse expanding in this film, and actually that without Tobey's Peter and Andrew's Peter being present for Tom's Peter at this very moment, he may not become the Peter Parker that he's supposed to become. I love that."[12]

The trio's family bond seemed to solidify in the scene where they realized they weren't going to prevail over the gathered multiverse villains unless they trusted their "tingle," focused on one villain at a time, and coordinated their attacks. Garfield's delivery of the line "Peter Three!" in that moment should have earned him an Oscar nomination and is the ideal evidence that he was fully embracing this unexpected opportunity to slide back into the Spider-Man suit and make the most out of much better material.

Holland referred to the trio as "a brotherhood," and that came across on-screen.

"It was so beautiful," Zendaya said. "[Tobey, Andrew, and Tom] care so deeply about the characters, and what their characters—what their *journey* had been as Spider-Man. It was so beautiful to see all of you guys connect on that and be able to talk to each other about such a special experience that very few people have been able to don the suit. It was great to see how much you guys all really cared and had each other's back. It was really sweet."[13]

"Honestly, being Spider-Man has changed my life," Holland concluded. "The roller coaster from the moment I got on to the moment we've gotten off has just been absolutely amazing. This film really is a celebration of three generations of cinema. I was delighted to kind of be at the helm and be the captain of the ship, which was awesome. It's been incredible. It's honestly been the best thing that's ever happened to me."[14]

"A Real Superhero"

The ending of *Spider-Man: No Way Home* could also be viewed as a new beginning for the franchise on numerous levels. The MCU's Peter Parker made the ultimate sacrifice, telling Doctor Strange to complete the spell that would wipe Spider-Man's secret identity from the world's collective memories. This isolated Peter from his girlfriend and his best friend and finally set him up in the classic underdog scenario that lifelong Spidey fans have been wishing on Holland since the moment he tried on the suit. Watts closed the movie with Holland in a sparse Manhattan apartment that mirrored Maguire's dumpy rental in *Spider-Man 2*. He's studying for his GED as his friends depart for the prestigious MIT. He's dogged by a relentless J. Jonah Jameson. He's broke, alone, but still compelled to be a friendly, neighborhood hero. The final swing for *Spider-Man: No Way Home*, therefore, can work as a fresh start for the MCU's Spidey, which explains why he's finally able to don a home-sewn, comic-accurate suit as he takes to the snowy skies over New York City's Rockefeller

Center at Christmastime. By the end of three Marvel movies, Holland's Peter Parker has fully evolved into the Spider-Man audiences know and love.

Garfield and Maguire snuck into Los Angeles movie theaters with Watts on opening weekend to watch audience reactions to their arrivals on-screen. Following the rush of their surprise cameos, though, the veteran Spider-Men said the dramatic heft of Holland's performance kept them in their seats. "I was in pieces," Garfield said. "This is a movie that is about a coming of age, an acceptance of loss, an acceptance of death, and taking responsibility for your gifts. I was torn open by the journey that Tom went on. . . . It's classic Peter Parker, but it felt totally fresh and totally reimagined. Tom's origin story was happening in his third movie rather than his first. There's something so profound [there]."[15]

The coda of *Spider-Man: No Way Home* caught Maguire off guard as well. Although he didn't really stop to process the enormity of the Spider-Man saga during his two weeks on set in Atlanta, Sony's first Peter Parker found it powerful and impactful to contemplate the different iterations of Spider-Man that Pascal and Feige shepherded to the screen as he watched them all interact in scenes. "I'd have these reflection moments, which were quite powerful and elegantly woven. Because you're thinking about taking 20 years of history and revisiting that. And how do you balance all of these things, and each of our series of films?" Maguire said. "It was pretty wild to witness the immensity of all of this history coming together and being put into what Andrew is saying is this standalone worthwhile story."[16]

Having seen how *Spider-Man: No Way Home* concludes, Holland's summation of the sequel made complete sense, as he said, "We were all treating [*No Way Home*] as the end of a franchise, let's say. I think if we were lucky enough to dive into these characters again, you'd be seeing a very different version. It would no longer be the *Homecoming* trilogy. . . . We were definitely treating [*No Way Home*] like it was coming to an end, and it felt like it."[17]

It's not coming to an end. Almost everyone associated with the ongoing negotiations between Disney, Marvel, and Sony confirm that Holland's Peter Parker will swing on for the immediate future. Opening up about the settlement that allowed Feige to collaborate on *No Way Home*, Tom Rothman noted, "We have one more reciprocal loan out as part of that deal, so there is one more movie in play right now. But it has been so successful for both companies that it's hard for me to believe it wouldn't continue."[18]

Amy Pascal processed *No Way Home*'s box office receipts and swiftly informed the *New York Times* that she loves collaborating with Feige, has a strong working relationship with Rothman, and hopes that the historic studio partnership "lasts forever."[19]

"At the end of [*Spider-Man: No Way Home*], you see Spider-Man make a momentous decision, one that you've never seen him make before," she said. "It's a sacrifice. And that gives us a lot to work with for the next film."

But the conclusion of *No Way Home* also opens interesting doors for the larger future of Spider-Man in both live action and animation as well as on television and the big screen. As Doctor Strange himself warns in the film, the multiverse is a concept about which audiences know frighteningly little. But Marvel and Sony continue to acquire a deeper understanding of its potential through longer-form projects like *Loki* on Disney+ or the feature-length sequel *Doctor Strange in the Multiverse of Madness*. And it could be the door that opens back up to Garfield, Maguire, or both, extending their respective runs as Spider-Man. Calls for both a Garfield-led *The Amazing Spider-Man 3* and a Maguire-led *Spider-Man 4* populated social media after *No Way Home*. And the mysterious way that the two Peters returned to their universes courtesy of Strange's spell leaves the possibility of either sequel coming to fruition. It's not hard to imagine a scenario where Holland continues to play Spider-Man in the MCU but Garfield or Maguire wear the costume once again, confronting the villains who were utilized in *Homecoming* and *Far from Home*, resurrected in *No Way Home*, or introduced in the SPUMC. In January 2022, while doing postrelease press for *No Way Home*, Garfield made it clear that he was open to returning for more Spider-Man projects as long as the creative approach felt right.

"I will say what I've always said, which is, having been at Marvel for 20 years, I wouldn't dismiss anything," Kevin Feige stated. "Or, I wouldn't rule anything out. When and how and where remains to be seen. Any rumor that you read online could happen anytime between tomorrow and never."[20]

What's certain is this: storytelling centered around Spider-Man isn't slowing down anytime soon. And Rothman's experience with the web slinger—both in live action and in animation—has helped the studio executive solidify his blueprint for Spider-Man success. "You must put creativity first. Creative issues have to dominate, and predominate, and come before any financial issues or any deal issues or any corporate issues," he said. "Let the creative lead. And if you follow the creative, you won't always succeed. But you'll give yourself your best shot at making great things."[21]

Rothman says he's observed the maturation of audience expectations during his stint as the head of Sony Pictures Motion Picture Group. His takeaways pertain to comic book movies and Spider-Man stories but really should be applied to every feature emerging from the studio system.

"This is maybe even different than when this journey started years ago, but it's certainly true now: that is, 'great' is the only thing that is possible for us," he said. "'Good' isn't good enough anymore. We have to make stuff that's great. Particularly when we're trying to make things that are theater worthy, and get people away from their cell phones and off their couches. Our content has to be great. And that means great filmmakers, great actors, great producers, and really great creative elements. That's what leads, and that's what led in [the *No Way Home*] decision. And I think that's why it's been fruitful. Creativity came before financial issues."

That mind-set informs the plans that have been in place for the continuation of Peter Parker's stories at Sony and Marvel both in movie theaters and on television sets. Feige confirmed active development on a fourth Holland film in the MCU. *Morbius* released in early 2022, followed by the animated *Spider-Man: Across the Spider-Verse*. Looking to the future, Sony circled three release dates in 2023 for unspecified features that will be part of the SPUMC. One is expected to be J. C. Chandor's *Kraven the Hunter*, with Aaron Taylor Johnson in the lead role. The other two slots likely belong to Olivia Wilde's untitled Spider-Verse movie and potentially *Venom 3*. No matter the choices, this road map demonstrates the stability of Sony's universe of Marvel characters and proves the film-industry value and cinematic drawing power of Spider-Man.

"The interesting legacy of Spider-Man is that Spider-Man just keeps going," longtime producer Matt Tolmach said. "He reinvents himself. He did in the books, and he does in the movies. And that's the amazing thing about that character, is that nobody gets to own him. I don't mean on a business level. I mean that no one actor, and no one filmmaker, can really claim to be the be all and end all. And that's kind of what's great about it."[22]

The feature films centered around Spider-Man are the tip of the iceberg. Like Marvel, Sony has figured out that longer-form television series housed on streaming services can expand on the mythology of a cinematic universe, serve as a testing ground for fresh storytelling voices, showcase lesser-known supporting characters, and free up a studio to explore riskier genres. Marvel Studios made the most out of the Disney+ streaming service by rolling out experimental (and Emmy Award–winning) story lines for *WandaVision*, *Loki*, *What If?*, and *Hawkeye*. Amy Pascal confirms that this type of experimentation will inform the decisions made at Sony regarding future Spider-Verse projects.

Immediate expansion will occur through Sony Pictures Television, which is producing live-action Marvel series for Amazon Prime Video. Pascal once again is collaborating with executive producers Phil Lord and Chris Miller on a full slate of TV series based on Sony's Marvel roster. Their first project, announced in 2020, is set to focus on the origin story of Cindy Moon, the superhero who calls herself Silk. As of June 2021, *Silk* had hired Tom Spezialy (HBO's *Watchmen* series) as its show runner, but no release date had been confirmed.

"We have a great team in place," Miller said in October 2021.

"We're working on it every day," Lord added.[23]

When new Spider-Man projects get announced, they also tend to clarify cryptic information Spider-Man collaborators have shared through exclusive interviews conducted over the years. Here's one example. During a daylong Disney+ marketing event held in November 2020, Marvel confirmed production on an animated series titled *Spider-Man: Freshman Year*, scheduled to arrive in 2022. Written by Jeff Trammel, the series will trace Peter Parker's journey through his early, in-canon days in the MCU, beginning with his spider bite and leading up to the moment Tony Stark recruits him for the events of *Captain America: Civil War*. It's assumed that over the course of this animated series, Marvel finally would address the mystery surrounding MCU Peter's Uncle Ben and whether Holland's hero was directly responsible for his surrogate father's demise.

That announcement reminded me of how *Captain America: Civil War* co-screenwriter Christopher Markus confirmed that he and his cowriter Stephen McFeely never considered Peter's spider bite or the loss of his Uncle Ben when they penned the scenes between Stark, May, and Peter in the hero's Queens home. And Markus said, at the time of our 2021 interview, "I kind of like wondering whether it's a different variation on the dynamic. And I'm sure, if he sticks around long enough in the MCU, you'll get what you want to know, but in a way you're not expecting to find out."[24]

Like in an animated series, produced exclusively for a subscription-driven streaming service.

Rothman also believes that television is guaranteed to be a strong component in Spider-Man storytelling as Sony maximizes partnerships with streaming services. But he's quick to confirm that the studio's Spider-Man movies will remain the straw that stirs the proverbial drink.

"Different stories are better suited for different storytelling structures and different mediums. But the heart and soul of our business is theatricality," Rothman said. "We believe that these movies, [because of] spectacle and relatability, can be culturally impactful events. And when you have a culturally impactful event, you have a chance for something to be theatrical. [But] there's no *WandaVision* if there's no *Avengers*. The movies plow the field, and then you can plant some other things in the wake of that."[25]

What can't be argued, though, is that Spider-Man plows more fields—to continue Rothman's analogy—than any other character in modern storytelling. No other individual superhero provides the same amount of content for an equal number of media platforms as the amazing Spider-Man. No superhero can boast the same merchandising reach, or claim the same cultural impact. From his lucrative live-action MCU movies at Sony and Marvel to his ambitious spin-off features in the SPUMC, from the Oscar-winning animated Spider-Verse franchise to the anticipated television projects in various stages of development, Spider-Man is a radiant sun around which numerous planets orbit. His ascent to the top of the superhero food chain was neither smooth nor direct. And his success can be attributed not to the work of any one individual but rather to a dedicated army of creatives who consistently stayed committed to the core traits that have defined Peter Parker and his masked, crime-fighting alter ego for the better part of six decades. Naturally, it's one of Spider-Man's "fathers," the inimitable Stan Lee, who has the perfect sentence to sum up the universal appeal of the character he helped create in 1962.

"That person who helps others simply because it should or must be done, and because it is the right thing to do, is indeed without a doubt, a real superhero."[26]

For generations—and for generations to come—that person is Spider-Man.

NOTES

CHAPTER ONE

1. Author interview with Tom Rothman, December 15, 2021.

2. Andrew Garfield interview with Andy Cohen on Sirius XM, September 16, 2021, https://www.youtube.com/watch?v=G7GheRx2xEI.

3. Deadline interview with Tobey Maguire, Andrew Garfield, and Tom Holland, January 26, 2022, https://www.youtube.com/watch?v=T0sRQ7N9XXc.

4. Kevin Feige, "A Fan's Guide to *Spider-Man: Homecoming*," DVD feature, June 17, 2017, https://www.youtube.com/watch?v=M43RNQ7emYU.

5. Ben Fritz, "'Spider-Man': A $175 Million Commercial for Disney Toys," *Wall Street Journal*, June 30, 2017, https://www.wsj.com/articles/spider-man-a-175-million-commercial-for-disney-toys-1498815005.

6. Brianna Reeves, "Marvel's Spider-Man Crossed 20 Million in Sales on PlayStation 4," *Playstation Lifestyle*, November 18, 2020, https://www.playstationlifestyle.net/2020/11/18/marvels-spider-man-ps4-sales-20-million.

7. Sanj Atwal, "Spider-Man: No Way Home Trailer Smashes Record; Tom Holland Reacts," Guinness World Records, September 2, 2021, https://www.guinnessworldrecords.com/news/2021/9/spider-man-no-way-home-trailer-smashes-record-tom-holland-reacts-673906.

8. Author interview with Amy Pascal, April 22, 2021.

9. Devan Coggan, "Simu Liu Suits Up in First Look at Shang-Chi and the Legend of the Ten Rings," *Entertainment Weekly*, April 19, 2021, https://ew.com/movies/shang-chi-and-the-legend-of-the-ten-rings-simu-liu-first-look.

10. Stan Lee interview with BBC Radio 4, November 18, 2015, https://www.bbc.co.uk/programmes/p038d4wr.

11. AMC Entertainment Holdings company release, December 17, 2021. https://finance.yahoo.com/news/amc-theatres-eclipses-box-office-124500112.html.

12. Scott Feinberg, "Oscars: 'Spider-Man: No Way Home' Team Plans Best Picture Push, Tom Holland Open to Hosting," *The Hollywood Reporter*, December 24, 2021.

13. Sony Pictures Entertainment press statement, September 27, 2019, https://www.cnbc.com/2019/09/27/sony-and-disney-reach-deal-to-continue-spider-man-movie-partnership.html.

14. Feinberg, "Oscars."

15. Owen Gleiberman, "I Hated 'Spider-Man: No Way Home.' But the Academy Should Absolutely Nominate It for Best Picture," *Variety*, December 31, 2021, https://variety.com/2021/film/columns/spider-man-no-way-home-oscars-analysis-best-picture-1235145184.

CHAPTER TWO

1. Sean Howe's Tumblr, "The Untold Story," October 8, 2013, https://seanhowe.tumblr.com/post/63464009133/producer-to-stan-lee-in-1975-maybe-elton-john.

2. Lord and Miller, interview.

3. *Marvel 616* on the Disney+ streaming service, episode titled "Japanese Spider-Man," https://www.disneyplus.com/video/99889682-8901-4816-811c-e04362ca4bf9.

4. *Marvel 616*, interview.

5. *Marvel 616*, interview.

6. Author interview with Nicholas Hammond, November 5, 2020.

7. Stan Lee interview with TelevisionAcademy.com, October 27, 2011, https://www.youtube.com/watch?v=RN2TDZa0Bhc.

CHAPTER THREE

1. Peter Galvin, "Mark Hartley Turns His Sights on the Infamous Cannon Films with Electric Boogaloo," *SBS Australia*, October 5, 2016, https://www.sbs.com.au/movies/article/2014/08/07/mark-hartley-turns-his-sights-infamous-cannon-films-electric-boogaloo-interview.

2. Author interview with John Brancato, December 3, 2020.

3. *Spider-Man* screenplay by Ted Newsom and John Brancato.

4. Author interview with Joe Zito, December 3, 2020.

5. Author interview with Scott Leva, December 7, 2020.

6. Ed Gross, "Spider-Man: From Cannon to Cameron," *Empire Magazine*, February 27, 2017, https://www.empireonline.com/movies/features/part-2-spider-man-cannon-cameron.

7. James Cameron, *Tech Noir: The Art of James Cameron* (Insight Editions, 2021), 332.

8. Author interview with James Cameron, December 4, 2021.

9. Tim Molloy, "Chris Claremont's Dream X-Men Movie: James Cameron, Kathryn Bigelow, and Bob Hoskins as Wolverine," *The Wrap*, March 25, 2012, https://

www.thewrap.com/chris-claremonts-dream-x-men-movie-james-cameron-kathryn
-bigelow-and-bob-hoskins-wolverine-3.

10. Spider-Man script treatment by James Cameron.

11. Cameron, interview.

12. Cameron's screenplay.

13. Cameron, interview.

14. Cameron's screenplay.

15. Cameron, interview.

16. Christian Moerk, "Cameron Delivers Spider-Man Script," *Variety*, September 1, 1993, https://web.archive.org/web/20090228064746/http://www.variety
.com/article/VR110100.html?categoryid=13&cs=1&query=cameron+spider-man.

17. Josh Wilding, "Leonardo DiCaprio Reveals How Close He Came to Playing James Cameron's Spider-Man," *Empire Magazine* (via SpiderManNews.com), December 30, 2015. https://spidermannews.com/2015/12/30/leonardo-dicaprio
-reveals-how-close-he-came-to-playing-james-camerons-spider-man.

18. Cameron, interview.

19. Tommy Cook, "James Cameron Talks Terminator, Terminator 2: Judgment Day, Casting Schwarzenegger, Spider-Man, Terminator: Genesis, and More," *Collider*, June 1, 2014, https://collider.com/james-cameron-terminator-genesis-spider-man.

CHAPTER FOUR

1. Kevin Feige interview with Rotten Tomatoes, July 12, 2021, https://www
.youtube.com/watch?v=aZZ_PWwbjb4.

2. Author interview with Avi Arad, March 23, 2021.

3. Dan Raviv, author of *Comic Wars* (Broadway Books, 2002), https://abcnews
.go.com/WNT/story?id=130357&page=1.

4. Arad, interview.

5. Jacob Oller, "David S. Goyer Details His Career Bringing Comics to the Big Screen at Comic-Con@Home," *SyFy Wire*, July 21, 2020, https://www.syfy.com/
syfy-wire/david-s-goyer-comic-con-at-home-panel-blade-crow.

6. Arad, interview.

7. Rothman, interview.

8. Arad, interview.

9. Ben Fritz, *The Big Picture* (Houghton Mifflin Harcourt, 2018), 42.

10. Arad, interview.

CHAPTER FIVE

1. Jeff Loeb, "Making the Amazing," DVD feature on YouTube, https://www.youtube.com/watch?v=-mVq1gsTxtQ.

2. Jack Matthews, *New York Daily News* film review via Rotten Tomatoes, https://www.rottentomatoes.com/m/spiderman/reviews?type=top_critics.

3. Matt Miller, "No Way Home Is Good, but Not the Best Spider-Man Movie Ever," *Esquire*, December 17, 2021, https://www.esquire.com/entertainment/movies/g28212557/best-spider-man-movies-ranked.

4. Author interview with Kevin Feige for CinemaBlend, August 27, 2021, https://www.youtube.com/watch?v=1xOSYfBYpHk.

5. Author interview with Matt Tolmach, April 28, 2021.

6. Author interview with John Dykstra, May 23, 2021.

7. Author interview with Don Burgess, May 26, 2021.

8. Arad, interview.

9. Tolmach, interview.

10. Michael Fleming and Claude Brodesser, "Maguire Spins Spider-Man," *Variety*, July 31, 2000, https://web.archive.org/web/20071012002038/https://variety.com/article/VR1117784384.html?categoryid=13&cs=1&query=spider-man.

11. Jay Boyar, "Stan Lee Offers His Spin on Spider-Man," *Orlando Sentinel*, May 3, 2002, https://www.orlandosentinel.com/news/os-xpm-2002-05-03-0205020436-story.html.

12. Tobey Maguire interview for *Spider-Man 2* on ScreenSlam's YouTube channel, April 14, 2015, https://www.youtube.com/watch?v=IpuAchsOi9U.

13. Pascal, interview.

14. Boyar, "Stan Lee Offers His Spin on Spider-Man."

15. Author interview with James Acheson, April 26, 2021.

16. Jason Wiese, "Every Live-Action Spider-Man Costume, Ranked," CinemaBlend, September 12, 2020, https://www.cinemablend.com/news/2554405/every-live-action-spider-man-costume-ranked.

17. Laura Ziskin on the DVD commentary track for *Spider-Man*.

18. Arad, interview.

19. Dykstra, interview.

20. Burgess, interview.

21. Acheson, interview.

22. Andrew Garfield in *Spider-Man: No Way Home*, 2021.

23. Spider-Man press conference footage, Movie FX Video Magazine on YouTube, August 1, 2020, https://www.youtube.com/watch?v=VUzZ0rFdqPk.

24. Boyar, "Stan Lee Offers His Spin on Spider-Man."

25. Tolmach, interview.

26. Acheson, interview.

27. Kirsten Dunst on the DVD commentary track for *Spider-Man*.

28. Arad, interview.

29. Burgess, interview.

30. Author interview with Josh Goldstine, December 16, 2021.

31. Tolmach, interview.

32. Tim Gray, "'Spider-Man: No Way Home' Director Reveals 'Therapy Session' Held for Tom Holland, Andrew Garfield, Tobey Maguire," *Variety*, January 26, 2022, https://variety.com/2022/awards/awards/spider-man-jon-watts-tom-holland-andrew-garfield-tobey-maguire-1235162454.

33. Burgess, interview.

34. Pascal, interview.

35. Tolmach, interview.

36. Goldstine, interview.

37. David Betancourt, "The Spidey Trailer That Changed the Game," *Washington Post*, May 3, 2014, https://www.washingtonpost.com/news/comic-riffs/wp/2014/05/03/spider-man-week-the-spidey-trailer-that-changed-the-game.

CHAPTER SIX

1. Tobey Maguire, "Behind the Scenes–Spider-Man 2," YouTube, https://www.youtube.com/watch?v=wcRu5xFLAa0.

2. Maguire, "The Amazing Andrew Garfield," *VMan*, May 9, 2012, https://vman.com/article/the-amazing-andrew-garfield.

3. Tolmach, interview.

4. Dykstra, interview.

5. Brady Langmann, "The Best Superhero Movies of All Time Show How Far the Genre Has Come," *Esquire*, February 23, 2021, https://www.esquire.com/entertainment/movies/g35509336/best-superhero-movies.

6. Laura Ziskin, "Behind the Scenes–Spider-Man 2," YouTube.

7. Tolmach, interview.

8. Arad, interview.

9. Roger Ebert's *Spider-Man 2* review, June 29, 2004, https://www.rogerebert.com/reviews/spider-man-2-2004.

10. Author interview with David Koepp, August 9, 2020.

11. David Koepp's *Amazing Spider-Man* script, https://davidkoepp.com/script -archive/amazing-spider-man-unproduced.

12. Koepp, interview.

13. Sam Raimi, "Behind the Scenes–Spider-Man 2," YouTube.

14. Tolmach, interview.

15. Sam Raimi, The Nerdist Podcast, December 30, 2014, via *Entertainment Weekly*, https://ew.com/article/2014/12/30/sam-raimi-spider-man-3-discussion.

16. Tolmach, interview.

17. Arad, interview.

18. Acheson, interview.

19. Tolmach, interview.

20. Arad, interview.

21. Raimi, The Nerdist Podcast.

22. Bob Mondello, "Spider-Man 3 Review," NPR, May 4, 2007, https://www .npr.org/templates/story/story.php?storyId=10259499?storyId=10259499.

23. Manohla Dargis, "Superhero Sandbagged," *New York Times*, May 4, 2007, https://www.nytimes.com/2007/05/04/movies/04spid.html.

24. Michael Booth, "Even with a Dark Twist, All the Fun's Been Spun Out," *Denver Post*, May 2, 2007, https://www.denverpost.com/2007/05/02/even-with-a -dark-twist-all-the-funs-been-spun-out.

25. Tolmach interview.

26. Sam Raimi interview with On Demand Entertainment, May 30, 2009, https://www.youtube.com/watch?v=9h1ejgvb-BM.

27. Tobey Maguire interview with David Poland, *DP/30*, January 11, 2010, https://www.youtube.com/watch?v=MUqxUMaLpzg.

28. Tolmach, interview.

29. Pascal, interview.

30. Acheson, interview.

31. Author interview with Jeffrey Henderson, May 27, 2021.

32. Tolmach, interview.

CHAPTER SEVEN

1. Andrew Garfield interview with CinemaBlend for *The Eyes of Tammy Faye*, September 12, 2021, https://www.youtube.com/watch?v=WYUEVjZNeYU.

2. Spider-Man 4 Actor Announcement on YouTube, July 1, 2010, https:// www.youtube.com/watch?v=O5sO5wotHew.

3. Matt McDaniel, "The Amazing Spider-Man Director Marc Webb Reveals How Andrew Garfield Won the Role," MovieTalk, April 16, 2012, https://www .yahoo.com/entertainment/blogs/movie-talk/amazing-spider-man-director-mark -webb-reveals-andrew-181735297.html.

4. Tolmach, interview.

5. Mike Fleming, "Matt Tolmach Discusses Exit as Sony Pics Prez and Segue to Producing Spider-Man," *Deadline*, October 29, 2010, https://deadline.com/2010/10/ matt-tolmach-discusses-his-sony-pictures-prexy-exit-to-produce-spider-man-80070.

6. Maguire, *VMan*, 2012.

7. Andrew Garfield interview with CinemaBlend, June 10, 2012.

8. Andrew Garfield, *VMan*, 2012.

9. Tolmach, interview.

10. Andrew Garfield on the *Amazing Spider-Man* DVD commentary.

11. Garfield, CinemaBlend, 2021.

12. Jamie Graham, "Andrew Garfield Talks Playing Spider-Man," *Total Film*, September 15, 2021, https://www.gamesradar.com/andrew-garfield-talks-playing -spider-man-i-knew-it-was-going-to-provide-a-gilded-prison.

13. Tolmach, interview.

14. Borys Kit and Lesley Goldberg, "*Comic-Con Winners and Losers*," *The Hollywood Reporter*, July 27, 2011, https://www.hollywoodreporter.com/news/general -news/comic-con-2011-winners-losers-216127.

15. Garfield, CinemaBlend, 2021.

16. Zaki Hasan, "Andrew Garfield Reflects on His Spider-Man Tenure," *Zaki's Corner*, August 29, 2015, http://www.zakiscorner.com/2015/08/interview-andrew -garfield-reflects-on.html.

17. Garfield, *VMan*, 2012.

18. Author interview with Jerome Chen, May 13, 2021.

19. Matt Donnelly, "Andrew Garfield on Loss, Art, Televangelism and Those Pesky Spider-Man Rumors," *Variety*, 2021, https://variety.com/2021/film/actors/ andrew-garfield-eyes-of-tammy-faye-tick-tick-boom-spider-man-1235057646.

20. Pascal, interview.

21. Marc Webb on the *Amazing Spider-Man* DVD commentary track.

22. Chen, interview.

23. Tolmach, interview.

24. Author interview with Christopher Markus, April 8, 2021.

CHAPTER EIGHT

1. Tolmach, interview.

2. Adam Rogers, "Kevin Feige Tells How Marvel Whips Up Its Cinematic Super Sauce," *Wired*, May 1, 2012, https://www.wired.com/2012/05/kevin-feige-avengers.

3. Tolmach, interview.

4. Chen, interview.

5. "Marc Webb Isn't Making a Sequel, He's Mapping Out a Massive Spider-Man Universe," CinemaBlend, January 29, 2013.

6. Dave McNary, "Sony Pushes Back Spider-Man 3 to 2018, Dates Sinister Six for 2016," *Variety*, July 23, 2014, https://variety.com/2014/film/news/spider-man-spinoff-sinister-six-dated-for-nov-11-2016-amazing-spider-man-3-back-to-2018-1201267269.

7. Tolmach, interview.

8. Sony press release, June 17, 2013.

9. Tolmach, interview.

10. Marlow Stern, "Andrew Garfield on the Evils of Capitalism, the Hacking Scandal, and Criticism of Spider-Man 2," *The Daily Beast*, April 14, 2017, https://www.thedailybeast.com/andrew-garfield-on-the-evils-of-capitalism-the-hacking-scandal-and-criticism-of-spider-man-2.

11. *The Amazing Spider-Man 2* DVD Featurette: Costumes, https://www.youtube.com/watch?v=B5WSTWLt8W8.

12. Scott, DVD featurette.

13. Chen, interview.

14. Christopher Rosen, "Emma Stone on Gwen Stacy & That Amazing Spider-Man 2' Ending," *Huffington Post*, May 5, 2014, https://www.huffpost.com/entry/emma-stone-amazing-spider-man-2_n_5228989.

15. Sara Vilkomerson, "Amazing Spider-Man 2 director Marc Webb on Gwen Stacy's fate," *Entertainment Weekly*, May 8, 2014, https://ew.com/article/2014/05/08/spider-man-marc-webb-gwen-stacy.

16. Rosen, "Emma Stone," 2014.

17. Chen, interview.

18. Tolmach, interview.

19. David Lieberman, "Sony Pictures to Shift Emphasis from Movies to TV, Will Cut Film Output for 2014," *Deadline*, November 21, 2013, https://deadline.com/2013/11/sony-pictures-to-shift-emphasis-from-movies-to-tv-640800.

20. Tolmach, interview.

21. Amy Pascal interview with CinemaBlend on the set of *Spider-Man: Homecoming*.

CHAPTER NINE

1. Shailene Woodley interview with Movies.com, July 18, 2013, https://www.youtube.com/watch?v=iXwoAODkuhY.

2. "Why Shailene Woodley Ended Up Out," *Los Angeles Times*, May 6, 2014, https://www.latimes.com/entertainment/movies/moviesnow/la-et-mn-amazing-spiderman-2-mary-jane-shailene-woodley-cut-20140506-story.html.

3. Andrew Garfield interview with SBS 2 Australia, April 7, 2014, https://www.youtube.com/watch?v=-1KIZnQIuCM.

4. Alex Kurtzman on the *Amazing Spider-Man 2* DVD features.

5. Tolmach, interview.

6. Frank Lovece, "The Amazing Spider-Man 2 Stars Talk Long Island's "Wild" Times Square Set," *Newsday*, May 1, 2014, https://www.newsday.com/entertainment/movies/the-amazing-spider-man-2-stars-talk-long-island-s-wild-times-square-set-1.7875942.

7. Tolmach, interview.

8. Marc Webb interview with Movies.com, via SlashFilm, April 30, 2014, https://www.slashfilm.com/531570/amazing-spider-man-2-mary-jane-deleted-scene/?utm_campaign=clip.

9. Woodley, Movies.com, 2013.

10. Steve Weintraub, "Andrew Garfield on 'Tammy Faye,' 'The Social Network,' 'Tick, Tick . . . Boom!,' 'Spider-Man' and Why Fincher Is Such a Great Director," *Collider*, September 13, 2021, https://collider.com/andrew-garfield-interview-tammy-faye-the-social-network-tick-tick-boom.

11. Tolmach, interview.

12. Weintraub, "Andrew Garfield," 2021.

13. Andrew Garfield to Amy Adams, Actors on Actors, *Variety*, November 29, 2016, https://www.youtube.com/watch?v=s7mQ1tWSNcg.

14. David Betancourt, "It's Time to Redeem Andrew Garfield's Spider-Man," *Washington Post*, January 11, 2022, https://www.washingtonpost.com/comics/2022/01/11/andrew-garfield-spiderman.

CHAPTER TEN

1. Tom Holland on the red carpet at the Empire Awards, April 3, 2013, https://www.youtube.com/watch?v=SQg6ogc6Fbo.

2. Markus, interview.

3. Rothman, interview.

4. Pascal, *Spider-Man: Homecoming* set visit interview.

5. Sony Pictures Entertainment press release, February 9, 2015, https://www
.sonypictures.com/corp/press_releases/2015/02_15/020915_spiderman.html.

6. Frank Pallotta, "Sony Makes Deal to Bring Spider-Man to Disney's Marvel," CNN, February 10, 2015, https://money.cnn.com/2015/02/10/media/sony
-brings-spider-man-to-disney-marvel/index.html.

7. Brian Truitt, "Spider-Man Joins Marvel's Movie Fold," *USA Today*, February 10, 2015, https://www.usatoday.com/story/life/movies/2015/02/10/sony-deal
-spider-man-marvel-studios/23157265.

8. Ryan Faughnder, "Inside the Deal That Brought Sony's Spider-Man Back to Marvel's Cinematic Universe," *Los Angeles Times*, June 26, 2017, https://www.latimes
.com/business/hollywood/la-fi-ct-sony-marvel-spider-man-20170626-story.html.

9. Arad, interview.

10. Fritz, *The Big Picture*, 2018.

11. Kevin Feige on the *Spider-Man: Homecoming* junket sound bites on You
Tube, https://www.youtube.com/watch?v=Z2cVQL2HsK0.

12. Corey Chichizola, "Yes, Kevin Feige Has Been Thinking about How Marvel Will Bring Mutants to the MCU," CinemaBlend, June 20, 2019, https://www
.cinemablend.com/news/2475308/yes-kevin-feige-has-been-thinking-about-how
-marvel-will-bring-mutants-to-the-mcu.

13. Pascal, *Homecoming* set visit.

14. Pascal, *Homecoming* set visit.

15. Pascal, interview.

16. Tom Holland interview with CinemaBlend for *Cherry*, February 25, 2021,
https://www.youtube.com/watch?v=o8Md8OPVy04.

17. Jonathan Heaf, "Tom Holland on His Darkest Role Yet, and Why *No Way Home* Could Be His Last Spider-Man Film," *GQ*, April 15, 2021, https://www.gq
-magazine.co.uk/culture/article/tom-holland-cherry-interview.

18. Tom Holland interview on the *Spider-Man: Homecoming* set.

19. Holland, *Homecoming* set visit.

20. Pascal and Robert Downey Jr. on the *Spider-Man: Homecoming* DVD
features.

21. Heaf, *GQ*, 2021.

22. Ramin Setoodeh, "Tom Holland Broke His Computer When He Found Out He Was Cast as Spider-Man," *Variety*, January 20, 2021, https://variety.com/
2021/film/news/tom-holland-spider-man-marvel-1234888202.

23. Heaf, *GQ*, 2021.

24. Tom Holland talks to Daniel Kaluuya for *Variety*'s Actors on Actors, January 20, 2021, https://www.youtube.com/watch?v=vRFTy9fdxwI.

25. Markus, interview.

26. Chris Cabin, "*Captain America: Civil War* Directors on Landing Spider-Man, *Infinity War* Shooting Schedule," Collider, January 14, 2016, https://collider.com/captain-america-civil-war-avengers-3-infinity-war-updates-russo-brothers.

27. Feige, *Homecoming* junket clips.

28. Markus, interview.

29. Kevin Feige interview with CinemaBlend for *Spider-Man: Homecoming*.

30. Markus, interview.

31. Jon Watts interview with CinemaBlend for *Spider-Man: Homecoming*.

32. Markus, interview.

33. Heaf, *GQ*, 2021.

34. Holland interview with CinemaBlend, June 26, 2017, https://www.cinemablend.com/news/1674299/one-way-tobey-maguire-inspired-tom-hollands-spider-man.

CHAPTER ELEVEN

1. Stan Lee on the *Spider-Man: Homecoming* DVD features.

2. Holland, *Homecoming* set visit.

3. Sam Raimi interview with MTV, July 16, 2015, https://www.youtube.com/watch?v=o3xNKWwojHY.

4. Author interview with Jonathan Goldstein and John Francis Daley, December 4, 2021.

5. Pascal, *Homecoming* set visit.

6. Holland, *Homecoming* set visit.

7. Watts, CinemaBlend.

8. Watts, CinemaBlend.

9. Goldstein and Daley, interview.

10. Watts, CinemaBlend.

11. Holland, *Homecoming* set visit.

12. Watts, CinemaBlend.

13. Pascal, *Homecoming* set visit.

14. Feige, CinemaBlend.

15. Feige interview with CinemaBlend at the *Spider-Man: Far from Home* junket, 2019.

16. Watts, CinemaBlend.

17. Chris Klimek, "Spider-Man: Homecoming Finds Its Footing with a Less Confident Spidey," NPR, July 6, 2017, https://www.npr.org/2017/07/06/535781802/spider-man-homecoming-finds-its-footing-with-a-less-confident-spidey.

18. Christopher Orr, "Spider-Man: Homecoming Is One of the Best Superhero Movies in Years," *The Atlantic*, July 6, 2017, https://www.theatlantic.com/entertainment/archive/2017/07/spider-man-homecoming-review/532737.

19. Tufayel Ahmed, "Spider-Man: Homecoming' Is the Best Spider-Man Movie to Date," *Newsweek*, https://www.newsweek.com/review-spider-man-homecoming-best-spider-man-movie-date-631246.

20. Goldstein and Daley, interview.

21. Feige, CinemaBlend.

22. Goldstein and Daley, interview.

23. Lucy Pavia, "'It's Time to Have Babies'—Up Close with *Marie Claire*'s July Issue Cover Star Kirsten Dunst," *Marie Claire*, May 31, 2017, https://www.marieclaire.co.uk/entertainment/kirsten-dunst-marie-claire-july-511120.

24. Goldstein and Daley, interview.

25. Jon Watts interview with CinemaBlend at the *Spider-Man: Homecoming* junket.

26. Feige, CinemaBlend.

27. Feige, CinemaBlend.

28. Jon Watts, CinemaBlend's ReelBlend podcast, https://podcasts.apple.com/lb/podcast/director-jon-watts-on-spider-mans-end-credits-scenes/id1332842638?i=1000443860682.

29. Watts, ReelBlend.

30. Watts, ReelBlend.

CHAPTER TWELVE

1. Markus, interview.

2. Anthony Russo in the Marvel Studios featurette "Choices," YouTube, https://www.youtube.com/watch?v=c6IrgVyTl6E.

3. Watts, ReelBlend.

CHAPTER THIRTEEN

1. Arad, interview.

2. Rothman, interview.

3. Lord and Miller, interview.

4. Andrew O'Hehir, "'The LEGO Movie': Plastic Blocks Fight for Freedom!,'" Slate.com, February 7, 2014, https://www.salon.com/2014/02/07/plastic_blocks _fight_for_freedom.

5. Rothman, interview.

6. Eric Francisco, "'Spider-Verse' Oscars: Brian Michael Bendis Opens Up on Miles Morales," *Inverse*, February 24, 2019, https://www.inverse.com/article/53518 -spider-man-into-the-spider-verse-brian-michael-bendis-opens-up-on-oscars-miles -morales.

7. Lord and Miller, interview.

8. Author interview with Rodney Rothman, December 19, 2020.

9. Adam Holmes and Jeff McCobb, "Jake Johnson's Not a Spider-Man Fan, but Has a Great Reason for Doing *Spider-Man: Into the Spider-Verse*," CinemaBlend, July 31, 2021, https://www.cinemablend.com/news/2571295/jake-johnson-not -spider-man-fan-great-reason-doing-spider-man-into-the-spider-verse.

10. Lord and Miller, interview.

11. Tom Holland's Instagram post, December 16, 2018, https://www .instagram .com/p/BrdX4NoHe_5.

12. Rothman, interview.

CHAPTER FOURTEEN

1. Faughnder, *Los Angeles Times*, 2017.

2. Adam B. Vary, "Will Spider-Man Ever Connect with Sony's Other Marvel Movies? 'There Actually Is a Plan,' Says Exec," *Variety*, May 28, 2021, https://variety.com/ 2021/film/news/spider-man-sony-marvel-kraven-sanford-panitch-1234984449.

3. Kevin Feige, Sony Pictures Entertainment press release, September 27, 2019.

4. Pascal, *Homecoming* set visit.

5. Author interview with Sanford Panitch, December 15, 2021.

6. Avi Arad interview with CinemaBlend at the *Venom* junket, 2018.

7. Jeff Pinkner interview with the Mutuals on YouTube, December 11, 2018, https://www.youtube.com/watch?v=o9ij2YOtc0E.

8. Josh Spiegel, "How Tom Hardy Transcends Venom," *The Hollywood Reporter*, October 5, 2018, https://www.hollywoodreporter.com/movies/movie-news/venom -tom-hardy-clearly-thinks-hes-a-comedy-1149683.

9. Ruben Fleischer interview with CinemaBlend at the *Venom* junket, 2018.

10. Tom Hardy interview with CinemaBlend for *Venom: Let There Be Carnage*, https://www.youtube.com/watch?v=Alv2mTZdORw.

11. Author interview with Kelly Marcel, September 22, 2021.

12. Tom Hardy interview with CinemaBlend at the *Venom* junket, https://www.youtube.com/watch?v=iLOok7iJ3e4.

13. Marcel, interview.

14. Adam B. Vary, "*Spider-Man: No Way Home* Screenwriters Explain All Those Surprises and Spoilers: 'This Wasn't Just Fan Service,'" *Variety*, December 29, 2021, https://variety.com/2021/film/news/spider-man-no-way-home-spoilers-tobey-maguire-andrew-garfield-aunt-may-1235144617.

15. Panitch, interview.

16. Vary, "Will Spider-Man Ever Connect," *Variety*, 2021.

CHAPTER FIFTEEN

1. Will Thorne, "Sony Pictures Chief on Spider-Man Split: 'For the Moment the Door Is Closed,'" *Variety*, September 5, 2019, https://variety.com/2019/film/news/spiderman-mcu-sony-pictures-chief-1203324907.

2. Sony Pictures Entertainment press statement, August 20, 2019.

3. Rothman, interview.

4. Steven Zeitchik, "Behind the Scenes of the Disney-Sony Fight for Spider-Man," *Washington Post*, August 23, 2019, https://www.washingtonpost.com/business/2019/08/23/behind-scenes-disney-sony-fight-spider-man.

5. Tom Holland interview with CinemaBlend for *Spider-Man: No Way Home*, December 8, 2021, https://www.youtube.com/watch?v=MDlSY7rDAfk.

6. Kevin Feige interview with Rotten Tomatoes, July 12, 2021, https://www.youtube.com/watch?v=aZZ_PWwbjb4.

7. Rothman, interview.

8. Bob Iger interview on *Jimmy Kimmel Live*, October 4, 2019, https://www.youtube.com/watch?v=kqtZQsbaxew.

9. Holland, CinemaBlend, 2021.

10. Tom Holland interview on *Jimmy Kimmel Live*, December 5, 2019, https://www.youtube.com/watch?v=1-NPFORuPCw.

11. Holland, *Jimmy Kimmel Live*.

12. Holland, CinemaBlend, 2021.

13. Aaron Couch, "How *Spider-Man: No Way Home* Was 'Shaped' by Its Secret Stars," *The Hollywood Reporter*, December 29, 2021, https://www.hollywoodreporter

.com/movies/movie-features/spider-man-no-way-home-andrew-garfield-tobey
-maguire-1235068153.

14. Bob Iger's Tweet, December 25, 2021, https://twitter.com/RobertIger/
status/1474783960324526089.

15. "Kevin Feige and Amy Pascal on the Future of Spider-Man in the MCU,"
New York Times, December 17, 2021, https://www.nytimes.com/2021/12/17/
movies/kevin-feige-amy-pascal-spider-man-no-way-home.html.

16. Pascal, *New York Times*, 2021.

CHAPTER SIXTEEN

1. Rothman, interview.

2. Frank Pallotta, "*Spider-Man: No Way Home* Is the First Film to Make $1
Billion since 2019," CNN, December 27, 2021, https://www.cnn.com/2021/12/26/
media/spider-man-no-way-home-box-office-billion/index.html.

3. Jon Watts on the *Spider-Man: No Way Home* electronic press kit, https://
www.youtube.com/watch?v=_F-FRWSRgS4.

4. Matt Donnelly, "Andrew Garfield Finally Spills," *Variety*, 2021.

5. Kevin Feige on the *Spider-Man: No Way Home* electronic press kit, https://
www.youtube.com/watch?v=hmiExlgZiS4.

6. Adam B. Vary, "*Spider-Man: No Way Home* Screenwriters Explain," *Variety*,
2021.

7. Tom Holland interview with Marvel.com, December 22, 2021, https://
www.marvel.com/articles/movies/spider-man-no-way-home-tom-holland-zendaya
-surprise-characters.

8. Deadline interview with Tobey Maguire, Andrew Garfield, and Tom Holland,
YouTube, January 26, 2022, https://www.youtube.com/watch?v=T0sRQ7N9XXc.

9. Deadline interview, 2022.

10. Donnelly, "Andrew Garfield Finally Spills," *Variety*, 2021.

11. Donnelly, "Andrew Garfield Finally Spills," *Variety*, 2021.

12. Deadline interview.

13. Zendaya interview with Marvel.com, 2021.

14. Tom Holland interview with Marvel.com, January 4, 2022, https://www
.marvel.com/articles/movies/tom-holland-zendaya-spider-man-no-way-home-love
-loss.

15. Deadline interview.

16. Deadline interview.

17. Devan Coggan, "Tom Holland Opens Up about *Spider-Man: No Way Home* and Facing Off against Alfred Molina," *Entertainment Weekly*, October 14, 2021, https://ew.com/movies/tom-holland-spider-man-no-way-home-preview.

18. Rothman, interview.

19. "Kevin Feige and Amy Pascal," *New York Times*, 2021.

20. Feige, Rotten Tomatoes, 2021.

21. Rothman, interview.

22. Tolmach, interview.

23. Phil Lord and Chris Miller interview with CinemaBlend at the Savannah Film Festival, October 2021.

24. Markus, interview.

25. Rothman, interview.

26. Stan Lee's quote, featured in *Spider-Man: Into the Spider-Verse*.

INDEX

Note: Characters are indexed by their first name. If applicable, the name is followed by their alter-ego and the actor's name who portrayed that character (examples include Ned (Jacob Batalon) and Adrian Toomes/Vulture (Michael Keaton)).